Wendland

# TRANSFORMING

# Performance
# Measurement

# TRANSFORMING

# Performance Measurement

## Rethinking the Way We Measure and Drive Organizational Success

**DEAN R. SPITZER**

American Management Association

New York • Atlanta • Brussels • Chicago • Mexico City • San Francisco
Shanghai • Tokyo • Toronto • Washington, D.C.

*This publication is designed to provide accurate and authoritative information in regard to the subject matter covered. It is sold with the understanding that the publisher is not engaged in rendering legal, accounting, or other professional service. If legal advice or other expert assistance is required, the services of a competent professional person should be sought.*

*Library of Congress Cataloging-in-Publication Data*

*Spitzer, Dean R.*
    *Transforming performance measurement : rethinking the way we measure and drive organizational success / Dean R. Spitzer.*
        *p.   cm.*
    *Includes bibliographical references and index.*
    *ISBN-10: 0-8144-0891-5*
    *ISBN-13: 978-0-8144-0891-9*
    *1.  Organizational effectiveness—Evaluation.   I.  Title.*
*HD58.9.S68   2007*
*658.4'013—dc22*

                                                                *2006020651*

*Printing number*

*10   9   8   7   6   5   4   3   2*

*To Cynthia, my wonderful wife*
*To David, my wonderful son*
*To Marjory Goldman, my wonderful mother*

# Contents

Acknowledgments      xiii

Introduction      1
    The Elusive Search for the Secret of Success      1
    Changing the Paradigm      2
    A Surprising Truth About Performance Measurement      3
    The Purpose of This Book      4
    The Transformational Measurement Questionnaire      5

Chapter 1: Why Measurement Is So Powerful      9
    The Pervasiveness of Measurement      10
    The Challenge of Organizational Measurement      11
    The Power of Measurement      12
    Performance Measurement Promotes Effective Management      13
    The Functions of Performance Measurement      15

Chapter 2: When Measurement Goes Bad      21
    The Problem of Measurement Dysfunction      22
    A Major Cause of Measurement Dysfunction      23
    How Rewards Increase the Potential for Measurement Dysfunction      23
    Fear Also Induces Measurement Dysfunction      26
    Measuring the Wrong Things      29
    Measuring "Looking Good" Rather Than "Being Good"      30
    Suboptimization      31
    Cheating      33
    Measuring Too Much      34
    Dysfunctional Measurement and Employees      35

Chapter 3: Why Measurement Goes Bad      36
    Motive and Opportunity      36
    How People Experience Measurement      38
    Employees' Attitudes Toward Measurement at Work      39
    The Context of Measurement      40
    Confusing Measurement and Evaluation      41

Purpose                                                         42
Disempowerment                                                  43
The "Motivational" Use of Measurement                           44
Distrust                                                        45
Negative Accountability                                         45
Resistance to Measurement                                       46
Opportunity and Motive Revisited                                46
The Challenge Ahead                                             47

Chapter 4: Beginning the Transformation                         48
The Transformational Vision                                     48
How to Realize the Vision: The Four Keys                        51
A Roadmap to Success                                            55

Chapter 5: Creating A Positive Context of Measurement           56
The Context of Measurement                                      56
The Formal Aspects of the Performance Measurement System        59
The Human Factor                                                60
The Context of Measurement Continuum                            61
A Sure-Fire Indicator of Positive Context of Measurement Change 62
Snapshots from the New Performance Measurement Paradigm         63
The Ongoing Transforming Power of Context                       67

Chapter 6: The Focus of Measurement                             68
The Importance of Focus                                         68
Selecting the Right Measures                                    69
Effectiveness First                                             71
How Value Is Created and Destroyed                              72
Business Models and Strategy                                    74
Measuring What Matters Most                                     76
Measuring Intangible Assets                                     78
High-Leverage Measuring                                         79
Emergent Measures                                               81
New Customer Measures                                           82
Don't Expect Perfection                                         84
The Next Step                                                   85

Chapter 7: The Integration of Measurement                       86
The Importance of Measurement Integration                       86
The Dis-Integrated Organization                                 87
Dis-Integrated Measurement                                      89
Dis-Integrated Data                                             90
Strategic Measurement                                           90

The Balanced Scorecard                                                     91
The Value of Measurement Frameworks                              93
Measurement Frameworks and Trade-Offs                        96
Developing Measurement Frameworks                               97
The Need for a CMO                                                       102
The Next Step                                                               102

Chapter 8: The Interactivity of Measurement                   103
The Importance of Interactivity                                     104
Data, Information, Knowledge, and Wisdom                    105
The Data-to-Wisdom Conversion Process                        108
Examples of Interactivity to Generate Wisdom               109
The Performance Measurement Cycle                             110
Dialogue: The Key to Measurement Interactivity            115
Assessing an Organization's Measurement Capabilities    116
The Challenge of Interactivity Today                             118
The Tendency to View Technology as the Panacea          119
Making Progress                                                          120

Chapter 9: Measurement Leadership                              121
The Importance of Measurement Leadership                   121
Why Measurement Leadership Doesn't Happen              122
The Tension Between Intuition and Measurement          122
What Happens in the Absence of Measurement Leadership?   123
Routine vs. Transformational Measurement                    126
The Challenges of Changing Measurement                     127
Leading Transformational Performance Measurement     128
Establishing an Environment Conducive to Change        128
Making the Transformation Happen                              132
Measurement Leaders                                                  134
Needed: The Role of Chief Measurement Officer (CMO)   139

Chapter 10: Learning About and from Measurement       140
Transformational Learning                                           140
The Process of Learning                                               140
The Learning Loop                                                       142
Transformational Measurement and Double-Loop Learning   144
Organizational Learning                                               145
Why Smart People Do Dumb Things                              147
How Performance Measurement Can Help                      148
Learning New Ways of Thinking About Performance Measurement   149
The Keys to Transformational Learning                          150
How Well Does Your Organization Learn About and from
Measurement?                                                             159

Chapter 11: The Uses and Abuses of Measurement Technology    160
    In Search of a Quick Fix and a Technology Breakthrough    160
    Technology Infatuation                                    161
    The Human Factor                                          162
    The Proper Role of Technology in Performance Measurement  163
    Business and Social Architecture                          164
    Failure to Address the Social Issues                      166
    Critical Issues in Adopting Measurement Technology        166
    Scorecards and Dashboards                                 168
    Adopting and Implementing Measurement Technology          171
    Steps for Successful Technology Investment                174

Chapter 12: Performance Measurement Maturity                 177
    The Concept of Maturity                                   177
    Assessing Transformational Performance Measurement Maturity  180
    Levels of Performance Measurement Maturity                188
    The Transformational Measurement Maturity Assessment      191

Chapter 13: Transformational Measures                        196
    Defining Transformational Measurement                     196
    From Exploration to Transformation                        197
    Traditional vs. Transformational Thinking                 197
    Taking the Lead in Transformational Measurement           199
    The Transformational Lens                                 201
    An Experimental Attitude Is Essential                     201
    The Challenge of Measuring Intangibles                    201
    Transformational Measurement of Intangibles               204
    Introducing the Transformational Measurement Action Plans 211
    Don't Get Discouraged                                     213

Chapter 14: Transformational Measurement Action Plans        214
     1. Customer Experience                                   214
     2. Customer Engagement                                   215
     3. Customer Delight                                      216
     4. Customer Loyalty                                      217
     5. Customer Relationship                                 218
     6. Voice of the Customer                                 219
     7. Customer Profitability                                221
     8. Customer Lifetime Value                               222
     9. Service Quality                                       222
    10. Brand Equity                                          223
    11. Intellectual Capital                                  225

12. Strategic Readiness of Intangibles                                226
13. Innovation Climate                                                227
14. Reputation                                                        228
15. Organizational Trust                                              229
16. Partner Relationships                                             232
17. Collaboration                                                     233
18. Productivity                                                      234
19. Organizational Agility                                            235
20. Waste                                                             237
21. Inventory                                                         238
22. Total Cost of Ownership                                           240
23. Activity-Based Costing                                            241
24. Economic Value Added                                              242
25. Organizational Intangible Value                                   243
26. Project Scheduling                                                244
27. Employee Engagement                                               245
28. Emotional Intelligence                                            247
29. Employee Safety                                                   249
30. Employee Presenteeism                                             250
31. Learning Effectiveness                                            251
32. Information Orientation                                           252
33. Information Proficiency                                           253
34. Knowledge Flow                                                    255

Epilogue: How to Begin Transforming Performance Measurement
in Your Organization                                                  257

Notes                                                                 262

Bibliography                                                          271

Index                                                                 277

# Acknowledgments

Even though I am the sole author of this book, there are more people than I can mention who contributed to it in one way or another.

My deepest thanks to Jim Spohrer, director of Almaden Services Research and a true champion of innovation at IBM, who has believed in my work on the "socialization of measurement" and protected my time so that I could write this book. I would also like to thank my colleagues in IBM Research, IBM Global Technology Services, and IBM Global Business Services, who have been invaluable sources of ideas, dialogue, and stimulation. I would also like to acknowledge all the clients over the years who have trusted my advice and provided me with the greatest laboratory there is—their organizations.

Thanks to the pantheon of performance-measurement thought leaders, many of them referenced in this book, who established the foundation upon which this book has forged new ground. However, without their contributions, there would be no ground.

Thanks in advance to all of those who will read this book, have the courage to at least begin transforming performance measurement in their organizations, and seize the opportunity.

Thanks also to Adrienne Hickey, executive editor at AMACOM, who believed in the importance of this book from day one and marshaled AMACOM's best resources to facilitate the publication process; to my editor, Niels Buessem, who did a wonderful job of trimming the excess but not the essence and sharpening my prose; to Mike Sivilli, AMACOM's outstanding associate editor; and to Vicki Weiland, my personal editor and friend, who provided much more than editing, including prayer, moral support, and great suggestions for improving the book.

Thanks to my family, to whom this book is dedicated, for their love and support. Special thanks to my wife Cynthia and son David who have forgiven me for neglecting them during the writing process. But most thanks are due to God for giving me meaning, purpose, wisdom, perseverance, and the strength to complete this book.

—Dean Spitzer

# TRANSFORMING

# Performance Measurement

# Introduction

What if I were to tell you that one of the most important keys to your organization's success can be found in a very unlikely place—a place many of you may consider to be complicated, inaccessible, and perhaps even downright boring? What if I were to tell you that this key to success is *already* one of the most ubiquitous and impactful forces in your organization? It's there, waiting for you to tap into it.

This key to success is MEASUREMENT.

Measurement done right can *transform* your organization. It can not only show you where you are now, but can get you to wherever you want to go. Don't believe me? Well, then, get ready to change the way you think about measurement. As you will see in this book, measurement is fundamental to high performance, improvement, and, ultimately, success in business, or in any other area of human endeavor.

## The Elusive Search for the Secret of Success

The search for the secret of success in business is an ongoing pursuit for each of us. We buy book after book, take course after course, and our antennas are constantly on the alert for the latest—and greatest—management trend. We're mentored, we're trained, and most often we're left more than a little drained by all of this information. We all strive to become better managers, better motivators, and better leaders of our organization, our Board, our unit, our department, our team. And our companies spend a lot of time and money helping us to do so—all with a view to improving the bottom line. Unfortunately, the results of most of this flexing of corporate resources are generally spotty at best. Sometimes the investment of time and money pays off, but mostly it doesn't.

Why? Because the root causes of organizational problems tend to remain unaddressed. Beyond all the hype and hoopla of these management "break-

1

throughs," there is one thing that can always be counted on: No matter how exciting or important or essential the latest management breakthrough might appear to be, it will turn out to be equally expendable as soon as the next big management solution comes around.

## Changing the Paradigm

It is my contention that there are certain performance measures and ways of measuring that can have a *transformational impact* on the way people in organizations view their work, their products, and their customers. Too many companies have tried to transform themselves by adopting short-term programs or changing superficial aspects of structure, systems, or technology without making the deep changes in the way people inside view their organization, as well as in the way their organization is viewed externally in the marketplace.

Actually, the transformation doesn't require a major change in your business structure or systems—but only in the way you think about measuring your organization. In order for this kind of deep change to occur, the existing paradigm of organizational measurement must change.

As you know, *paradigms* are widely accepted "mental models" that determine how we see the world. A paradigm is said to *shift* when there is a change in that model. In business, most change occurs when people start looking at the same things differently. As I will explain in Chapter 1, performance measurement represents the fundamental *lens* through which people "see" the performance of their organizations. When we use the same ways of measuring things, we are operating with the same lens, the same perspectives. If we are focused on the wrong measures, then we might very well miss the things that are most important—and, because business is so dynamic, what is important continues to change. Since measurement is a lens and, to a large extent, it determines how we view things, organizational transformation is what happens when people begin to see their organization through a new lens.

But the first step I am proposing is that you begin to view measurement *itself* through a new lens. Measurement is potentially one of the highest leverage activities any organization can perform. However, despite its importance, we tend to treat it as peripheral or superfluous in much of what we do. This is because most of us have failed to realize the *true power of measurement* in our lives, both at work and outside of it. We have taken it for granted, frequently implemented it poorly, and consider it, for the most part, to be a highly specialized undertaking—better delegated to specialists, such as accountants, financial analysts, and operational measurement staff.

When most people think about measurement, they think about the *technical aspects* (collecting data, calculations, analyzing data, statistics, etc.).

However, performance measurement is a lot more than tables of numbers and scorecards. Measurement may use numbers, but it is not *about numbers*; it is about *perception, understanding,* and *insight.* Measurement, when done well, can have an enormously positive and transformational impact on your organization.

## A Surprising Truth About Performance Measurement

Perhaps the most surprising truth covered in this book is that the "context of measurement" will largely determine its effectiveness. The context of measurement is actually more important than the measurement itself! One of the major reasons why performance measurement is seldom able to deliver on its positive potential is because it is almost never properly "socialized," that is, built *in a positive way* into the social fabric of the organization. It is this building of a positive environment for performance measurement that I believe is the missing link between basic, workmanlike performance measurement and the truly transformational kind I will be proposing and helping you implement in this book.

It should not come as a great surprise that most employees don't particularly like or trust the measurement systems in their organizations. And while 93 percent of organizational leaders believe that measurement is important in influencing business outcomes, only 51 percent are satisfied with their current systems and only 15 percent are very satisfied. Even accountants don't like them—a recent study showed that only 35 percent of respondents rated their organization's performance measurement systems as effective or very effective.

Additionally, it is an interesting paradox of measurement that, while so many employees wince at the mere thought of being measured at work, these same people would be horrified at the prospect of golfing (or, for that matter, bowling, playing baseball, tennis, football, or any other sport) without keeping score. In fact, measurement is probably the single most motivating aspect of sports and games. Even people who flunked math in school and are intimidated by their tax returns spend hours collecting and comparing sports statistics, and discussing them with anyone who will listen.

Why is the attitude toward measurement *at work* so different—ranging from ambivalence to outright hostility? Because too many people are accustomed to measurement's negative side, especially the judgment that tends to follow it—too much traditional performance measurement has been seen as "the reward for the few, punishment for the many, and a search for the guilty."

In contrast, on those occasions when measurement is used for the purpose of improvement rather than to make judgments or place blame, and when it is focused on the right measures, its true power is revealed. On a personal level, I'm sure you will agree that it feels very different to get on a scale and be told that you are overweight than it is to use the scale proactively to enable weight loss. It is the same scale, but, in the first case, it is being used to judge, while, in the second case, it is being used to motivate and empower. The context in which measurement is *used* makes all the difference!

## The Purpose of This Book

This book is *not* about *doing* measurement; it is about *creating an optimal environment* (context) for its effective use. Large organizations collect millions of data points every day, but few are able to establish the right environment for the effective use of that measurement. Most organizations have very competent people crunching and keeping track of numbers and have made massive investments in technology to deal with this data deluge. But almost none have done anything to improve the social and organizational context to make measurement enjoyable and productive for all the people in the organization—from those who ultimately determine what to measure and how to measure it, to those who interpret the data, communicate about it, and learn from it. That's the real challenge. In fact, as you will see, measurement is not something that should be reserved for the select few; in a high-performing organization, measurement is *everybody's* job. Unfortunately, if the "context of measurement" issues are not addressed, then the efficacy of performance measurement will change very little, and performance measurement will continue to be a drudgery and it will continue to be viewed through the same old lens.

When performance measurement *is* done right—the way that is being advocated in this book—both the organization itself *and* the people within it will be impacted positively. For the organization, transformational measurement leads to improvements in virtually every aspect of organizational performance from Accident reduction to Zero defects, including: improved strategy execution, better investment decisions, increased value creation and value capture from diverse assets (tangible and intangible), improved relationships (customers, employees, suppliers, partners, and others), increased synergy and synchronicity of the supply chain, increased forecasting accuracy, enhanced employee motivation and performance, greater organizational learning, and much, much more.

For the people who work in the organization, transformational measurement makes people feel good about measurement, and it improves their morale, their engagement, their loyalty, and makes them more eager to continuously improve their performance. Instead of an activity to be avoided or feared, measurement becomes an activity that people actually can enjoy, and measurement data become information that people look forward to receiving. Sound too good to be true? By using measurement *transformationally*—and creating the right *context* for its effective use—benefits such as these can be achieved by any organization.

I wrote this book as a manifesto and a guide for helping you to *at least begin* the journey toward transforming performance measurement in your organization. I have endeavored to provide you with a resource that will increase in value as you use it over time to create and stimulate the kind of *properly socialized* performance measurement that will transform the way your team, department, business unit, or entire organization thinks about and does performance measurement.

Once you have read this book, you will probably be surprised at how simple the basic concepts are, but doing it right isn't necessarily easy. That's why this book focuses on the most important and highest-leverage strategies, tactics, and action proposals you can use for releasing the *power* of your organization's measurement system to achieve truly *transformational* results. So, let's get started!

But before you start reading Chapter 1, you might want to answer the questions in the Transformational Measurement Questionnaire (TMQ) below. It will provide a quick assessment of your organization's need for transforming performance measurement.

---

### Transformational Measurement Questionnaire

**Instructions:** Please answer the following twenty questions "Yes" or "No" according to your *honest* assessment of the current state of performance measurement in your organization. A quick scoring guide appears at the end of the questions.

1. Are you confident that the most important factors for the present and future success of the organization are being effectively measured? __ Yes __ No

2. Is there any ongoing process of continually aligning and re-aligning performance measures with strategy? __ Yes __ No

3. Is the importance and value of performance measurement widely acknowledged throughout the organization? __ Yes __ No

4. Do people in the organization proactively seek and welcome measurement-based feedback? __ Yes __ No

5. Do employees have positive attitudes toward performance, trust it, and are confident that it will not be used against them? __ Yes __ No

6. Is performance measurement information in the organization timely and easy to understand? __ Yes __ No

7. Is performance measurement data being routinely converted into knowledge, deep insight, and wisdom? __ Yes __ No

8. Are projects and initiatives in the organization measured for effectiveness (not just for cost and timely completion)? __ Yes __ No

9. Does the organization's performance measurement system foster decisiveness, candor, transparency, and collaboration? __ Yes __ No

10. Does the organization's performance measurement system foster cross-functional collaboration? __ Yes __ No

11. Do organizational stakeholders understand the cause-and-effect relationships, dependencies, and trade-offs among key performance measures? __ Yes __ No

12. Do organizational stakeholders feel confident that the organization's performance measurement system is providing the insight and foresight to guide high quality decision-making? __ Yes __ No

13. Has significant progress been made to integrate data (especially customer data) to enable more holistic decision making? __ Yes __ No

14. Is continuous improvement of the performance measurement system and updating performance measures an organizational priority? __ Yes __ No

15. Is there progress being made in measuring difficult-to-measure sources of intangible value (e.g., talent, knowledge, innovation)? __ Yes __ No

16. Is the organization open to experimentation with new, innovative, and cross-functional performance measures? __ Yes __ No

17. Is there frequent interactivity and positive dialogues about performance measurement in staff and management meetings? __ Yes __ No

18. Is the organization's performance measurement system dynamic and flexible enough to adapt quickly to increasing complexity and changing circumstances? __ Yes __ No

19. Is measurement used at least as frequently for improvement and learning as it is for monitoring, reporting, and rewarding? __ Yes __ No

20. Is there a major effort in the organization to educate employees about performance measurement? __ Yes __ No

**Quick Scoring Guide:** Use this scoring guide to give you a quick snapshot of your organization's Transformational Measurement Quotient. Score 1 point for a "Yes" and 0 points for a "No." Then interpret your organization's score using the following guidelines:

| | |
|---|---|
| 15–20 points | Congratulations! Your organization is doing a good job of transforming performance measurement. This book should be a great refresher and help you build on your strengths. |
| 10–15 points | Your organization is making progress in transforming performance measurement. This book should help your organization take performance measurement to the next level. |
| 0–9 points | Performance measurement in your organization is still very much in need of transformation. But don't be discouraged. This book will help you develop a blueprint for the transformation. |

# CHAPTER 1

# Why Measurement Is So Powerful

M easurement is not something new. It has been around since the beginning of time. In primitive, self-contained villages, there was little requirement for measurement. Advances in measurement were driven by powerful needs, such as the needs for social interaction and to move beyond subsistence living, which led to trade and commerce, and the need for understanding and mastery of the physical environment, which led to science. Trade and commerce have been such a crucial part of world history that they have become virtually hard-wired in our DNA—and it is trade and commerce that gave rise to most of early practical measurement, including weight, size, quantity, and monetary measures. Early measurement was based on human body parts—for example, the ancient cubit was the length of the pharaoh's arm plus the width of his hand—and a variety of natural artifacts (such as flowers, stones, and shells), which were used in exchange for goods and services. Over the centuries as more sophisticated needs emerged, more sophisticated measures were developed.

Thus, measurement arose because of the *uniquely human* needs for social interaction, trade and commerce, and the drive to understand the world around us. Most measurement today continues to facilitate the formation and operation of our current social activities and institutions. An important thesis throughout this book is that measurement is, at its roots, a *social* phenomenon—not a detached calculation of numbers. In fact, measurement was created to facilitate socialization, and its further development and effectiveness depend on a socialization process.

The social nature of measurement is well exemplified by how the measurement of time evolved from social need. In early cultures, time was not very important, and the position of the sun in the sky was sufficient for the level of time-consciousness needed at that time. As people became more *conscious* of time, they started *valuing* it more, requiring more time *discipline.* This led to more precise measurement of time, including the appropriate measurement tools, such as clocks and watches. David Landes said, "It can be persuasively argued that improvements in the measurement of time . . . were the most important physical advances in the history of Western Civilization, without which few of the other advances would have been likely."[1]

In fact, all scientific and industrial progress has depended on measurement and the continuing development and refinement of increasingly more sophisticated measurement devices—telescopes, microscopes, x-rays, atomic clocks, etc. As Louis Pasteur said, "A science is as mature as its measurement tools."[2]

## The Pervasiveness of Measurement

Today, if we were consciously aware of the pervasive impact of measurement on our lives, we would be very surprised just how ubiquitous measurement is. Almost everything in modern life is based on some form of measurement. Think for a moment about the critical role of measurement in your daily life.

Literally hundreds of *measurement incidents* trigger much of what we do during the course of a day—from the moment our alarm clocks wake us up in the morning. We spend much time each day measuring things: time (clocks and calendars), finances (paychecks, bank accounts, budgets, credit, investments, retirement plans), shopping (price comparisons, product quality ratings), weather (temperature, precipitation, wind velocity, humidity, barometric pressure), vehicle operation (speed and gas gauges, maintenance records, specifications), travel (schedules, fares, locations, directions, distances), quantities (lengths, volumes, weights), food (size of portions, recipes, calories, fat content), education (grades, test scores, graduation requirements), health (vital signs, lab tests, cholesterol, blood pressure, weight), sports (scores, batting averages, records), politics (votes, opinion polls)—and hundreds of other measures we use almost daily. Just think of how much measurement goes on as you drive your car or play a round of golf! As Herbert Arthur Klein so rightly said: "Man is a measurer of all things."[3]

However, most of our daily measurements are so habitual we hardly notice them, much less label them as "measurement." Because of the pervasiveness of measurement and its integration with so many other activities, it often blends into the background, and we tend to take it for granted. But it is rather obvious that, especially in today's complex world, we would be in great trouble if we didn't have measurement to guide our decisions. Consider just a few possible consequences of *not measuring* in our personal lives: We would never be on time, our health would be at risk, our finances would be a shambles, and we would be constantly running out of gas!

Geniat and Libert say (with only slight exaggeration), "Without the capacity to measure, we would be uncertain, literally, as to where we stood and where we are going. We would not know if we are rich or poor, hot or cold, old or young. The very word 'measure' pervades all fields. . . . You can't make decisions, connections, money, or music without true measurements."[4] To a large extent, the way we measure success determines the success we will achieve. Unmeasured things cannot be easily replicated, or managed, or appreciated.

Of course, while measurement is a necessary condition for success, it alone is not sufficient for it. *We still must take action.* A blood pressure reading is not very useful if we ignore it. If we pay attention, however, and take appropriate action, it can change our life—or perhaps even save it.

What makes measurement so potent is its capacity to instigate informed action—to provide the opportunity for people to engage in the right behavior at the right time.

## The Challenge of Organizational Measurement

There is no area of human endeavor so much in need of effective measurement as are organizations. Organizations are probably the most complex entities in the universe—composed of thousands, even millions, of components. In fact, nothing has more "moving parts" than a large business or government enterprise!

The challenge is to manage those parts strategically, synergistically, and with appropriate alignment and synchronicity to attain the desired results. Measurement is the connecting fiber that can make all the parts work together. Achieving this kind of coordination and alignment is impossible without exceptional performance measurement.

Of course, smaller, simpler businesses can get by with much less sophisticated measurement. But even the sole proprietor or small business owner needs some measurement, and as small organizations grow in size and complexity, the role of measurement becomes increasingly vital.

Furthermore, the intensely competitive marketplace today demands a level and quality of performance measurement unlike any that ever existed. In the not too distant past, making money and winning at business was much easier: Companies could establish a competitive advantage quite easily and keep it for a very long time; market strength was virtually unassailable; customers were much less demanding; and leaders could manage relatively effectively with good-enough strategies and mediocre execution. But today, "good-enough" is *not* good enough.

Achieving and sustaining success in today's hyper-competitive marketplace is an ultimate challenge for any company and business leader. This is an era of unprecedented change, complexity, volatility, and risk—when everything seems to be moving at warp speed. There is very little room for error. The business imperative today is not just to perform *excellently*, but to perform excellently *consistently*. Organizations that understand and can use performance measurement to manage their strategy, systems, and processes more effectively and more consistently have found that it provides a tremendous competitive advantage.

As organizational change expert Daryl Connor said, "Never before has there been so much change so fast with such dramatic implications for the entire world."[5] Ironically, in order to adapt to change, organizations must become *even more* complex—and the more complex they become, the more difficult it is for them to be managed. And the more complexity and change there is, the more crucial measurement is. Managing a business without effective measurement is like piloting an airplane through a stormy sky without instruments. In any organization that wants to succeed today, top-notch performance measurement is no longer optional.

## The Power of Measurement

There are some who say that rewards are the most powerful force in organizations. According to Michael LeBoeuf, the world's greatest management principle is "What gets rewarded gets done."[6] He said that he reached this conclusion after hearing the following parable:

> A weekend fisherman looked over the side of his boat and saw a snake with a frog in his mouth. Feeling sorry for the frog, he reached down, gently removed the frog from the snake's mouth and let the frog go free. But now he felt sorry for the hungry snake. Having no food, he took out a flask of bourbon and poured a few drops into the snake's mouth. The snake swam away happily, and the man was happy for having performed such good deeds. He thought all was well until a few minutes passed and he heard something knock against the side of his boat and looked down. He was stunned to see that the snake was back—with two frogs!

Sound familiar? We have all experienced analogous situations where employees do something that is inconsistent with the goals or values of our organizations, and we can't understand for the life of us why they did it. The fact is that people do these things because their managers often inadvertently apply LeBoeuf's principle of "What gets rewarded gets done," but they fail to implement an effective system of measurement to support it.

Every day, I see or hear of disturbing behavior by individuals in organizations as a result of how they (and their performance) are rewarded: Sales managers who alienate key customers because they need to close a sale by the end of the month so they can get their quarterly sales bonus; corporate executives who allow expenses to be deferred to a subsequent period because they are rewarded for profits during the current period; employees who fail to share knowledge with others because knowledge sharing isn't counted in their performance appraisals. The list of reward-motivated abuses goes on and on.

So, was Michael LeBoeuf right? Is "What gets rewarded gets done" the greatest management principle in the world?

No—I think not.

Rewards are indeed extremely powerful, and people will naturally tend to do the things for which they are rewarded. But despite the plethora of books and articles (including several I authored) that promote rewards and recognition as the solution to every conceivable organizational failing or management woe, simply implementing a system of rewards is only one part of the solution, and it isn't even the most important part. In fact, this book resulted from my realization that *no matter how important and powerful rewards are, they are no better than the measurement system they are based on*.

But rewards aren't the only management system that can be problematic without good measurement. Measurement underlies every system in an organization—and that's why performance measurement is so important!

While "What gets rewarded gets done" may very well be *one* of the world's greatest management principles, there is another principle that is even *more* fundamental. In fact, it determines what people choose to do (and reward) on the job, and in their lives. This principle is: "*You get what you measure*" and its proper application will help you not only to use rewards better, but also manage *everything else* you do more effectively.

## Performance Measurement Promotes Effective Management

Effective management is based on a foundation of effective measurement, and almost everything else is based on that. Bain & Company director emeritus and customer loyalty expert Frederick Reichheld unequivocally put it this way: "Measurement systems create the basis for effective management."[7]

As Figure 1-1 illustrates, measurement determines what management does, and it works—through management—to touch every part of the organization, including compensation and rewards.

Organizations are conglomerations of many systems. Measurement is actually the most fundamental system of all. When the "measurement system" works well, management tends to manage (and reward) the right things—and the desired results will occur. The measurement system—for

FIGURE 1-1. MEASUREMENT: THE MOST FUNDAMENTAL
MANAGEMENT SYSTEM.

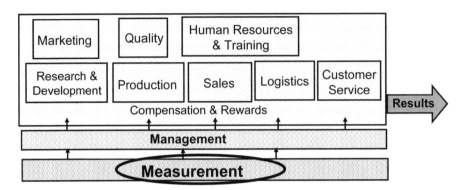

good or ill—triggers virtually everything that happens in an organization, both strategic and tactical. This is because all the other organizational systems are ultimately based on what the measurement system is telling the other systems to do. Unfortunately, as we will see, most organizations do not have one integrated measurement system, but rather many measurement systems located in functional "silos" and not well interconnected.

I am continually amazed how many leaders pursue the wrong things—and it almost always comes down to what is being measured. The wrong measures tend to trigger the wrong activities—because they represent what people "see." Then these wrong activities generate the wrong results—no matter how well-executed the activities are. *Most individuals and organizations don't get what they want because they don't measure what they really want!*

If your measurements are out-of-whack, everything else will be as well. This is a real problem, because no organization can be any better than its measurement system. Here is just a small sample of bad things that happen to good companies that don't measure well:

- Strategy isn't well executed, because managers and employees don't know what the strategy means for their jobs.
- Operational performance can't be appropriately managed, because management becomes (at best) a set of educated guesses.
- Priorities are vague and conflicting, and goals can't be set because goals require the right measures.
- People don't understand what's expected of them, and when they do figure it out, it's often too late.
- Managers don't really know how well their functions, their people, and their initiatives are performing.

- There's frenetic behavior, lots of activity, but little seems to get accomplished, and nobody really knows what is paying off, and what isn't.
- There are Herculean efforts at problem-solving and performance improvement, but problems don't really get solved and nobody really knows which improvements are working or what caused the problem in the first place.
- The wrong things are rewarded, and the things that should be rewarded are not.

Do any of these symptoms sound familiar?

Nothing is more frustrating and futile to observe than the chaos and waste that proliferates in a *poorly measured* organization.

## The Functions of Performance Measurement

Even if we don't always measure well, we tend to measure *often*. That's why this book is about how to measure *both often and well*.

You would be amazed to know how many times on an average workday you are involved in some form of measurement. It is the ubiquity of measurement that makes it almost invisible, and we have come to think of it as routine—as part of the standard infrastructure of the organization—and it has been allowed to evolve. But this is a mistake. Organizational performance measurement is much too important to leave to chance and evolution. Measurement at work serves a great many vital purposes, and the extent to which it serves those purposes is the extent to which organizations like yours will realize its true value.

Let's look at some of the major functions of performance measurement:

- *Measurement directs behavior.* According to Eliyahu Goldratt, author of the business classic, *The Goal*, all behavior can be predicted by what is being measured: "Tell me how you measure me, and I will tell you how I will behave."[8] The most frequent question I get from clients is: "What can we do *immediately* to improve performance in our company?" My response is invariably: "Change one key measure that is currently driving the wrong behavior."

- *Measurement increases the visibility of performance.* You can't manage what you can't measure. Because most of what happens in organizations (processes, capabilities, and performance) is not directly visible, measurement then becomes "our eyes." This book will show you how to measure *anything*—even those difficult to measure intangibles like innovation, relationships, and knowledge—so that everything *important* in your organization can be effectively managed. In our far-flung and virtual enterprises, where onsite managing is becoming increasingly difficult, measurement is what makes the "virtual organization" and self-management possible.

• *Measurement focuses attention.* Because people are faced with so many competing demands on their time and resources, what is measured tends to get their attention—particularly when what is measured is linked (even tangentially) with the reward system. Furthermore, in the absence of good measurement, it is human nature to pay attention to the unusual or the annoying. That's why the squeaky wheel often gets the grease—even if it's the *wrong* wheel.

• *Measurement clarifies expectations.* One of the most important roles of management is to communicate expectations to the workforce. It is well known that people will do what management *inspects* (measures), not necessarily what management *expects!* Too often management is vague about what it expects, resulting in considerable confusion:

"We want our supply chain to be more agile!"
"We are committed to being the most innovative company in our industry!"
"We aim for maximum customer service and total customer satisfaction."

What do these statements mean? Twenty people will interpret them in twenty different ways. Some people are adamant that "I'll know it when I see it!" But, will they really? As we will see, well-defined measures cut through the layers of vagueness, and get right to the point.

• *Measurement enables accountability.* Accountability is really nothing more than "measurable responsibility." Measurement tells you how well you and your employees are performing against commitments—the essence of accountability. Without measurement, it's difficult to hold yourself—or anyone else—accountable for anything, because there's no way to determine that whatever it is you're supposed to do has actually been accomplished. Unfortunately, accountability traditionally has negative associations. In this book, I will differentiate between "positive accountability" (an opportunity to perform and improve) and "negative accountability" (merely doing what is necessary to get rewards or avoid punishment).

• *Measurement increases objectivity.* One of the major points of this book is that people actually like *measuring* and even like *being measured*—but they don't like *being judged*, especially based on subjective opinions. How measurement is experienced depends on its *purpose*—and the highest purposes of measurement are to learn and to improve. As measurement expert Bob Frost has explained, objective measurements "enable you to manage by fact; without them, you're left to lead with charm and personality."[9] Few employees appreciate that kind of "charm and personality!"

• *Measurement provides the basis for goal-setting.* Everybody knows that goals are the means by which most organizations define success. The goals that a company sets will depend on what the company measures. However, few people realize that a goal is really nothing more than a "target value" established on a particular measurement *scale*. But, first you must define that scale. The measurement scale can be net profits, customer satisfaction, sales, productivity, etc. Most people are familiar with the SMART acronym for the qualities of good goals—Specific, Measurable, Actionable, Relevant, and Timely. They are all important, but the most crucial one is the "M"— *Measurable*. Remember: *You will get what you measure!*

• *Measurement improves execution.* You won't be able to reach your goals—whatever they are—without good execution. And you won't be able to execute well, *consistently,* without measurement. Even the greatest plan in the world can be ruined by poor execution. If you doubt the importance of measurement in execution, consider what execution guru Larry Bossidy says about those who don't do it: "When I see companies that don't execute, the chances are that they don't measure."[10]

• *Measurement promotes consistency.* Above, we talked about the imperative to manage well, consistently. Inconsistency (high variability) is a characteristic of unmeasured and poorly measured systems, and it is the antithesis of true quality. Outstanding performance is not about success in a quarter or year; it's about consistent success over the long-term—and this requires more than occasionally pulling a rabbit out of a hat or making a single hole-in-one. Examples from both business and sports show us that winners don't just win: They win *consistently,* and they use effective measurement to do so.

• *Measurement facilitates feedback.* You won't be able to execute anything or reach the goals you set consistently without good feedback. Feedback is the basic navigational or steering device of any individual or organization. Remember the childhood hide-and-seek game when you were blindfolded? "You're cold!" "Now you're getting warmer." "You're hot!" You had to depend on others for feedback. When you received clear and timely feedback, you could usually reach the hidden object very quickly and minimize zigzagging and frustration—but when feedback was not given, or was inaccurate or late, you were in trouble.

Similarly, without good measurement your organization is flying blind, and it will take a lot of good luck to take you anywhere near your destination. Many organizations, like ships or airplanes with faulty instruments, gradually—*often imperceptibly*—drift off-course. A missile can be only a fraction of a degree off-course and miss its target by hundreds of miles. Ask any of your employees about the quality of feedback they receive from your measurement system, and I think you will be surprised at how low they rate it. Quality expert H. James Harrington describes it this way: "Measurement is the lock, feedback is the key. Without their interaction, you cannot open the door to improvement."[11] Great measurement-based feedback might even be the key to unlocking high performance in your organization.

• *Measurement increases alignment.* Consistent behavior and performance across any organization is impossible without an aligned measurement system. I'm sure you have noticed the amount of self-interested behavior in organizations today. In fact, some organizations appear to be composed of a collection of functional silos that operate so independently that there seems to be little connection among them at all. That doesn't mean that people aren't trying to do a good job—but they define a "good job" as maximizing their own functional measures of success. The key to making self-interest coincide with organizational interest is the kind of fully-aligned, holistic measurement system you will learn how to develop in this book.

• *Measurement improves decision making.* As Bain & Company consultants Paul Rogers and Marcia Blenko say, "The hallmark of any highly effective organization is making good decisions and making them better, faster, and more consistently than their competitors."[12] Unfortunately, few managers have ever formally learned how to make decisions, much less to make *data-based* decisions. This is why Dr. Paul Nutt, author of *Why Decisions Fail*, contends that two out of three managers use "failure-prone" decision-making practices, and that as many as 50 percent of all managerial decisions fail.[13]

One of the major reasons for failure-prone decisions is over-reliance on intuition, that is, on an individualistic combination of experience, opinion, mythology, power, politics, and probability, all of which are highly susceptible to bias and personal blind spots. In the absence of data, anyone's opinion is as good as anyone else's—but usually the *highest ranking* opinion wins! We would be wise to remember the proverb: "One accurate measurement is worth a thousand opinions." Intuition is good, but by itself, it isn't good enough. Among other things, this book will show you how measurement can improve your business intuition and significantly increase your "decision-making batting average."

• *Measurement improves problem-solving.* According to Will Kaydos, "It's not the 95 percent that's right that makes something work; it's the 5 percent that's wrong that messes everything up."[14] If you don't have ways of finding that 5 percent, then the 95 percent that you and your people do well can be undermined—but if you do, then the full potential of that 95 percent can be realized. When people do see "problems," most of what they are really seeing are just "symptoms," because, in most organizations, only the obvious symptoms are being measured. To make matters worse, because of time delays built into organizational systems, it often takes a long time for the symptoms to manifest themselves.

Peter Senge cautions us to "beware of the symptomatic solution," because you cannot solve a problem by merely removing a symptom.[15] When a serious-enough problem is identified, the *root causes* need to be diagnosed and validated by collecting actual performance measurement data using a disciplined process. If you are already systematically measuring performance, problems will be much easier to discover, prioritize, and solve.

• *Measurement provides early warning signals.* No matter how right the solution, what good is a problem that's solved too late? Many people don't recognize a problem until it reaches a crisis level. This is the same situation with a business. If crucial problems are not identified and addressed early on, the longer-term consequences can be quite severe. Companies need to calibrate their measurement systems for both their internal and external environments to recognize changes. Sometimes small but significant changes, which normally might be overlooked, can become visible with the right measurement. For example, companies that fail to keep monitoring their customers in new and innovative ways are those most likely to be asking, "What the heck happened?" as they watch their stock prices fall. The sooner problems can be diagnosed the better. Good measurement is a lot less expensive in the long-run than major overhauls, business recovery, or bankruptcy.

• *Measurement enhances understanding.* Quality guru W. Edwards Deming based much of the methodology he used to help transform Japanese industry on deep understanding through systematic process measurement, which he called "profound knowledge." Measurement can provide a deeper understanding of virtually anything. Quality expert James Harrington has said, "If you can't measure something, you can't understand it. If you can't understand it, you can't control it. If you can't control it, you can't improve it."[16] Famous physicist Lord Kelvin was well known for saying that if you can't measure something, your understanding of it is "meager."

In any area of an organization, without good measurement, it is impossible to know what is working and what is not. If used appropriately, "properly socialized measurement" (the kind this book is about) will provide you, your employees, and your partners with the kind of growing understanding essential to managing the difficult-to-measure sources of real value creation in your organization—and, in the process, help you to be a much more effective manager and a better leader. What is most remarkable is that the mere *effort* to measure a difficult-to-measure construct can lead to a much deeper understanding and more effective management of that dimension or asset.

• *Measurement enables prediction.* There is an adage that states, "Looking back is helpful, but looking forward is essential." In *The New Economics,* W. Edwards Deming pronounces unequivocally that "management is prediction."[17] Of course, prediction is not entirely new to management; companies make predictions regularly. What I am talking about in this book is how good "predictive measurement" can be used to *lead* an organization, not just attempt to extrapolate data for spin or reporting purposes. This book will show you how you can use dialogue to improve predictive measurement, including estimating and forecasting accuracy. While no prediction is ever certain, using predictive measurement appropriately by building, and continually refining, measurement models or frameworks can make your organization's management more proactive, forward looking, and much more effective.

• *Measurement motivates.* Measurement tends to make things happen; it is the antidote to inertia. We have all experienced, for example, how milestones in a project plan get people moving energetically toward a goal, while open-ended timeframes inevitably lead to complacency and low energy. Measurement also helps people see their progress, which is highly motivating. Give people measurable goals (even ambitious ones), in a relatively nonthreatening environment, help them track their progress, and they will be strongly motivated. On the other hand, when improvement goals are vague, unmeasurable, and cannot be objectively tracked, people often lose interest and disengage from the improvement efforts—in favor of what can be measured.

In addition, measurement releases powerful motivational forces—including initiative, pride in accomplishment, peer pressure, and competitiveness. One of the most remarkable examples of the motivational function of measurement is how dedicated athletes use measurement to motivate themselves to ever higher levels of performance. You can mobilize that same kind of dedication in your organization.

However, despite its enormous potential to motivate intrinsically, measurement is often linked with rewards that are so powerful that they overpower the value of measurement. As we will discuss in Chapter 2, while the alignment of measurement and external consequences—both rewards and punishment—is desirable, linking performance measurement too tightly with rewards and punishment is one of the contributing factors to measurement dysfunction and undesired behaviors. This is just one of the many problems that organizations face "when measurement goes bad"—and what keeps organizations from fully realizing the positive power of performance measurement.

# When Measurement Goes Bad

As we have seen, measurement has the potential to be a very *powerful*, highly *functional*, and extremely *positive* force in organizations and for their employees. When used well, no other single aspect of management provides greater functionality than performance measurement.

But there is a flip side. Unfortunately, when used poorly, not only does it not live up to its positive promise, but performance measurement can be highly *dys*functional. This is the "dark side" of measurement's enormous power. Everything that is powerful for good, if misused, can be powerful for bad. Because measurement is the *lens* through which most performance is viewed, because it is *the most fundamental management system* upon which other management systems are based, and because it is the *triggering mechanism* for most of what happens in organizations, it should be apparent that there is the potential for both unintentional and intentional distortion and manipulations. If your lens is out of focus or focused on the wrong things, if your most fundamental management system is being poorly used, and if your triggering mechanism is triggering the wrong actions, then bad things are virtually guaranteed to happen.

In this chapter, you will learn what happens when measurement goes bad so that you will be able to proactively address the problem rather than waiting for bad measurement to continue to undermine your organization's or your function's effectiveness.

Without a vision for *both* the positive and negative sides of performance measurement, you might be lulled into a false sense of complacency, thinking that any problems can be taken care of through routine maintenance or by delegation to technical measurement specialists. No organizational leader today can afford to take their measurement system for granted.

The good news today about performance measurement is that organizations are finally discovering the importance of measurement. The bad news is that most organizations are still using it very poorly. In *The Agenda*, Michael Hammer puts it this way:

> A company's measurement systems typically deliver a blizzard of nearly meaningless data that quantifies practically everything in sight, no matter how unimportant; that is devoid of any particular rhyme or reason; that is so voluminous as to be unusable; that is delivered so late as to be virtually useless; and that then languishes in printouts and briefing books, without being put to any significant purpose. . . . In short, measurement is a mess."[1]

But, as you will see, Hammer's indictment of organizational measurement systems is not nearly strong enough!

While most people are aware that "something is wrong" with their organization's measurement system, few can pinpoint the causes, much less the solution. That is why dysfunctional measurement continues to persist. Performance measurement is complex, and we still do not understand it very well; you can't fix something that you don't understand. As a result of ignorance about performance measurement, many executives try to fix *everything else* in their organizations *except* measurement, and find that the problems are never solved—because the source of so many organizational problems is a defective measurement system.

## The Problem of Measurement Dysfunction

What is commonly referred to as "measurement dysfunction" occurs when the measurement process itself contributes to behavior contrary to what is in the best interests of the organization. When measurement dysfunctions occur, specific numbers might improve, but the performance that is really important will worsen.

While some of the most egregious examples of measurement dysfunction in the history of business were at companies like Enron, WorldCom, and Tyco, its more mundane manifestations are being played out virtually every day in almost every organization around the globe. Because of the failure to address the root causes of the problem, most organizations are full of examples of measurement used for self-aggrandizement, self-promotion, and self-protection; measurement used to justify pet projects or to maintain the status quo; and measurement used to prove, rather than improve. Although the more routine cases of dysfunctional measurement might not appear to be very serious individually, the collective consequences of small doses of measurement dysfunction can be profound.

## A Major Cause of Measurement Dysfunction

Probably the biggest problem with measurement is not the flaws in the system, but with the consequences that so often follow flawed measurement. There are two major types of measurement, based on how they are used:

1. *Informational measurement*—measurement used for informational purposes
2. *Motivational measurement*—measurement used for rewards and punishment

When measurement is used as a source of information for organizational members to improve management and the work that is done, it is enormously valuable. However, when measures are tightly linked with rewards or the threat of punishment, the informational value of the measurement becomes subordinated to its use for inducing people to exert more effort. This is where the major problems begin.

Most organizations have very strong contingencies that tell employees, either explicitly or implicitly, "If you do this (behavior) or achieve this (result), you will get this (reward, punishment)." Because, in most organizations, behavior and results can't be directly observed, these performance expectations are operationalized by how they are measured. The performance measures become the way to achieve rewards and to avoid punishment. No matter how many other things might be measured, what is rewarded or punished becomes the focal point.

Striving for rewards is one of the most important aspects of life and work. But when rewards are at the end of the line, measurement becomes a means to that end. Furthermore, the greater the rewards that are offered, the less attention is paid to the information that measurement can provide. When the focus is on the carrot, it's difficult to see anything else! And human beings are very adept at doing whatever it takes to get a reward. Because measurement is so powerful, especially when coupled with contingent rewards, measurement dysfunctions are quite prevalent and widespread. Furthermore, when people are being rewarded by the existing measurement system, they will resist any changes that will reduce their rewards, even if the changes are in the best interest of the organization.

## How Rewards Increase the Potential for Measurement Dysfunction

The weaknesses of most measurement systems together with the need to base rewards on measurement cause a lot of measurement dysfunction. As Frederick Reichheld explains, "Many companies are shooting themselves in both feet with their rewards systems. They pay on results that are easy to measure rather than on the right results."[2] I could literally fill this book with examples of the dysfunctions that can and do happen when rewards become too closely linked with the wrong performance measures.

One of my favorite stories comes from the world of sports. Vasili Alexeyev, a famous Russian super-heavyweight weight lifter, was offered an incentive for every world record he broke. The result of this contingent measurement was that he kept breaking world records *a gram or two at a time* to maximize his reward payout! Can you imagine what would happen in almost any business organization if the measures and rewards encouraged that sort of behavior?

There is little doubt that striving for rewards affects the way we respond to measurement. When individual people or groups are highly incented, the measurement system becomes a tug-of-war between opposing interests: those who are trying to do the best for the organization, and those who want to do the best for themselves. But even "doing the best for the organization" is based on the interpretation of whatever measures are being used. Given the defects in almost every measurement system, strong rewards are bound to significantly increase the probability that these defects will be used for personal benefit and give rise to measurement dysfunction.

While you might find some of the following examples of dysfunctional measurement unbelievable—even *unbelievably stupid*, at least in retrospect—sadly these situations are all true and surprisingly common:

• A manager of a fast-food restaurant striving to achieve an award for attaining a perfect 100 percent on the restaurant's "chicken efficiency" measure (the ratio of how many pieces of chicken sold to the number thrown away) did so by waiting until the chicken was ordered before cooking it. He won the award, but drove the restaurant out of business because of the long wait times.

• A company's measures showed a near-perfect delivery record, yet some 50 percent of customers complained of their products arriving late. To attain rewards the company had adopted a measure of on-time delivery that only reflected whether the product had *left* its plant on-time.

• An automobile industry executive explained that to receive his quarterly bonuses "all that mattered was meeting production quotas and getting the cars out of the factory." What happened after that was somebody else's problem.

• In the race to meet revenue goals and get their commissions, salespeople are often adept at doing whatever they need to do to make the sale, without really caring whether the company is losing money on every sale. This behavior is often justified by totally illogical reasoning, e.g., "We can make up for our negative margins on these sales with higher volumes."

• Many training managers get rewarded and win awards for measuring training effectiveness by the number of training hours and by trainee satisfaction ratings, rather than by any real measure of effectiveness.

• I regularly hear a variation on the following theme: "Here the ultimate goal is not customers—it's the scorecard." One senior manager said, "The people I work with aren't thinking about anything except the bonuses and points they receive at the end of every quarter." Another manager explained it this way: "We don't worry about strategy; we just move our numbers and get rewarded."

Here are some more all-too-common real-life business examples of incentive-based dysfunctional measurement:

• A company reported a 7 percent productivity gain that reflected positively on managerial performance, and earned significant bonuses for the production manager. However, later, long after the bonuses had been awarded, it was discovered that there had actually been a 1 percent productivity *decrease*, when a more widely accepted productivity formula was used.

• A company paid bonuses to its central warehouse spare parts personnel for maintaining low inventory. As a result, necessary spare parts were not available in the warehouse, and operations had to be shut down until the parts could be ordered and delivered.

• Manufacturing companies everywhere have learned how easy it is to hit their quarterly sales revenue targets. They just produce plenty of inventory and offer great prices, huge discounts, unwise rebates, over-promotions, attractive financing or other methods that together are virtually guaranteed to generate a large amount of *unprofitable* sales.

• Purchasing departments are too often measured and rewarded on price discounts negotiated. Purchasing managers know that the best way to get a low price is to buy in large lots, even if production is stuck with huge inventory. Unfortunately, no one is measuring the cash flow that is eaten up by the inventory, the space it takes up, the maintenance it requires, or that much of it is ultimately written off as waste.

• To make its profit numbers at the end of a period, some plants ship high-margin goods ahead of schedule at the expense of the on-time delivery of low-margin goods, and at the risk of dissatisfied customers.

• In order to win awards and certificates, some companies have developed quality bureaucracies that contribute more to loss than to profit or quality. Companies spend enormous amounts of money for elaborate preparations for audit team and examiner visits. Research has shown that 80–90 percent of ISO certifications are not cost-effective in improving quality. One company spent 14,000 labor hours to prepare an award application.

• Rather than investing in better performance, many companies meet their numbers by selling off valuable assets, often at fire-sale prices, and go to great lengths to get as much "milk" as they can from their "cash cows."

As these examples illustrate, people tend to do what they are paid to do—even if it's the wrong things. When managers and employees are striving for rewards—anything from "employee of the month" to a pay raise or stock options—they will often revert to self-serving behaviors, even when they know the behaviors are harming the customer, the company, or both. Even when there is minimal dysfunction, very rarely does measurement with strong incentives lead to healthy outcomes or continuous improvement.

People tend to behave in their own self-interest, especially when their self-interest is being generously rewarded. British business journalist Philip Slater adds, "Getting people to chase money . . . produces nothing except people chasing money."[3] And others I know have described highly incented people as "coin operated"—certainly not the kind of response to measurement that most smart business people want. But it's not just greed that makes people respond that way.

## Fear Also Induces Measurement Dysfunction

Incentives and rewards aren't the only organizational influences that encourage measurement dysfunction. This is particularly true for the majority of employees who are more likely to encounter sticks than carrots. Fear is a major cause of measurement dysfunction, as many employees become hapless victims of a measurement system over which they have no control.

Negative measurement messages abound in most organizations:

"You're 20 percent behind on this week's shipments."
"Customer complaints are up 8 percent."
"This project is $128,000 over budget."
"We can't afford to record another accident."

Messages such as these are more likely to elicit negative reactions, rather than problem-solving behaviors. This is particularly true when employees see the threat potentially affecting their job security. Much traditional measurement focuses on inducing employees to meet targets with an actual or implied threat attached.

Negative pressure tends to compel people to do whatever it takes in order to comply with measured performance expectations. Goals or targets, in and of themselves, are not bad; it depends on how they are used. According to quality guru W. Edwards Deming, when faced with measurement targets, an untold number of companies give their employees direction such as the following: "Make this quarter look good. Ship everything on hand at the end of the month (or quarter). Never mind its quality; mark it shipped. Show it as accounts receivable."[4] Forced compliance with what most employees know is wrong robs them of pride in workmanship, diminishes intrinsic motivation, and reduces commitment to the organization.

If avoiding failure means attaining a particular score, then people are good at doing what is necessary to achieve that score. Employees learn that they must do whatever it takes to make the numbers, and that the ends justify the means. W. Edwards Deming has explained that people will do what they need to do to meet their targets, "even if they have to destroy the enterprise to do so." As someone once said to me, "Never underestimate how clever frightened human beings can be when faced with a numerical target."

In many cases, employees will meet the letter of a law, but violate its spirit; or they will grudgingly do *just enough* to stay out of trouble and keep managers off their backs; this is what is referred to as "passive resistance" or "malicious compliance," which are very common reactions when people are forced to make their numbers—*or else*. Lastly, this type of measurement not only encourages mindless conformity, but it also tends to put a cap on performance—as people commonly reach their goal or quota, and then stop. When you push people, they will do one of two things: They will go in the direction that you push them, or they will push back. Unfortunately, both situations often lead to negative behaviors, and damage to the organization as a whole.

One of the most egregious examples of the negative use of measurement is the production manager at a large manufacturing plant who, with considerable insight into the controlling power of measurement, posted the names and productivity levels of employees who were performing *below standard* outside the cafeteria on what he referred to as "the wall of shame." The productivity targets were met in record time, but every other production indicator (including quality and safety) suffered, as did morale—and you can bet that performance measurement wasn't enthusiastically embraced in this plant.

Here are some other examples of fear-induced measurement dysfunction:

• Plants refusing to receive shipments of raw materials at the end of each month, so that month-end inventory targets will be met—even if production suffers and customer orders are not filled.

• Workers reporting "pallets loaded" as a major measure of productivity, whether the pallet contains one or fifty items.

• Airline crews routinely miscoding takeoff or landing delays to avoid being blamed for them; luggage handlers leaving bags on the tarmac once they were unloaded, since they were being measured on the time taken to *unload* bags.

• Plant employees shipping products before customers' desired delivery dates in order to reduce inventory, and make their numbers.

• Companies rotating inventories to various plants right before audits were taken, making it appear that inventory levels are at appropriate levels—when they really aren't.

• Companies shipping incomplete orders to make critical on-time delivery dates, or sacrificing one very important late shipment for the sake of others that might be delivered on-time.

Do these things sound illogical? People often behave in seemingly illogical ways when they feel that the system of measurement is stacked against them. And, regardless of the organizational consequences, they will do whatever it takes to ensure that the results do not have a negative impact on their jobs, their careers, or their income. Here are a few more examples:

• Help desk agents being measured on the number of calls they handle and on time taken to resolve customer issues have been "spectacularly successful" in cutting customers off before their issues are actually resolved, and prematurely closing cases. They didn't do these things to be rude, but because they were only doing what the measurement system is telling them to do.

• Software quality inspectors reporting *many* defects—even if it means debating whether every small problem is truly a defect—because they are being rated on the *number* of defects they find, while those whose performance evaluation depends on how many defects *inspectors* find in their products fudge the data, spend excessive time perfecting the product before releasing it for inspection, or do whatever they can to avoid inspections altogether.

• More egregious is employees under-reporting (and even hiding) accident data, because "accident-free days" or "lack of recordable incidents" are being measured, and "unsafe employees" being identified rather than being encouraged to find out what happened and therefore reducing future accidents.

• A health management organization was successful in meeting its commitment to reducing the number of people on hospital waiting lists by pressuring doctors to treat smaller problems before larger ones.

• We are all familiar with the practice of booking sales *at the right time* to make a quota this year or next. Salespeople are notorious for delaying processing orders if they have already made their quota or will fail to do so, so they can have an additional sale in the next period.

• And there is the common practice of pre-paying vendors so that budget money is not lost or so that expenses are booked in a previous period.

## Measuring the Wrong Things

Under conditions of both strong reward and strong threat, it is very common for organizations to measure the wrong things. Sometimes this is due to intentional malfeasance, but most of the time it is due to lack of knowledge about the system that is being measured. In most cases, those involved genuinely believe that they are doing the right thing for the organization, but coming up with the right measures of performance is no easy task. Too much reliance on numbers typically leads management to manage what is easiest to quantify—causing people to do what *you count*, not necessarily *what counts*. And, ease of measurement and triviality are highly correlated.

The measurement "hall of shame" is full of organizations that do a *good job* of producing "results" on the *wrong measures* of success. For example:

• A hotel chain responding to a cash flow crisis by mercilessly cutting costs when it should have been focusing on occupancy rate. This resulted in a short-term increase in cash, but a further deterioration of the business.

• A retail store chain that wanted to increase customer satisfaction using a "smile index" to measure employees on the extent to which they smiled at customers. Customers knew the smiles were phony, and the morale of employees, forced into unnatural acts, plummeted.

• Stores measured on product variety carried thirteen different toasters (even though two of them produced 85 percent of sales), and their sports department carried forty different fishing reels—contributing to high costs and low profits.

• Call center measures are most commonly used to drive quick response and low costs, rather than customer insight and cross-sales to grow the business. Ironically, by the existing measurement system, the faster they hang up on customers, the better their performance!

• One company was measuring everything related to production, but failed to measure anything related to delivery to customers.

And we all know how many dot-com companies went out of business because their focus was on the number of website visits and not on revenue or profits.

Dysfunctional measurement is often caused by organizations doing the *wrong things* for the *right reasons*. In order to reduce customer wait time, an insurance company, known for its customer-focus, invested in a device to measure average customer wait time for each call center team. They mounted a digital scoreboard above the office cubicles for all to see. This caused employees to get their customers off the phone quickly, even if their issues had not been completely resolved, just so that the customers in the queue wouldn't have to wait! It also compromised customer service behaviors (like empathy for a customer who had recently experienced a death in the family). To his credit, when he realized the problem, the CEO immediately acknowledged it and replaced the "wait time" measure with one that measured the percentage of customers who completed their business on the first call, with no need for follow-up.

## Measuring "Looking Good" Rather Than "Being Good"

Because of measurement system weaknesses, measurement is particularly flawed and often quite subjective—especially in the areas of nonfinancial and intangible measurement in support functions and relating to knowledge work. When organizations have difficulty identifying and measuring what is really important, many functions, and the employees in them, begin to believe that the most important thing is to "look good," so that they appear to be effective and successful. The operant question is: "How good can I make myself, or my function, look?"

We have all experienced the "uncanny" ability of organizations and individuals to perform well, just at the right time, when they are being measured. A recent experience illustrates this well. At a medical clinic I occasionally have to visit for check-ups and routine health care, on-time performance and friendliness improved dramatically because service quality was being measured. However, after the "measurement exercise," service reverted back to its normal low levels. You probably have your own favorite stories of a similar nature.

Too many measurement systems are designed and used to placate top executives. This is why measurement so often degenerates into a contest of appearances—too often a *beauty* contest. Rather than aiming at managing and improving the real business and focusing on the customer, measurement is often used to sell and posture internally. And, people in these organizations become very skilled at using deficient measurement systems to help cast themselves and their business units in the best possible light, pursuing the appearance of success (rather than real success), highlighting the good news, and hiding bad news—at least until the truth becomes known, usually long after the measurements have been recorded and, even more insidiously, after the responsible persons have been promoted or have moved on.

We all know people who have used the measurement system to get ahead. In such an organization, often the "best employees" are the ones that are *best* at putting their "best foot forward" on performance appraisals. On this topic, one colleague remarked: "Organizations must realize that people with shinier shoes don't walk faster!"

As one would expect, in such an environment there is also an enormous amount of filtered and distorted measurement information, whereby great pains are taken to share only the good news and suppress the bad news—after all, nobody wants to be "the messenger who gets shot." Even accountants are encouraged to show the numbers in the most favorable light. As former Securities & Exchange Commission chairman Arthur Levitt explained, "Corporations were playing with their earnings calculations until they arrived at the best possible numbers."[5]

In this kind of "look good" environment, *activity measures* abound: number of employees hired, number of training programs implemented, number of help desk calls, number of machines repaired, number of inspections, number of audits, number of invoices processed, number of sales calls, number of clinical trials, number of patent applications, etc. Activity measures often produce an illusion of progress, as well as what has been called "the activity trap."

Another example of "look good" measurements is the huge investments in technology and improvement projects that organizations can't or won't measure. It is amazing how often the actual costs of these projects far exceed the promised benefits, but when the measure of success is that the project implementation was "successfully completed on-time and on-budget," nobody knows or wants to acknowledge that they are actually destroying value. Project champions are often good at making bad projects look good by creatively overestimating benefits and underestimating costs.

Without any standard approach to measuring nonfinancial value creation and intangibles, it is easy to "declare success" on whatever criteria one wishes to use. Organizations everywhere are finding it easy, in the short-term at least, to look good on the wrong measures of success!

## Suboptimization

"Suboptimization" is the practice of focusing on, or making changes to, one component of a total system, without consideration of the impact on the whole. This leads to the optimization of the one component—that is, the individuals and functions will do well on their own measures of success—but it leads to damage to others, and the organization as a whole is likely to suffer. In fact, most organizational measurement systems are made up of many disparate measurement "silos." These "mini measurement systems" (such as sales measurement, marketing measurement, or finance measurement) actually work at cross-purposes—attempting to optimize their own numbers—rather than optimizing the whole.

Nothing exemplifies both measurement dysfunction and suboptimization as much as the abuse of the annual budgeting process. Although it doesn't have to be this way, organizational budgeting tends to devolve into a time-consuming, adversarial "tournament" in which each group competes for its "fair share" of the organization's budget pie—too often resulting in bloated budgets and inflexible performance commitments. Budgeting, at least the way it is typically done today, is more of a political activity than a business function—disconnected from strategic plans, with the not-so-hidden agenda of gaining the maximum share of resources for one's unit or department (including camouflaged "pots of resources" that can be drawn upon when needed), committing to as little as possible in return ("so that we can make our numbers"), and then spending as much of the budget as possible ("so we don't get less money next year"). According to former CEO of General Electric, Jack Welch, "The budget is the bane of corporate America. It should never have existed." As business journalist Simon Caulkin has said, "It is no exaggeration to say that budgets corrupt."[6] Furthermore, because it is so central to operations, too often, it's the budget that gets managed, rather than the business. At the end of the year, too often the biggest winners are those who have destroyed the most value!

Another classic case of suboptimization is the proliferation of projects in organization. In *Connecting the Dots*, Benko and McFarland explain, "Individually, each project may appear be to be adding value to the organization. But when projects are examined together, a different picture emerges. Some may be working at cross-purposes, others may be needlessly duplicating each other, still other projects may be aiming to meet outmoded objectives—but all are competing for scarce resources."[7] Measuring pieces of an interrelated system separately will always lead to suboptimization. Here are some other, quite common examples of suboptimization:

• Salespeople in a manufacturing company took orders from customers at the end of the quarter, but some customers couldn't pay for all of the product they had been "encouraged" to order. Because the unpaid portion was not delivered by the customer's desired date, all of the orders got counted as "late deliveries." In this case, everybody was doing their own thing to meet their own measurements. Sales never properly flagged the questionable credit-worthiness of the customers but could have cared less, because it wasn't part of their scorecard!

• Marketing departments often generate an enormous number of leads for their scorecard that result in few sales—and they keep getting away with it because there is no way to measure "how qualified" the leads are.

• After a cost audit, a company cut its inter-building mail runs by 50 percent, thus saving the mail room a significant amount of operational cost. These cuts resulted in functional groups supplementing the mail runs by having their own personnel deliver mail from building to building, at a cost far exceeding the mail room's savings. "Optimizing" mail room expenses actually increased the total cost to the organization.

Organizations today are bastions of suboptimization because they are full of functionally-focused, unaligned measures.

## Cheating

When striving for rewards in sports or in business, "players" will often do whatever they can get away with to win. In sports, we see players committing fouls or faking catches or injuries—hoping that the deception won't be detected by the distracted referees. Of course "cheating" comes in all sizes. Most cheating in business is so minor that we have come to accept it as normal—we have even come to call it "gaming." For example, project teams are known to build in sufficient slack in each task estimate so that they are virtually guaranteed of meeting project milestones. And, almost everyone has been involved in the practice of setting goals as low as possible, so that they can be exceeded.

In the recent bestselling book, *Freakonomics*, authors Levitt and Dubner ask and answer the question: "Who cheats? Well, just about anyone, if the stakes are right."[8] In other words, when the motive is strong enough, almost everyone will game the measurement system.

People in organizations become very good at managing to the numbers, reporting the numbers, "tweaking" the numbers, fudging the numbers (if necessary), and obtaining acceptable scores almost every quarter. All of these tactics are perceived as acceptable, while *real cheating*—whatever it is—isn't. Cable pioneer Craig McCaw said: "Lots of companies manage their earnings, and I think it's okay within reason." General Electric CEO Jeff Immelt has also endorsed the practice. But consulting firm Stern Stewart demurs: "When decent men endorse indecent behavior something is terribly wrong." And they add, "Fudging financial results has become so ingrained in corporate culture that even ethical business leaders have succumbed to the temptation to mislead the public."[9]

At the extreme of cheating is criminal activity. Of course, it is often difficult to determine where cheating the measurement system becomes "crime." But, whether cheating or crime, this kind of measurement dysfunction will continue to exist and seriously impede organizational effectiveness. We are all aware of examples of the truly egregious forms of cheating—actual criminal activity—mostly second-hand through the news stories that play themselves out in courtrooms throughout the world. But here are some fairly common examples of routine measurement cheating:

• Experienced case workers in a government agency work on the easiest cases and leave the difficult ones for the inexperienced staff members, because they are measured on the "number of cases closed."

• When required to have a succession plan in place in order to be promoted themselves, divisional executives at a company reverted to what has been dubbed "The Roger Jones Phenomenon." When they had trouble developing their own successors they simply put down the name of one of the company's superstar performers. However, when the plans were rolled up, a single employee, Roger Jones, was found to be the potential successor for most of the key jobs at the company!

• To reach their numbers, inflate their stock price, and get their bonuses, many company managements rely on "aggressive" accounting, the selective application of accounting principles to achieve better looking results, including earning management, premature revenue recognition, deferring expenses, use of special charges, capitalizing operating costs rather than expensing them, and other deceptive, if not illegal, practices. Sunbeam Corporation's accounting gimmickry is legendary. The company took a huge restructuring charge ($337 million before taxes), so that the next year could show a fabulous sales and earning rebound.

• While many companies inflate profits to drive a higher stock price, one highly-regulated company reported *lower profits* than they had actually earned to "smooth out" their year-over-year profit picture to avoid government scrutiny.

• Software inspectors have been known to plant bugs in software programs, because they are measured on finding a certain number of them.

• A company instituted a productivity measure for stenographers based on number of keystrokes and was surprised to find some stenographers tapping random keys or the space bar while eating lunch. I don't know why they were surprised!

## Measuring Too Much

Today, some organizations seem to take measurement to an extreme. However, measuring *too much* can be as dysfunctional as measuring *too little*. One employee described the situation in her organization in the following way: "We measure everything that moves, but little that matters!" Elliott Jaques explains why in *Executive Leadership*: "In a play-it-safe environment, there is a tendency to measure everything."[10]

It seems as if every function, every area, and even every team in an organization has its own scorecard, instrument panel, and idiosyncratic measures of success. That means that many organizations can have literally hundreds of different sets of measures.

Michael Hammer shares the following comment from a corporate manager about excessive and unnecessary measurement: "We measure too much and get far too little for what we measure."[11]

Too often measurement becomes an end in itself, disconnected from the larger purposes of the organization. In one company, the R&D department was told to create a list of measures, but to limit them to one page. In order to comply, those who were in charge of measurement in that department crammed approximately sixty disjointed "innovation measures" onto a single page, an exercise described by one measurement expert as "useless and probably harmful."[12]

As a result of today's data collection mania, some companies have become buried in their own "data mines." Furthermore, measuring the wrong things or unnecessary things brings with it high costs of measurement, both in terms of actual cost and opportunity cost. Certainly, there is enough real work to do today without inundating employees with needless data that confuses more than clarifies.

It is a sad fact that much of the measurement data being collected today is never acted upon because organizations don't know what to do with it. As Dow and Cook say, "If you don't translate measures into action, you may as well throw them out the window."[13] For example, one supermarket chain collected 340 million different data points per week, but used only 20 percent of the data.

Why are leaders so reluctant to change the measurement system, even if it is not working? Because they are deeply invested in the existing measurement system and being rewarded by it, they don't know how, and they are afraid that they might create an even more dangerous monster—better the devil that you know!

## Dysfunctional Measurement and Employees

The problems discussed above are not the actual measurements themselves but rather how they are used and interpreted by employees. Art Kleiner explains the seemingly irrational behavior of many employees this way: "Measure something and the organization moves to produce it—especially if you set up incentives accordingly."[14]

Given the examples cited, it is no wonder that employees are cynical about measurement and its positive potential. For most, the promise of the positive power of measurement remains just an unrealized promise. But those who avoid or criticize measurement are really just reacting to the way they have traditionally experienced it. In the next chapter, we will explore the reasons why people feel so strongly about measurement and why it is so often perceived as "the enemy" at work.

# CHAPTER 3

# Why Measurement Goes Bad

Why is it, considering all the incredible positive power and functional potential of measurement, that performance measurement seems to go so wrong? Why is it that good people in organizations so often do such detrimental things as those we saw in Chapter 2? This chapter provides the answers to these questions, and shows you how you can reduce measurement dysfunction and cynicism and begin to move your company toward a more positive measurement future.

## Motive and Opportunity

There are two factors that contribute to measurement dysfunction—and, unfortunately, usually also translate into negative, or undesirable, behaviors. The first is *opportunity*. Opportunity is presented by flaws endemic in virtually every measurement system. Because measures are surrogates for actual performance, performance measurement will always be imperfect—and these imperfections will only increase as progressive organizations experiment with new measures in the future. The kinds of measurement dysfunctions described in the previous chapter are negative side-effects of defective measurement systems. However, the defects themselves are not the biggest part of the problem, although they do "open the door" to misbehaviors.

Like flaws in computer software programs, *people* can use defects for nefarious purposes (such as "hacking"), or they can report the defects so that they can be fixed. A positive example is the Linux operating system, where the community of users have been working together collaboratively to "plug the holes" in the software, rather than to exploit them. Of course, they recognize that there will always be hackers—the question is how many. So it is with measurement system defects, which can similarly promote either dysfunctional behavior—unintentional or intentional—or lead to continuous measurement system improvement.

The second factor is *motive*, which determines whether intentional dysfunctional behavior will occur. Motive is the "reason *why*" people take advantage of the weaknesses in the measurement system, and in order for this kind of intentional measurement dysfunction to occur, there must be *both* opportunity *and* motive.

When I was growing up in New York City, there were self-service newsstands outside various shops, and, rather than go inside and pay, people would take a newspaper and place money right on the newsstand. That money was readily available for other passers-by to steal, but, for the most part, they didn't. There was opportunity, but not motive. The prevailing "honor system" caused people *not* to exploit the opportunity.

In any system, those who stand to "win" or "lose" because of the defects in the system certainly have an incentive to use the system for their own personal benefit—but the questions is: What makes them do so? Why did the people in New York City almost never steal from the newsstands and why do the Linux users focus on fixing the problems with the operating system, rather than exploiting its weaknesses? The answers that follow will provide insight into *why* dysfunctional measurement occurs—and why it is endemic in most organizations today.

As revealed in the examples presented in Chapter 2, there are pressures and incentives that too often provide a strong motive for people to exploit the defects in the system. This is exacerbated by a "conspiracy of silence" that results in the problems not being detected and fixed. What is so incongruous about this situation is that almost nobody really *wants* dysfunctional measurement—not even those who benefit from it.

Few people wake up in the morning and think about how they can manipulate the measurement system of their organization for personal benefit. Most of us don't scheme about how we can defraud our employers. But, sadly, most of us have been guilty of unintentional, if not intentional, "measurement crimes." Have you ever done anything at work that you *knew* wasn't the best thing for the organization? Of course, you have. We all have. However, you have probably also done many other things *unintentionally* that were not best for the organization.

Whether measurement dysfunctions will occur has less to do with the *number* of defects and more with how people *respond* to the defects. As with the Linux users, the positive response to flawed measurement is to acknowledge the limitations, fix the problem or report it to those who can fix it, and contribute to continuously improving the system. The negative response is to ignore the limitations, take advantage of the defects for personal or functional benefit, avoid reporting the problems (because you are benefiting from it), and fail to contribute to the solution. When measurement goes bad, it too often devolves into a "game" by people who have the knowledge and position to take advantage of the measurement system flaws.

Too often this gaming tends to pit employees, managers, and the organization against each other in an adversarial relationship. As Leonard Greenhalgh explains, "When the relationship is adversarial, people will be motivated to outwit the control system."[1]

## How People Experience Measurement

People tend to refer to what they perceive as negative and threatening as the enemy. When I ask participants in my workshops about their personal measurement experiences, the enmity is obvious. The negative responses far outnumber—and, more importantly, outweigh—the positive ones. Even more distressing is that, even when I probe deeply, most people can't even think of *any* positive experiences!

We first come in contact with measurement at a very early age. For many of us, parental measurement resulted in punishment more often than reward. In school, measurement meant tests. Teachers measured our value by the number of mistakes we made, usually with red marks highlighting our mistakes and points subtracted from our scores. In fact, most people have years and years of miserable memories about being "measured" by parents, teachers, employers, bankers, credit agencies, government bureaucrats, doctors, and a host of others. By the time we attain adulthood, we have had hundreds (or thousands) of measurement experiences.

Almost everybody has, at one time or another, experienced *negative measurement* used to expose negative things—errors, defects, accidents, cost overruns, out of stock items, exceptions of all kinds—and to trigger negative emotions—like fear, threat, fault-finding, blame, and punishment. They also know how dangerous measurement can be in the hands of those who don't use it well or benevolently. Although negative measurement can get results, it is mostly short-term compliance, and it leaves a bad taste in people's mouths.

Almost every employee, initially at least, perceives performance measurement from a traditional "command-and control," top-down perspective: "These are your measures; follow them!" Too often measurement is used to control, justify, audit, and determine *who* went wrong, rather than *what* went wrong—to find fault rather than to provide useful feedback or trigger positive reinforcement. Unfortunately, employees often associate measurement with time-and-motion studies, being judged, humiliating comparisons, and a restrictive work environment—none of which are inherently linked to performance measurement. Most employees naturally assume that data has a strong likelihood to be used against them.

There is so much negativity associated with measurement that we often fail to consider the positive side of measurement: the many times measurement has guided us safely to our destinations in cars and airplanes, or helped us manage our finances, solve problems, or maintain or regain our health. Most people don't associate positive experiences with measurement, while they tend to remember negative ones.

## Employees' Attitudes Toward Measurement at Work

For most employees, measurement is viewed, at best, as a "necessary evil." At worst, it is seen as a menacing force that is greeted with about the same enthusiasm as a root canal! When most people think of performance measurement at work, they tend to think of being watched, being timed, and being appraised. It only takes one snakebite to make someone fearful of snakes for the rest of their lives—and many people have been bitten more than once by measurement at work. As a result, they tend to see it as a nonproductive cost, as bureaucratic overhead.

The environment of measurement tends to have a major influence on how measurement is perceived by employees and therefore how they respond *emotionally* to it. Even if people aren't directly involved in measurement, almost everyone *feels* strongly about it. And yet, very few people *talk* about it—which, as we will see, is one of the primary problems with the way performance measurement is implemented in most organizations.

As previously discussed, measurement is powerful, and—for better or for worse—*what is measured tends to get managed.* Most employees also seem to intuitively understand that measurement is important because their success, their rewards, their budgets, their punishments, and a host of other things ultimately are, directly or indirectly, based on it.

At work, people are typically being measured *against* goals imposed upon them ("These are the targets you are responsible for hitting." "I will be measuring you on . . .") and forced into rating categories they feel they don't deserve. Managers often go ballistic when they see data points that fall below a particular level, and, instead of viewing this as a problem-solving opportunity, they take preemptive action, and sometimes cause heads to roll. Numbers are used, often without being fully understood, to compare departments, teams, or individuals; and employees react by following the numbers—even if it means going in the wrong directions. The negative use of measurement is deeply engrained in most cultures.

As John Sedden describes the conventional scope of measurement: "Managers are preoccupied with the number of calls they've got coming in, the service levels they're achieving, they monitor their people's adherence to scripts and procedures and they perform inspections to make sure people have 'done as they should.' Managers call these inspections 'quality monitoring,' but most people realize it has little to do with quality."[2]

Just consider how the employees in your organization would react if a group came by and said, "We're from the Measurement Committee and we're here to help you do your work better." How enthusiastically do you think they would be received?

In recent years, measurement has become increasingly associated with the manipulation of results as evidenced by the number of accounting scandals. But nothing represents the context of measurement so negatively as the annual performance appraisal, one of the most despised aspects of organizational life—which, even when it occurs only once a year, typically casts a pall on work throughout the entire year.

Peter Hunter agrees that the kind of behavior he sees occurring in employee performance measurement is often quite horrendous: "At school this behavior is called bullying. . . . At work this behavior is what we have to put up with every day if we want to continue being paid."[3] This certainly doesn't add up to an environment that is likely to encourage openness and transparency. On the contrary, a colleague once expressed it this way: "For some reason, the mere sound of the word 'measurement' coming from someone's mouth causes me to run far and fast in the opposite direction."

These painful experiences of arbitrary and capricious instances of measurement linger long after the event has passed, and they only serve to reinforce the feeling that measurement is not just a negative force, but something to be avoided altogether. Indeed, in a recent survey of 2,600 working people by Mercer Human Resources Consulting, only 29 percent of respondents reported that they felt they had been rewarded for good performance in their performance appraisal.[4] That leaves *a lot* of people who experienced the negative side of measurement on the job—*up close and personal*. Of course these fears and bad experiences aren't universal—some people are very comfortable with measurement and others know how to benefit from the flaws in the system—but they are widespread enough to make it very difficult to implement effective performance measurement.

Despite all the so-called employee performance measurements, few managers really know how their employees are performing, or how to enhance their talent assets. And, on the employees' side, few know how they are performing or how to do a better job. Almost no one knows what their "score" is on a monthly, much less weekly or daily basis. Bottom line: In most organizations, "people measurement" is in the pits—at a time when it should be leading the pack.

## The Context of Measurement

In a previous book, *SuperMotivation: A Blueprint for Energizing Your Organization From Top to Bottom*, I made the distinction between work "tasks" (the specific technical activities performed) and the "context" (everything else that surrounds and affects the task).[5] Measurement is a task. But when most people think of measurement at work, it is much more than the technical *task* that they are reacting to. It is the task, *plus* the context.

The prime example I used in *SuperMotivation* to illustrate this point is the task of using an elongated instrument to get a small round object into a hole 18 times. Clearly most of you will recognize this "task" as golf, one of the most popular games in the world. Why is it that such a task would probably be quite painful if performed *at work*, while millions of people spend incredible amounts of time and money happily performing the same task on golf courses around the world?

It's a matter of *context*. Like the "small-object insertion task" described above, measurement is viewed positively or negatively depending on the context. The prevailing negative attitudes toward measurement create the *motive* and provoke the accompanying negative behaviors in response to it. In a positive context, there is no motive to cheat; in a negative one, there tends to be plenty of motive to manipulate the flaws in the system. If you felt that golf was being used against you, I am sure that even if you love the game, your orientation toward it would be quite different.

Most of the attitude problems that cause people to take advantage of system flaws for personal advantage are largely due to a handful of management practices that wreak havoc on the best-intentioned performance measurement system. Many of these negative attitudes about measurement at work are due to its association (and confusion) with evaluation. Few people, including corporate executives, know the difference between *measurement* and *evaluation*—and there *is* a very significant difference!

## Confusing Measurement and Evaluation

The word "evaluation" is really composed of three component parts: "e," "value," and "ation." The central element of the concept of evaluation is *value*. When you evaluate, you *place a value* on whatever you are evaluating. Most people don't mind measuring, or even being measured; they just don't like *being measured upon*. And that's what most evaluation is—having a value placed by an external agent on us and our performance.

The outcome of an evaluation is a *judgment*. Evaluation is essentially about making value judgments. People don't like being judged—especially when they are suspicious about the fairness of the evaluation process and the motives of those who are doing the judging. As we go through life we get bombarded by negative measurements—too short, too fat, not aggressive enough, too slow, and so on. This is why Eliyahu Goldratt says that "the issue of measurement is probably the most sensitive issue in an organization."[6]

Although measurement can be a valuable input into evaluation, it should never be equated with it. As soon as judgment is introduced into a situation, there will be almost inevitably be some degree of defensiveness. Because of the widespread use of evaluation in organizations, many people fear that any measurements can be used against them. Because of previous experiences, people are often suspicions about management's motives. What does this mean for me? How will they be using the data? In addition, evaluation has become inexorably linked with demotivating organizational processes and issues such as organizational politics, perceived unfairness, and internal competition for scarce resources. It is unfortunate that measurement is more often viewed as an instrument of control than of empowerment. But, there is nothing about measurement that is inherently that way.

Measurement should actually be a *nonjudgmental* process of collecting, analyzing, and, most importantly, using information for understanding whatever is being measured. Measurement is inherently neutral. No matter what the function of measurement, it should be based on a desire to *better understand* what is happening—and, at least initially—without judging. Effective measurement should precede any judgment or decision-making—although it all-too-rarely does. In order to be credible, evaluation should always be based on a solid foundation of measurement.

Evaluation without good measurement data is very likely to be highly subjective and judgmental, and that's what most people confuse with measurement. And that's why so many people hide from measurement. Judgment makes people feel vulnerable. Says James Champy, author of *Reengineering the Corporation*, "People want to shield themselves from judgment, deflect it . . . muddle it . . . anything to avoid standing in the glare of a clear, unequivocal measure of their worth."[7] And, who can blame them when measurement is used to drive an organization's system of rewards and—its system of punishments.

When faced with the choice of either measuring something or evaluating it, we will almost always bypass good measurement in favor of evaluation. Why? Because evaluation is very natural and measurement is not. It is not surprising which one people use as the default. Making snap judgments is easy, while undertaking systematic measurement is hard work.

We may even believe that, as managers, it's our job to make rapid judgments—no matter how uninformed they may be—and we may encourage those who work for us to do the same. This is a mistake. For as long as measurement is associated with judgment, there will be fear. And as long as there is fear, measurement will be always be viewed as a negative force.

## Purpose

The purpose for which measurement is used is the single most powerful determinant of employee reaction to it. Is it being used to provide real understanding, helpful feedback, and to foster learning and improvement—or for justification, reporting, judgment, control, and reward?

Most people in organizations are accountable for hitting targets. The reaction to hitting targets tends to be quite different from striving to improve one's score. Hitting targets leads to a command-and-control orientation and compliance, especially when there are rewards or penalties associated with it. In such an environment, everything is focused on hitting the desired number—often by whatever means are available, even if it means bending the rules.

At a recent CEO summit on innovation, hosted by IBM's Sam Palmisano, Dartmouth University professor Vijay Govindarajan pointed out that one of the biggest mistakes companies may make is tying managers' incentives too directly to specific innovation measures. He warned that linking pay too closely to specific measures may tempt managers to, for instance, achieve a high "percentage of revenue from new products" by encouraging a lot of incremental brand extensions rather than true breakthroughs.[8]

Contrast this with a situation in which the purpose of measurement is to provide high-quality information to assist in learning and improvement. In this latter case, measurement will be perceived as a much more positive force—to enable continuous improvement, rather than just monitor goal achievement (that the target score was attained). Later, in this book, we will discuss the learning purpose of measurement in more detail, and explore how it promises the best long-term benefits.

Measurement tends to be much more positively embraced by the workforce when it is used as a *steering tool*, rather than as a *grading tool*. Unfortunately, measurement has for too long been an instrument of control.

## Disempowerment

If you ask employees and managers in your organization, "How's it going?" how many of them could answer that question with accuracy or confidence? Most of the time, you'll get vague answers, like "Not bad" and "Yeah, we're making progress." But, ask for specifics and most people will be lost. Without good measurement-based feedback, there is simply no way to accurately determine how well individuals or the entire company are performing. Many organizations make the mistake of setting goals without having a way to track their progress, but how can you deliver on what you can't effectively measure? How do you know you are doing well if you don't define upfront what doing "well" means? "We had a very successful . . . (fill in the blank)." How do you know unless there is a measurable goal to compare your performance with?

When people do not feel empowered to succeed, or if the measurement is not perceived to be instrumental to success (such as when the measurement data is not relevant, understood, and timely), these same measurement tools become nagging reminders of a sense of impotence. Like a frustrated golfer or discouraged weight watcher, too many employees view organizational measurement as an ever-present reminder of their inability to win. Clearly, if employees felt confident about the efficacy of measurement, they would seek even more opportunities to keep score!

When people are in a situation in which they feel empowered to change, they will likely feel positive about the measurement associated with it. In contrast, when people are being *compelled* to change or if they are in a situation that is similarly disempowering, they will very likely feel quite negatively about measurement—even if the same measurements are being used.

## The "Motivational" Use of Measurement

The motivational use of measurement is not inherently bad—after all, the measurement system is the foundation of all the other systems, including compensation, rewards, and discipline. Unfortunately, too often it tends to take precedence over the other functions of measurement, such as the informational value of measurement. When you add rewards or the threat of punishment to a measurement system, the informational value of the measurement becomes subordinated to its use for control. Alfie Kohn, in his book *Punished By Rewards*, points out that incentives and rewards can be just as controlling as threats and punishments.[9] If rewards for good performance and penalties for poor performance are too great, it can also encourage situational and inaccurate measurement and reporting, which can negate the accuracy and trustworthiness of the information.

The following is an example of how defective measurement interacts with motivational measurement to cause problems. Let's say that you have a car with a speedometer that isn't working quite right, and you doubt its accuracy. You will very likely keep your speed slightly below the speed limit, use the other traffic to pace yourself, and arrive at your destination safely and close to the schedule. That is the positive response: Knowing the limits of measurement, and adapting your behavior appropriately. However, let's say that you are being rewarded for getting to the destination quickly, or punished if you don't arrive right on time. There would very likely be an incentive for you to err on the high side of speed, and slow down quickly if you see a police car. If you have a radar detector, you will very likely exceed the speed limit until the alarm goes off, and then quickly decelerate. Then you will accelerate again after "the danger" has passed.

This is analogous to what happens too often in an organization with strong rewards and/or threats of punishment. People tend to do what it takes to obtain the reward or to avoid the punishment. Consider how you might respond at work "driving" with a strong incentive and a defective speedometer (measurement system). You will very likely be self-conscious (even paranoid) about your speed, focusing on the prize, perhaps getting tired from playing the "speeding" game, and waste "gas" (or other resources) speeding up and slowing down. It certainly wouldn't be best for your (or your company's) reputation if someone you know (like a customer) happens to see you driving this way. And while this strategy is not necessarily the best one from a "balanced perspective," we all know what wins! I sure wouldn't want to run a business this way. But, unfortunately, this kind of behavior at work occurs every day when highly incented employees strive for their coveted rewards.

## Distrust

Trust is an essential ingredient of effective measurement, and it is currently seriously lacking. If people feel that those in a position of authority over the measurement system are trustworthy, then they will trust measurement. Because of the sensitivity of measurement that we have been discussing, trust is crucial. Fear is often an employee's first reaction to measurement—fear that the measurements will be used against them. Fear is antithetical to trust. David Meador explained that when he was involved in measurement at Chrysler, "To win people's trust, we had to keep measurement away from management."[10]

When people distrust and fail to respect measures, they will have no qualms about ignoring or manipulating them. If people don't trust the measurement system, they are likely to view it as an enemy. For example, a sales executive said that he didn't trust any opportunity in the pipeline below a 90 percent win probability, which means he didn't trust most everything in the pipeline. It's difficult to manage a pipeline, or any measurement system, when you don't trust its content. Measurement doesn't have to be perfect to be trusted. However, there must be honesty. The capabilities, and especially, the limitations of measurement must be openly acknowledged—only then can something be done to improve the situation.

People find all kinds of ways to evade or obstruct a measurement system that they don't like or trust. Here is an important piece of advice I give chief executives: If you try to remove cheating by creating a cheat-proof measurement system, you waste a lot of time and will probably go broke. If you remove the *need* to cheat, then cheating will be much less likely to happen, and it won't cost you anything. It will save you a lot of money and is guaranteed improve your organization in the long run."

## Negative Accountability

The term "accountability" has gotten a bad rap. There should be no fear of accountability, since it is really just the basis for sound management. It is an agreement to be *held to account*. It is more than mere responsibility. I define accountability as *measured commitment*, because you can't have accountability without measurement. This is "positive accountability." Interestingly, the real fear is *not* of accountability, but of the visibility that measurement provides to people who are not accustomed to having to deliver on their commitments.

In contrast, "negative accountability" is when measurement is used to *force* performance and *punish* nonperformance. Because of the flaws in measurement and distrust for those administering it, there is the constant fear that measurement will be misused. When employees do not feel prepared, are poorly enabled, or view the measurement as threatening, they will naturally be fearful of the accountability that measurement provides. In addition, measurable accountability will tend to expose those who have traditionally succeeded because of their ability to hide from, manipulate, or finesse the defective measurement systems.

## Resistance to Measurement

If you ever wondered why so many people are willing to muddle through rather than measure their way to success, the reasons should now not be too hard to understand. Many of the points already raised make it clear why employees are reluctant to use measurement or decide to use it to advance their personal agendas.

When I ask people (even executives) why they often prefer to manage "by the seat of their pants" rather than use measurement, their comments are predictable:

- It's too difficult, time-consuming, and tedious ("It's too much work." "It's boring." "By the time we do the measurement, the data is obsolete.")
- It's someone else's job ("I just leave it to the accountants and other specialists.")
- Lack of understanding ("I don't know what to do with the data.")
- Lack of resources ("I can't do everything!")
- Bad experiences ("We've already tried it, and it never worked before.")
- Lack of accuracy ("I don't trust the data." "It's too subjective." "It's too political.")
- Lack of involvement ("Why should I do it? Nobody cares about my input.")

Some people think that, without measurement, there is no failure. But, in fact, without good measurement, bad measurement will fill the void. And that's just what I see happening in organizations everywhere—the worst of both worlds: bad measurement in a negative context resulting in all kinds of dysfunctional behaviors.

## Opportunity and Motive Revisited

There will always be opportunity for dysfunctional behaviors because performance measurement is inherently flawed and will always be many steps away from perfection. You can go out and plug some of the holes in your technical measurement system, but you won't be able to plug them all. Also, as measures change and evolve, and as new, transformational measures are adopted, there will be new opportunities for people to exercise their personal and functional agendas. So, the solution to measurement dysfunction continues to lie with motive. Reduce the motive, and the opportunities for gaming and cheating won't be nearly as significant and problematical.

In order to realize the potential of performance measurement, organizations will have to do a lot more than improve its technical aspects. It is like any other organizational advance—ultimately it is about the people who need to use the advances. Attempts to advance the technical side, without sufficient attention to the human side, have always failed. Let's not make this mistake yet again!

## The Challenge Ahead

Despite enormous advances in the technical areas of performance measurement (especially in scorecards, dashboards, analytics, and technology support) and some progress on the human side (for example, with Lean and Six Sigma), the "content of measurement" has not changed very much—and neither has the experience of the average employee. For the most part, performance measurement continues to make people feel helpless, rather than empowered. Employees in most organizations are still more likely to receive defect reports, be reprimanded for poor quality, and not have the tools or authority to improve things. Employees are further demoralized when they see how widespread measurement dysfunction still is, with new cases emerging seemingly on a daily basis. Despite the proliferation of scorecards and dashboards, for most employees the company's measures are *management's scorecard,* not theirs. If anything, the numbers are used to tell them why they won't get a pay increase this year. And it should be no great surprise that most employees still don't eagerly embrace performance measurement!

Before moving on to the next chapter, why not try to get a quick "gut check" on how well your organization is truly engaging the hearts and minds of its employees: Ask them about the measures they use, how they are related to the strategic measures of the business, and how they use these measures in their work. Chances are you will get blank stares, or very superficial or dismissive responses.

Despite isolated progress, most companies still have a long way to go to make measurement both useful and relevant to their employees. It is a challenge, but a worthy one. How to start the journey toward positive *transformational* performance measurement is the subject of the next chapter.

# CHAPTER 4

# Beginning the Transformation

We have just left behind some content that was distinctly negative in tone and painted a fairly dismal picture of the current state of performance measurement in most organizations. Despite that, this book carries an extremely optimistic message, starting with this chapter, which gets us onto the transformation path toward realizing the "transformational performance measurement" vision.

In this chapter, I introduce the "Four Keys" that are the foundation for *realizing* the transformational performance measurement vision. Then, in Chapters 5 to 8, I describe each of these keys in detail. In Chapters 9 to 13 I share knowledge and tools that will help your organization achieve and sustain the transformation. As you proceed on the transformation journey laid out in this book, you will continue to gain additional insight and perspective on the transformational potential of performance measurement for your organization.

## The Transformational Vision

The transformational performance measurement is a *visionary* destination that does not yet exist. However, there is a path with some clear markers along the way—especially in the early stages—that will serve as a guide.

Earlier I discussed how transformational measurement leads to improvements in virtually every aspect of organizational performance. In this next section I will be considerably more specific about what transformational measurement might look like.

Let us now consider an organization that is well on its way to the vision, one where all of the functions of performance measurement are being well used; where measurement is relevant, practical, and understandable; where measurement is simplified, making it more usable and less burdensome; and where most of the routine functions of measurement are automated, but where people understand what the numbers represent.

Everyone is involved in performance measurement from the lowest level to the highest level of the organization. All employees have scorecards (a set of measures for their individual work), have a clear line-of-sight between their own scorecards and the measures of the larger functional units or teams, and know how their own measures relate to each next set of measures. As such, they don't need much external feedback, because the feedback is provided by their own scorecard. Employees have continuing personal involvement in creating their own scorecard and are *empowered* to take action on their measurements.

There is extensive interaction around measurement. Everyone realizes that, although measurement is a surrogate for actual performance, it is the only way to "see" what is actually happening and to trace the impact of the performance drivers on desired outcomes. Through the positive use of measurement, employees at all levels have great visibility into virtually everything that is happening and virtually everything that they can impact. They know what to do to make a difference. They realize that performance measurement is not primarily about the numbers, but about providing clearer perception and greater shared insight and knowledge.

New measures appear on scorecards regularly, at least on an experimental basis, to supplement or replace obsolete measures to drive internal and external innovation.

Communication and open discussion of measurement are strongly encouraged. There are regular "dialogue" meetings within teams and among functions to discuss existing measurements, develop actions plans, review measurement frameworks, and consider transformational measurement issues. Employees feel strong ownership in measurement, and they increasingly realize that it is a key to their, and the organization's, success.

Measurement is built into the social fabric of the organization, and is no longer just a program or an add-on. Measurement, which had been programmatic in the past (like Six Sigma), is now infused throughout the culture.

Measurement is less tightly connected with judgment and rewards. Evaluations are much more data based.

There is much more self-management. Managers no longer have to be "supervisors" and are able to focus more on empowerment, providing resources, helping to remove constraints, and on ongoing development and succession planning. Virtually everyone is part of a self-managing high-performing work team, and managers no longer need to micro-manage, because performance is highly visible to everyone.

There is no "tampering," nor are there inconsistent knee-jerk reactions to measurement data. A wide variety of scorecards are in use, even into the extended value chain. With the increased emphasis on supply chain performance, companies are finding that supplier scorecards help supply chain members collaboratively monitor performance and results and improve key aspects of their own performance.

The measurement paradox is being bridged, and measurement at work is becoming more like measurement in sports. Employees enjoy tracking the statistics of teams and high-performing individuals, who are finally getting recognized for their actual accomplishments, rather than just their image.

Attitudes toward measurement are changing in a positive direction. Although performance measurement is used for a variety of purposes, the focus is on improvement and learning. Everybody in the organization is being educated about measurement on an ongoing basis. There is no longer any secretiveness about measurement.

While there is widespread acknowledgement of the power of measurement, there is open acknowledgement of its limitations. Internal measurement specialists are available for those who don't want to get into the technical aspects of measurement. This allows everyone to focus on the meaning of the measurements, rather than on the calculations.

The gaming of measures has almost disappeared, along with most other dysfunctional behaviors. Accounting abuses aren't happening because employees have become knowledgeable and are willing to "blow the whistle" quickly on those who are abusing the system.

There is now only one, *fully-integrated* measurement system. Many of the traditional barriers of functional "silo" management have crumbled because of the widespread use of cross-functional measurement. Cross-functional measures are viewed as a key to collaboration across the organization, and new cross-functional measures are being regularly adopted.

The organization is able to tap into its wealth of data, mining its business intelligence to retain and attract customers, develop new products, and retain key employees. Measurement consumes much less time and yields much richer insights.

Measurement specialists work with business line people to make the best use of statistics and modeling, resulting in payback in essential management functions.

Planning and forecasting are becoming increasingly accurate. The total cost of investments is becoming more visible, as are the actual (rather than the idealized) benefits. Using "multiple-gate" assessment and "real options," better investment decisions are being made and continually reassessed based on actual data. Because real value is now being tracked, even better investment decisions can be made in the future.

Perhaps most crucial of all, employees and managers view the focus of measurement as enabling high performance and improvement. Employees trust measurement, and feel confident that it won't be used against them.

And there is *commitment* throughout the organization to continuous improvement of measures and the measurement system. And although managers and employees realize that there is potential for continuous improvement, they know that transformational measurement is more of a journey than a destination.

What follows next will give you an overview of what is needed to achieve all or part of the vision I have articulated, and take performance measurement from mere functionality to being a truly transformational force.

## How to Realize the Vision: The Four Keys

The four keys to making progress on the transformation path are *Context, Focus, Integration,* and *Interactivity,* as shown in Figure 4-1. At the base of the diagram is "basic performance measurement," which is the probably the current level of performance measurement in your organization—even though there might be some enlightened measurement projects underway.

If you were to use the traditional criteria for evaluating performance measurement, then you and your organization would be looking pretty good. The organization might have a Balanced Scorecard (perhaps even a technology-enabled one) and dedicated specialists well-trained in financial and nonfinancial performance measurement. At this basic level, organizations can take advantage of at least some of the functionality that performance measurement has to offer. However, in order to tap into its *real power,* it is important to progress far beyond this level.

As the diagram shows, the extent to which an organization can make effective use of the four keys is the extent to which it can tap into the true

FIGURE 4-1. FOUR KEYS TO TRANSFORMING PERFORMANCE MEASUREMENT.

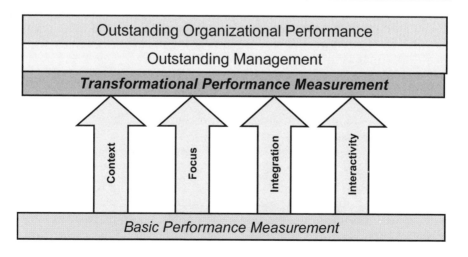

potential of transformational performance measurement, which will enable "outstanding management," and which will, in turn, enable "outstanding organizational performance"—the ultimate goal of both measuring and managing.

## Context

The first key, *Context,* is everything that surrounds a task, including the social and psychological climate in which it is embedded. Although measurement can be an extremely positive and empowering force, its real power can only be realized in a *positive context*. A positive environment can be truly transformational—both in terms of the internal climate of the organization and externally as demonstrated by much better results.

Most of you are familiar with performance measurement-related initiatives such as Balanced Scorecard and Six Sigma. When they are done well, they can contribute to impressive, if isolated, performance improvements. But how effective they are depends, to a large extent, on the context in which they are implemented. The procedure for programs like Balanced Scorecard and Six Sigma is essentially technical, including only some prescribed social interaction.

The context of measurement tends to reflect how measurement is perceived by employees and therefore how they respond *emotionally* to it. Interestingly, even if it is accomplished with great technical skill, it can still carry a negative implication. How people respond to measurement is largely a function of how it is used—that is, what is *done* with the data that is collected. For example, measurement is experienced much differently when used to inspect, control, report, or manipulate—compared to being used to provide feedback, to learn, and to improve.

The context of measurement can make the difference between people being energized by measurement or people just minimally complying with it, and even using measurement for their own personal benefit. That is why the first key to progressing toward transformational measurement is to change the context in a positive direction.

## Focus

The second key to making progress is *Focus*. Because of the validity of *"You get what you measure,"* it is vital to select the right measures. If the right things are measured, the right things will happen. But what are the *right* things? As we saw in Chapter 2 , organizations measure too many things, described by performance measurement experts as varying from "the measurement mess," to "a dog's breakfast." In addition, most of what organizations measure is routine—the hundreds or thousands of measures that permeate every nook and cranny of organizations. This dilutes performance measurement—like trying to boil the ocean! As I said, when everything is important, then nothing is really important. When this happens, an organization has very little focus, and performance measurement has very little power.

This focus on the wrong things, or the lack of focus, tends to do little more than perpetuate the status quo. However, in today's competitive marketplace, organizations need to have very clear focus. Not only do companies need to do the routine things well, they must do those things better and better. They must also find new measures that are high-leverage so that they can achieve competitive advantage. This can be done by focusing on a critical few *transformational measures*—measures that will make a real difference to competitive advantage, that will differentiate the organization from the others with which they compete. But even great isolated measures aren't enough.

## Integration

The third key to transformational performance measurement is *Integration*. As powerful as individual measures are—even transformational ones—they can be poorly used if they are not integrated into a larger "measurement framework" that shows how each measure is related to other important measures, and how the constructs (which the measures represent) combine to create value for the organization. Focusing on isolated functional measures causes suboptimization and tends to build functional "silos" that focus exclusively on their own self-serving measures.

It is my contention that measurement frameworks provide a vital "big picture" view of the impact of one measure on another. For example, too much focus on profitability can actually undermine customer loyalty, while too much emphasis on customer loyalty can undermine profitability. It is all about overall trade-offs and balance. The proper trade-offs and balance among several different factors will create an optimal configuration of measures. Of course, what is optimal at a particular time might not be optimal a month or so later. Businesses and the marketplace change, and therefore so must a measurement framework.

In addition, the cause-and-effect logic between measures (especially between drivers and outcomes) must be understood. The payoff of doing this well is that organizations will be able to predict with greater confidence what should be done to *create optimal value* for the organization and its stakeholders—and that's what outstanding management is all about!

Measures must be aligned with strategy, and then integrated across the entire organization (even the extended enterprise), or dis-integration will occur. In addition, measurement frameworks will spotlight the potential of "cross-functional measures"—measures that can help to integrate functions and lead to higher levels of collaboration.

## Interactivity

The fourth key to transformational performance measurement is *Interactivity*. This book emphasizes that measurement isn't primarily about calculations, data collection, or analysis—it is about the *ongoing interactions* that should occur throughout what I call the "measurement socialization process." In order for the full power of performance measurement to be realized, there must be considerable interaction at each phase of the process, leading to new insights about what to measure and how to measure it.

Transformational performance measurement is not a static, technical process of identifying standard measures and collecting and analyzing data on them. It is much more of a *social process*. If it is to be done well, the processes of selecting and creating key measures based on the organization's business model and strategy and utilizing the feedback loops that are necessary at every phase will all be highly social and interactive.

This is not to say that the technical aspects of measurement are unimportant, but they are only one part of an effective system of performance measurement—and they are the easiest part. For example, developing, validating, and aligning of measurement frameworks requires a deep understanding of the business model, strategy, and operational imperatives that can only occur with a strong "social infrastructure." The difference is that you can purchase a technical infrastructure, but you can't purchase a social one!

## Why Four Keys?

Some organizations excel at one or two of the keys. However, for any organization to achieve superior results, it is essential that all four keys work in tandem with each other. For example, without the right *focus*, the other keys will be meaningless—because if you don't measure the right things, you won't be able to manage the right things, and you won't get the right results—no matter how well you might measure them technically. On the other hand, even with the right focus, without a positive *context,* people won't be motivated to measure the right things, will tend to focus on what will bring them the largest personal rewards, and will tend to have an adversarial posture toward whatever it is that is measured. When measurement has the wrong focus *and* a negative context, a multitude of things can go wrong.

Without the right *integration*, measures will stand alone, functional silos will be perpetuated, individuals and functions will not be properly aligned, and there will be a natural tendency to maximize individual measures, often at the expense of other parts of the organization or the organization as a whole. In fact, the individual measures may actually work against each other, and even cancel each other out. Measurement can be a potentially strong force toward integration or dis-integration.

Without frequent *interaction* relative to measurement, none of the other keys can really work. Without frequent and effective interactivity, you will have a technical engine without a social engine, which is like having a Ferrari but not being able to drive it. In addition, you might develop a scorecard or a measurement framework, but who is going to maintain it and keep it up to date? Without adequate interactivity, it is impossible to sustain any gains from the other three keys.

When all four keys are working together synergistically, amazing things can, and will, happen to enable the awesome power of measurement to make a real difference—a *transformational* difference—in your organization!

## A Roadmap to Success

Once you have begun to start implementing a more *positive context,* there will be a growing enthusiasm for measurement throughout the entire organization and a natural increase in commitment to doing it in the right ways. As you continue to improve the context of measurement in your organization, the positive aspects of performance measurement will gradually emerge. There will be heightened trust and a dynamic appreciation of how measurement can benefit both the individual and the organization. In addition, measurement governance will become a vital aspect of management leadership.

Following the roadmap presented in this book is both the right thing to do *right now* and the most effective solution *in the long-run.* This will lead not only to immediate positive results—but, more importantly, it will promote commitment to continuous improvement and increased measurement maturity throughout the organization.

# CHAPTER 5

# Creating a Positive Context
# of Measurement

In this chapter, we will explore how the "context of measurement" (the social and organizational aspects) largely determines the effectiveness of performance measurement, and how the context of measurement is actually *more* important than the technical aspects of measurement.

Measures come and go, but the context is always there! Unless you do something about it, a negative context can undermine whatever attempts you make at improving the technical aspects of your measurement system; without a positive context, much of the potential power of performance measurement will not be realized.

## The Context of Measurement

The context of measurement is foundational to the other three keys. As shown in Figure 5-1, it touches everything else and influences everything it

FIGURE 5-1. CONTEXT OF MEASUREMENT.

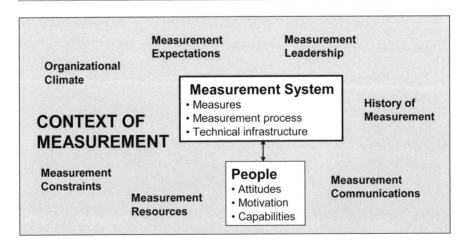

touches—most prominently the technical aspects of the measurement system and the people who use it. The factors listed in the diagram are those that most strongly influence performance measurement.

## Organizational Climate

The first factor, *organizational climate,* is the prevailing "atmosphere" of the organization, the social-psychological environment that profoundly influences all behavior, and it is typically measured by employees' perceptions. The climate is what best "defines" the organization to employees. It reflects perceptions on a variety of dimensions, including, among others:

- The extent of formality (hierarchical structure) versus informality
- Inward-looking versus outward-looking
- Past focus versus future focus
- Trust versus distrust (and cynicism) of employees
- Open versus closed communication
- Task-focus versus people-focus
- Controlling versus collaborative decision making
- Meritocratic rewards versus entitlement
- Change versus rigidity
- Risk-taking versus risk aversion

Clearly, many of these organizational climate dimensions are relevant and closely connected to performance measurement. Organizations with a climate that is most conducive to transformational performance measurement tend to be rated highly in such dimensions as openness, trust, honesty, collaboration, customer-focus, and flexibility.

## Measurement Expectations

*Measurement Expectations* describes the organization's measurement practices, and the "rules" of conduct relative to measurement. These expectations are not always explicitly documented, and are often unwritten, but that makes them no less real. These expectations tend to reflect the organization's assumptions, its deeply-held beliefs about performance measurement. For example, expectations will prescribe what types of measures are most credible. In most organizations today, financial measures are still much more highly valued than nonfinancial ones. In some organizations, nonfinancial measurement is still just an afterthought, or even actively resisted. Although most organizations have highly structured expectations about which financial measures to use and how to use them, including accounting rules, the budget process, and reporting cycles, expectations regarding nonfinancial measurement tend to be much less formal, and are typically left up to the individual function to decide. This kind of measurement expectation tends to reinforce functional silos and hinder cross-organizational integration. Obviously, because of the importance of non-financial measurement in transformational performance measurement, organizations with a stronger financial measurement bias will have more difficulty in affecting the change.

Other expectations relate to such issues as the prescribed roles relative to performance measurement, the relationship between measurement and rewards and punishment, the role of technology in performance measurement, and the importance of the social aspects. But no expectation is more important than the purposes for which performance measurement is used. Organizations that tend to focus on the monitoring, justifying, and reporting purposes of performance measurement are very likely to struggle with transformational measurement. While all of these purposes are legitimate, it is really a matter of emphasis and balance. One thing is certain: In order to be transformational, the purpose of measurement must be separated as much as possible from judgment—especially from performance appraisal. As I continue to stress: "The most powerful purpose of measurement is to *improve*, not to prove."

## Measurement Leadership

*Measurement Leadership* relates to roles, responsibilities, and practices of measurement leaders in the organization as a whole and in the functional areas. Without effective measurement leadership, no major change is likely to occur. To a large extent, leaders establish expectations about performance measurement. This factor also pertains to how organizational leaders view the opportunities and threats involved in performance measurement. Many executives are still oblivious to the serious problems that measurement dysfunction is causing in their organization. On the other hand, there are other so concerned about the potential misuse of measurement that they err on the side of extreme caution, and fail to use the transformational power of measurement. Neither orientation is optimal. Suffice to say that measurement leadership is a key factor in making transformational measurement happen.

## History of Measurement

*History of Measurement* relates to the organization's experiences with performance measurement. Both individuals and organizations are creatures of habit. Our experiences tend to shape what we do subsequently—what we will embrace and what we will avoid—and the same is true for organizations. History tends to send powerful messages regarding expectations for present and future practices. Clearly organizations with positive measurement experiences are going to be more open to transformational measurement than those with negative experiences. But it is also a matter of what kinds of experiences have taken place (i.e., routine versus innovative), which affects how performance measurement is being used today. One of the major determinants of how eagerly members of an organization will embrace transformational measurement is how the "consequences of measurement" have personally affected people in the organization.

## Measurement Communications

*Measurement Communications* describes the amount and type of interaction—if any—that is occurring around performance measurement. This factor is obviously closely associated with one of the keys to transformational performance measurement: Interactivity. Particularly important are the levels of openness, honesty, and the sharing of measurement-related communication.

## Measurement Resources

*Measurement Resources* include any available support for performance measurement activities (such as funding, software, facilities, and training). These resources are important, but they are no substitute for a climate that is conducive to transformational measurement. Of course, an organizational climate conducive to transformational performance measurement is also more likely to provide the resources to support it.

## Measurement Constraints

*Measurement Constraints* is essentially the flip side of all of the other contextual factors mentioned above. It is an umbrella term that can cover anything that inhibits or impedes transformational measurement, such as lack of resources, lack of time, lack of data sharing, and any pressures that make effective performance measurement more difficult.

# The Formal Aspects of the Performance Measurement System

As shown in Figure 5-1, the formal or technical "Measurement System" is composed of three basic components:

1. Measures
2. Measurement process
3. Technical infrastructure

The *measures* are the variables to be measured. The *measurement process* describes the step-by-step process of how measurement is implemented.

The *technical infrastructure* typically includes the computer hardware and software (such as databases and analytical software) to support the measurement process. Although technology is often an important *enabler* of successful performance measurement, it is rarely one of the most crucial factors for transformational performance measurement. Chapter 11 deals with the proper role of technology for transformational performance measurement, but for now it is sufficient to say that, even with the greatest technology, without a positive context and without the presence of the other three keys to transformational performance measurement, organizations will only be able to use a minuscule proportion of technology's full potential.

The truth is that the technical parts of performance measurement don't—and won't—work very well unless the social aspects are in place. Many organizations have great technical infrastructures chock-full of data, but produce little or no insight. Organizations everywhere are stuck with measurement systems that aren't working very well—and, for the most part, the problem isn't technical.

## The Human Factor

The final component of the context of measurement depicted in Figure 5-1 is "People." It is people who will ultimately determine the effectiveness of the measurement system, because measurement data is of no value without human involvement. It is human beings, not machines, who turn data into information, information into insight, insight into knowledge, and knowledge into wisdom. Without people, measurement data would just sit in a repository or in a report and be good for nothing.

As shown in Figure 5-1, people bring attitudes, motivation, and capabilities into their use of the measurement system. These factors are crucial. Let me explain briefly.

### Attitudes and Motivation

Every person has certain *attitudes* about measurement based primarily on past experiences. When people have had negative experiences, their attitudes tend to be negative, or neutral at best. Some people do love measurement, but they are a small minority. Most people either tolerate it from a distance, or shy away from it. For the most part, those who love measurement are those who come from scientific or financial disciplines for which measurement is a fundamental component. However, those who feel comfortable with scientific measurement might still not feel comfortable with performance measurement.

Our attitudes determine our preferences. These attitudes, along with the emotions with which they are infused, shape *motivation*, the energy that is made available for any activity—in this case, measurement. Emotions are very closely associated with motivation. That is why negative feelings about measurement can be such a problem. The good news is that attitudes and related emotions are not permanent. Any negative attitudes can be turned around, although that will not happen by itself. When people have positive experiences with measurement, new attitudes can form that replace the old attitudes. While our positive and negative experiences profoundly influence our attitudes and motivation, most of us prefer activities that cause us to experience positive consequences. And in anticipation of positive experiences, we are likely to become highly motivated; the reverse, of course, is true when we anticipate negative experiences.

## Capabilities

Capabilities—a person's aptitude, skills, knowledge, and experience—establish the readiness for effective performance. These capabilities are primarily based on previous education and practical experience. The level of technical capability level will be highly dependent on the employee's function and discipline. Obviously some disciplines (like accounting and scientific areas) are more naturally associated with technical measurement than others, and this factor alone will likely affect individual employee attitudes and propensity to embrace performance measurement. As we all know from our personal experience, the more capable we feel, the more motivated we will be, because capability makes us feel competent. As psychiatrist David Krueger has explained, "The experience of mastery of being effective may well be the most powerful motivating force in an individual's work."[1]

## The Context of Measurement Continuum

Like any major organizational change, changing the context of measurement in an organization is not something that will happen overnight. It should be viewed as a continuous improvement process. The context of measurement is a continuum. It is not a matter of being either positive or negative—but rather the *degree* to which it is positive or negative.

Obviously, it isn't possible to negate all the past experiences that employees have had with measurement. But you *can* change their experiences with measurement *from this day forward*. Much of the rest of this book will show you what you can do to change those experiences in order to move your organization along the context of measurement continuum. You will be able to track your progress using the Transformational Measurement Maturity Assessment in Chapter 12. It doesn't matter where your organization is now, and there is no better starting point for improving performance measurement than with the context of measurement.

## A Sure-Fire Indicator of Positive Context of Measurement Change

There is one "sure-fire" indicator that tells me that an organization's context of measurement is changing in a positive direction. That indicator is *increased self-management,* enabled by greater empowerment and increased employee ownership and involvement in measurement. Self-management is impossible without highly effective measurement and at least an *increasingly* positive context of measurement.

When people want to change, they commonly use measurement to help them to do so. In fact, when people feel good about their performance potential, they tend to want as much information as possible about how they are performing. They realize that—win or lose—measurement is the key to improvement. Remember our discussion of the "measurement paradox"? Most golfers, for example, are aware that, no matter how modest their current performance might be, a better score is just a stroke away. When people are serious about losing weight, a scale is an empowering feedback tool.

The same is true at work, when employees feel empowered to improve. Measurement tools, like scorecards, provide essential information—and they actually *intrinsically motivate* improvement. They enable people to set goals, help them monitor progress toward the goals, and make them feel good about what they are accomplishing, even without external incentives and rewards that can so easily causes dysfunctional behaviors. Almost everyone will embrace measurement when they see real value in it for the organization and themselves, and believe that it won't be used against them.

One of the changes that is radically reshaping measurement is employee involvement in determining at least some of what should be measured to help them understand, manage, and improve the work they do. Increasingly organizations are involving employees in the design of scoring systems that are *meaningful* to them in their work—scorecards that reflect actual performance relative to some comparative data, such as past performance or a goal level. In addition employees have clear *line-of-sight* between the measures at their level and important organizational measures. Gary Hamel and C. K. Prahalad add, "Every employee must have a personal scorecard that directly relates his or her job to the challenge being pursued [and] links individual achievement to the firm's overall strategic intent."[2]

Accountability and effective performance measurement are also crucial for self-management. In today's complex, knowledge-intensive, and often virtual workplaces, self-management is essential to organizational success. Command-and-control approaches are becoming increasingly obsolete. Empowerment, rather than control, is the order of the day. But the control mentality dies slowly. As Michael Hammer advises, "If they are given the information and tools that they need to perform, if they are provided with an understanding of customer requirements and of the big picture of the work, if they are guided by clear measurement systems . . . then they will do what needs to be done without being 'managed'."[3]

Self-measurement is a necessary condition for self-management. It is also a major milestone for any measurement program and a key to sustainable performance improvement. One of they major recommendations in this book is: Give the power of measurement to every employee. But this will only work in a positive context.

## Snapshots from the New Performance Measurement Paradigm

When a positive context for measurement is established, amazing changes in attitudes, motivation, and performance are not only possible, they are probable. As John Case reminds us, "The human dimension of business—the wanting, the caring, the enthusiasm, the problem solving and initiative taking—is where more and more competitive battles are being won or lost."[4]

The following vignettes are from organizations that are at least beginning to win the battle. They are "snapshots" of what performance measurement looks like when the context of measurement starts to change in a positive direction. They are called snapshots because they are isolated pictures from a variety of organizations. Someday soon, I hope to be able to report entire "photo albums" from the same organizations that vividly show the full transformation. And I hope that soon, snapshots such as these will be the rule, rather than the exception:

• One of the most astonishing sights is formerly disenfranchised factory workers who have been empowered to use Statistical Process Control (SPC) to manage the quality of their processes. Instead of having someone down the line complaining about the poor quality of components, they control the quality themselves—by constantly monitoring the indicators of when the "control limits" are being crossed, and by being able to do something about it without having to ask permission. They are no longer helpless; they control the quality of *their* process and *their* product with measures they understand and can directly influence, resulting not only in more accurate process measurements, but also in a "no-fault" measurement climate.

• When employees can clearly see their own performance in a way that is meaningful to them, they are much more likely to take positive action. Referring to a dip on the latest performance graph, an employee at a processing plant remarked, "We ain't gonna let that happen again. . . . We already took care of that problem."

• Executives in a sales department were accustomed to responding to gaps in the sales pipeline by admonishing the sales force to "sell harder," and, if necessary, by increasing incentives. After finally acknowledging that this approach was not working, they are now more focused on using sales data to help the sales force sell more effectively. According to one of the executives, "The way we traditionally used sales measurement was like squeezing a little more juice from the oranges we already have. Now we are focused on picking new oranges, growing new trees, and, better yet, planting new orchards!"

• In another company, when penalties for mistakes were eliminated, a wonderful thing happened. Workers who had been reporting flagrantly bogus numbers began to tell the truth about their performance. They began reporting accurate levels of quality and productivity even when they were poor, so that the problems could be addressed. Managers in this company were truly astounded that workers whom they once saw as recalcitrant were actually *telling on themselves*!

• In one company I recently visited, scoreboards and graphs are everywhere. They range from roughly drawn tables and charts posted on bulletin boards or drawn on whiteboards, to elaborate computer dashboard displays. Previously, workers tended to avoid (and hide from) measurement. But now that measurement is used positively, everybody, it seems, wants to keep score.

• One company CEO was inspecting a steel manufacturing plant when he stopped to count the ingots. Without saying anything, he wrote "78" on the hearth with a piece of chalk, and then continued on to other areas. The next day, he returned to the same work area, and beside it, the employees had written "80." One day later, it was "85." And this positive competition to increase production continued daily.

• In another organization, when a team of employees failed to achieve its own self-imposed production target, there were no recriminations or blame. Instead they used data to find out what had happened, and find a solution. Based on this data-based problem-solving, the team was able, over a three week period, to dramatically improve the process, resulting in a process cycle time reduction from 8.5 hours to only 1 hour. In addition, during this period of time, the team actually generated 74 suggestions for improving the process.

• Examples of positive work measurement also occur in some companies that practice Open-Book Management. In these companies, employees have access to all financial and operating measures and understand what most of them mean. Although they call it "the game of business," they take it very seriously. They are educated about measurement, and they know many of the key causal relationships. In "huddle" meetings they discuss with managers and with peers what they can do to make a difference to move the numbers in the right direction. And they treat the company's money like it was their own—because they have real involvement, understanding, and a genuine stake in the company's success.

• One company decided to make their performance scorecard into a game. Eighteen organizational measures were identified and the employees were encouraged to help the firm maximize its total score by achieving "eagles," "birdies," "par," or "bogies" on each of their own performance measures. This unusual and playful approach has generated a lot of excitement around measurement.

• In another company I visited, I kept hearing performance measurement conversations like the following: "Customer complaints are up 8 percent. What are we going to do about it?" "Let's look at the data." "It looks like shipment delays are way up." "What caused the delays?" "How often was the warehouse out of stock?" "How much equipment downtime occurred on the second shift?" When people start asking the *right* questions, they are on the path to *improving* whatever they are doing.

• Another company has invested significant efforts to provide education for all employees aimed at reducing the mystery around both financial and non-financial performance measurement. Employees throughout the company are learning a common language around measurement that is helping them communicate more effectively about performance issues. All managers participate in the learning sessions with their teams and employees are given plenty of time to learn and to apply their learning in on-the-job projects.

I hope that these vignettes have given you a glimpse of what kinds of transformations are taking place within the context of measurement in some selected organizations throughout the world—and that you may even have "caught" some of their enthusiasm! Equally exciting are the following examples from companies that are just beginning the process of transforming performance measurement—and are starting to see positive results:

• In a company with an extremely defective technical measurement system, despite improvements, there are still a profusion of opportunities for managers and employees to distort the measures for their own benefit. What is most interesting is that nobody does! This is because a context exists in which measurement is trusted, there is open and honest communication about performance, and everyone has input into what is being measured. Most importantly, there is demonstrated commitment to continuous improvement throughout the company.

• In another organization, managers came to the realization that maximizing their own functional measures might benefit them, but it would actually hurt the organization as a whole. Instead of relying on their self-serving measures, they have decided to adopt new cross-functional measures—even though adopting the new measures might reduce their short-term incentive pay.

• A company that previously had used measurement as part of a "blame game" to identify poor performers (rather than poor performance) decided to change its approach. Now, when a performance deficiency is identified, the data triggers problem-solving, not a search for the guilty. Employees are beginning to see data as a friend, rather than as their enemy, and they are becoming more eager to learn from it. One of the most surprising changes to those who remember the "old regime" is that now bad numbers are actually being considered "good news" because they represent *opportunities* for improvement and learning.

• In a company where functional directors had for a long time jealously guarded their data as their own property, it was rather surprising to see them willingly pooling their databases. Collaboration around measurement was helping to bring down the traditional protective walls between functional silos. This was enabling the identification of cross-functional measures to be adopted to reflect cross-functional reality, and the company is beginning to consider the customer, and not the internal functions, as the center of gravity.

• Another company has moved away from its rigid, adversarial, and internally-focused annual budget planning process (which rewarded functional managers for hitting their budget numbers) toward a more flexible, collaborative, customer-focused, ongoing planning process, aiming at achieving relative improvements in functional performance and optimizing the total organization. This has significantly reduced the traditional planning bureaucracy, increasing collaboration across the organization, and providing resources where and when they are most needed.

• In another company, the finance function is transforming itself from its traditional role as "bean counters" and "financial police" to being more of a collaborative partner with the firm's operating units. Now the emphasis is on working together proactively to come up with the best—often innovative—answers, rather than just the standard accounting ones.

• Finally, here's how a senior vice president at one company describes his organization's experience with transformational measurement: "We are on a journey from measurement *confusion* to measurement *clarity*—but we still have a long way to go. We're learning that measurement isn't about reacting to isolated data points, or tables of numbers, or even balanced scorecards. We're learning to combine numbers with observations, questions, models, visualizations, and intuition, and helping everyone understand 'the story' behind the data that used to be hidden in the abstract numbers. Furthermore, when our measurement system includes the right measures that reflect our strategy, then I am confident that our people will know what they have to do and how they can contribute even more effectively to our results—and we won't even have to tell them!"

## The Ongoing Transforming Power of Context

We have seen how "context" is critical in transforming performance measurement. Think about it this way: Consider each of the functions of measurement, described in Chapter 1. Each one can be experienced in a *positive* or a *negative* way—depending on the context of measurement. For example, each and every function will be experienced quite differently in a command-and-control climate, or in one that is self-directed. If employees perceive that measurement is in place to help them to become more successful (rather than to monitor and judge them) and to empower them (rather than manipulate them), then measurement will become a powerfully positive force in the organization. Everything will feel better in a positive context, and everything will feel worse in a negative one.

As Paul Strassman points out, "The essence of a corporate culture is the firm's measurement system. It is the lens through which reality is perceived and acted on."[5] The context of measurement is actually the most important aspect of the measurement system, and therefore it impacts both the culture and the lens. Making sure that the right context is in place is a superb investment, since the context affects all aspects of the measurement system across the entire organization. It is the importance of context that will bring us back to this topic again and again as we continue our journey.

However, let me emphasize one more thing: Transforming the context of measurement will take time, and may have to start small. Some areas of your organization are likely to be more receptive to change than others. Sometimes change is driven strongly from the top, and the rest of the organization falls in line and follows. A more likely model is change that begins in one area of the organization, driven by a visionary person, as a "proof of concept." Once the concept has been shown to be effective, the rest of the organization will be more receptive to broader change.

One thing I have learned from my years of organization leadership and consulting: Don't try to change those who clearly resistant to change—nothing will frustrate you more than that. Look for those visionary leaders who "get it"—people who are likely to be the "early adopters" of the concepts we have discussed. Enlist the sponsorship of those who are the candidates for the kind of "measurement leadership" discussed in Chapter 9.

# CHAPTER 6

# The Focus of Measurement

The second key to transformational performance measurement is Focus. To repeat: *What gets measured gets managed and what gets managed gets done.* Selecting the right measures can create enormous leverage for any organization. And, of course, the things that get measured command management attention, one of a company's most important resources. But as management expert Geoffrey Moore asserts, "Nothing is wasted more in a Fortune 500 corporation than management attention."[1] If management is paying attention, are they paying attention to the *right* things? Unfortunately, too many organizations appear to be "majoring in the minors."

## The Importance of Focus

Clearly it is critical to focus measurement efforts on the *right things*. The right measures will provide laser focus and clarity to management. As Napier and McDaniel say, "Much of the power of leadership is bound up in what leaders pay attention to. Measurement is focused attention."[2] Unfortunately, most leaders don't differentiate between the *critical few* measures that will have the greatest impact and the hundreds, or thousands, of other measures—the *trivial many*—that permeate every area of their organizations. There is an infinite variety of things that can be measured in any organization, and a lack of focus can be very dangerous. Even among senior executives, the "focus" of measurement is too often tactical, functional, and diffused. Further, the recent emphasis on addressing the concerns of shareholders, customers, regulators, and the variety of societal constituencies has further diffused attention.

As a consequence, most organizations measure a hodge-podge of things, hoping to capture the important things in the process. However, this only leads to a waste of resources that should be focused on the critical few high-leverage drivers of the most important results—*if they were only known.* Ask people at all levels and in all functions what is most important, and you will probably get almost as many answers as the number of people you ask. This unfocused proliferation of measures has led to what former General Electric CEO Jack Welch has described as "measuring everything and understanding nothing."

## Selecting the Right Measures

While most organizations realize that measurement is essential for managing, they don't realize how important the selection of their measures is. What a company (or a functional unit) measures, to a large extent determines how its people behave.

Too many executives and other managers think it is sufficient just to track generic or standard *industry-approved* measures. These are what I call "routine measures," and they are satisfactory for maintaining the status quo, but not for taking the organization to the next level. They are like your body's "vital signs"—important, but they won't get you to the pinnacle of health; they are not differentiators. Similarly, an organization's routine measures are not differentiators (unless the organization's strategy focuses on "operational efficiency," and then certain routine measures can be highly strategic). How can any organization differentiate itself from the competition while measuring exactly the same things as the competition? There is nothing wrong with routine measures—every organization needs them to survive—but that's not what we are concerned with here.

Management needs to focus its attention on the measures that really drive the performance of their particular organization. When "everything" is important, there is nothing that is *most important*. According to Bob Phelps, "Most managers are in fact overwhelmed by measures and data— but these have not improved their performance. Why? Because companies have taken the easy option and selected lots of poor measures instead of a few good ones."[3] Also, when we choose to measure a particular object of interest, we are—at least by default—choosing to ignore other things.

Just look at your own organization's measurement system and you will probably find a vast array of measures that keep your business running— but few, if any, that will help get your organization to the next level. Furthermore, do you even know which the most important measures are? But identifying these measures and socializing them throughout your organization is one of the most important things you can do.

Many organizational measures are labeled "metrics," and have become so institutionalized that they are virtually impossible to change or delete. That is one of the reasons why I resist using the term "metric" for just any measure. I believe that this is more than a linguistic issue. When a measure is first introduced, I recommend calling it an "indicator or emergent measure." Call it a "measure" when it has been well defined and you are confident that it is ready for widespread use. Only use the term "metric" when the measure has been validated for use organization-wide as a "key organizational performance measure." Having a consistent language of performance measurement is an important step toward measurement maturity.

Of course, doing the routine well—the basic blocking and tackling—is necessary for winning in any arena—in business as well as in sports—but it isn't sufficient for sustainable winning performance, like winning championships. For example, all companies need to measure revenue, cost, profit, and customer satisfaction; manufacturing companies need some way to measure raw materials' costs, productivity, and quality; insurance companies can't stay in business if they don't measure risk; banks have to measure deposits and return on their investments. The list of *important but routine* measures is virtually endless.

If you measure what everyone else is measuring, your business will be well on the way to commoditization. However, if your organization strives for more than that, you might want to consider rethinking the measures that are currently populating your measurement system.

I am reminded of the story of the man who was vainly looking for his lost keys on a dark night under a particular light post; when asked why, he said it was because that was the only place where there was light! Similarly, many managers are forced to manage only the things that are currently being measured because those measures are the only "lamp posts" casting light.

Just as nonsensical are organizations that are so concerned about not measuring the right things that they try to measure every thing. Obviously some things don't need much measurement. You don't need to measure everything! Too often, much of what is measured in organizations today is analogous to someone who thinks he needs a thermometer to tell that water is boiling!

Since performance measurement is about viewing things through a lens, the operant questions are: Is it the right lens? Are we viewing the right things in the right ways? Is the view clear enough? If they are being honest, most of the time, managers must answer these questions, "No." In today's highly competitive and increasingly services-oriented marketplace, it is vital to be measuring more than just the same old, routine measures. Not only is almost all measurement routine, but almost all of it has derived from a commodity manufacturing mindset. It is amazing how few *new* measures have been developed since the industrial revolution!

Deciding what *not* to measure is almost as important as deciding what to measure. Measuring something that isn't *really* important to a key stakeholder is a waste and time and resources. Furthermore, as management experts Eccles and Nohria state, "There is the temptation to turn every measure deemed relevant into a crucial part of an official measurement system."[4] This is because it is much easier to add measures than to get rid of them once they have been adopted. This tendency has led to bloated "legacy" measurement systems (most based on a mass production model) that actually reduce the agility of most organizations, compared to what a lean, focused, and customized set of measures could provide. Most measurement data is clutter—very little ever gets used! I call it "waste of time measurement." If you don't believe me, do a measurement audit to find out what measures are actually being used and contribute to better decision making.

Realizing the dangers of unfocused measurement, smart organizations are significantly reducing the number of variables they measure, and making sure that they are the right ones to focus attention on. Ask yourself: "How long have we been measuring this?" and "What successful actions have we taken based on this measure?" That might help you identify many of the trivial routine measures that are taking time and attention away from what is really important to measure.

If you and your organization continue to measure what you have always measured, you will very likely continue to get what you have always gotten—except probably *less* of it—because the marketplace is getting so much more competitive. Most companies certainly do not need *more* measures—in fact, they need fewer measures—but we all need *better* measures.

## Effectiveness First

Focused measurement is about being *effective*, getting the *right things* done. In contrast, efficiency—which is too often the primary focus of management—is about minimizing resources—as organizations desperately try to drive out cost. While efficiency is important, effectiveness must come first. As Peter Drucker has pointed out, "What value is there in doing efficiently those things that should never be done at all? Anything that isn't *effective* is waste, and reducing waste is, in turn, a key to increasing efficiency."[5]

The danger of selecting the wrong measures should be obvious, but here is a little anecdote that conveys the issue pretty clearly: Hours after the last familiar sign, the taxi driver kept up a steady pace. "We're lost, aren't we?" asked the passenger. "Yes," said the driver. "But we're making good time, don't you think?"

Six Sigma has worked well where there have been specific problems that needed to be solved. Six Sigma has done remarkable things to drive out variance, even if not to Six Sigma levels! But the traditional Six Sigma methodology and its practitioners will struggle with transformational measures that are more qualitative, subjective, and flexible. Six Sigma and transformational measurement *can* succeed together, but only if a less rigid approach is taken. Six Sigma is one of the greatest things that ever happened to *traditional* measurement, but it needs to be adapted if it is going to work with the more transformational challenges.

So, when clients ask me, "What should we measure?" I usually respond by asking them, "What does success look like for *your* organization?" That is when we begin the critical reexamination on value creation—before we even get to the subject of measurement.

## How Value Is Created and Destroyed

Nothing is more important today than the concept of "value creation," and it has become the benchmark criterion for success. Ultimately, all organizations exist to create value for their stakeholders. Value is created when the benefits provided to stakeholders exceed all the costs incurred. All businesses, government agencies, and nonprofits should be focused on *creating value* for their stakeholders, whoever they are.

In business, value creation is typically measured by profitability and long-term growth. In order to achieve those goals, a company must establish a continuing process for developing and delivering a steady stream of products and services, based on its business model, that offer unique and differentiated benefits to a chosen set of customers. Just because an organization has created value for shareholders in the past doesn't mean that it will be able to continue to create value in the future. Long-term value creation is a challenge that requires extraordinary management capabilities.

Organizations that do not create value, by definition, *destroy* it. Unprofitable companies are wasting the money of their shareholders, who could have invested it elsewhere. The same is true of government agencies that waste the money of citizens, or nonprofits that waste the resources of their donors. Some describe value destruction more euphemistically as "allowing value to leak or evaporate"—but however it happens, too often the value of an organization's resources and assets is lost.

Since value creation of some kind is the key to organizational success—and what you measure is what you get—it is vital that this value creation process be measured. Very few people really know how value is created in their organizations, or even seem to care. Furthermore, business leaders who invest and manage resources in projects that do not pay off destroy value. In a large organization, there are literally thousands of opportunities to create value or destroy it every day. Unfortunately, few organizations have value creation mindset or the measurement system they need to support value creation.

This results in serious mismanagement and misdirected behavior. That is why organizational measures should, first and foremost, capture "the story" of value creation for the particular organization. Lack of focus and clarity causes confusion, lack of alignment, and eventually value destruction. What's more, anybody in an organization, at any level, can contribute to creating value or destroying it. Employees who waste time or are otherwise unproductive destroy value. Much of today's workforce is composed of knowledge workers, whose productivity is difficult to "see," much less measure. Measurement is becoming an even greater challenge as performance is becomingly increasingly invisible. But that is precisely why transformational measures are needed. The old measures just don't work well anymore, at least not in complex services and for knowledge work. Most of the "raw materials" from which we create value are intangible.

Value is created when the right actions are taken and the right investments are made. Value is destroyed when the wrong actions are taken and the wrong investments are made. Value leaks or evaporates when nothing is done. Sadly, too much decision-making in organizations is driven by individual advocacy and self-interest, and not by what creates measurable long-term value. As Napier & McDaniel say, "It is hard to overemphasize how powerful measured attention can be when it is well conceived and deployed, or how destructive it can be when done poorly."[6] Too much traditional measurement focuses—*very precisely*—on the wrong things!

A generic model of the value creation/destruction process is illustrated in Figure 6-1.

Most organizations don't even have a reliable definition of value creation. However, they do establish some "bottom line," typically some measure of profitability—such as gross profits, net profits, EBITDA, ROI, EVA, EPS, stock price, P/E ratio, cash flow, CFROI, ROA, ROE, etc. But, as Paul Hawken explains, "The bottom line is down where it belongs—*at the bottom*. Far above it in importance are the infinite numbers of events that produce the profit or loss."[7] Do you know how value is created in your organization? Could you map out the value creation process? Can you measure it?

FIGURE 6-1. VALUE CREATION AND DESTRUCTION.

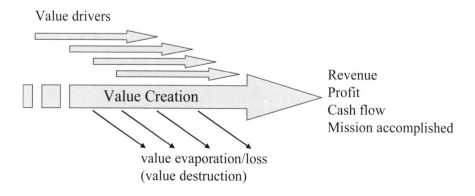

Value drivers

Value Creation

Revenue
Profit
Cash flow
Mission accomplished

value evaporation/loss
(value destruction)

Although, as Hawken says, there are a great many possible value-creating activities, every successful organization has relatively few key "value drivers"—factors that drive the most value creation. Strategy should be focused on *making best use of the value drivers to create optimal value from resources for stakeholders*. Measurement is one of the most crucial aspects of value creation, because without good measurement, value creation cannot be managed. That is why the poor, routine, manufacturing-legacy measurement systems are hobbling organizations that are trying to be innovative and create more value. The failure to adequately measure any resource or asset is likely to retard its development, impair its conversion into value, and allow waste, in the form of leakage or evaporation.

## Business Models and Strategy

Business strategy expert Ram Charan cautions all business leaders to "simplify the business and get to the fundamentals."[8] When that is done, the value creation (or destruction) process becomes quite visible, and then it can be effectively managed. A company's "business model" is the basic logic of how the organization *creates value* for itself (and shareholders) by *delivering value* to customers.

But if you don't know what drives your success, you're in trouble. For example, where most clothing stores consider merchandising their core competency, The Men's Wearhouse knows that its business is about *sales*, not buying merchandise, and that's why its sales per employee are so much higher than its competitors. What are the keys to success in *your* business? If you don't know them, you better find out. And, if you *do* know, then you had better figure out how to measure them well!

The organization's "strategy" is its *specific plan* for applying the business model to create "competitive advantage" in a particular marketplace at a particular time. Even if you are a leader in a government or non-profit, you still need to be focused on how best to manage your "business." Whatever your business, it's all about competitive advantage. Even if you don't have any direct competition, your competition is someone deciding not to use your product or service, to seek an alternative, or to cut your budget. Value is created when the business model is properly leveraged through the effective execution of the strategy to produce the right operational performance. This is illustrated in Figure 6-2.

When a business is able to use its strategy to leverage the basic economics of its business model, good things tend to happen. In contrast, when the basic economics of the business (the cake) are poorly understood and managed, then everything else is just "icing without a cake." For example, one hotel chain didn't realize how important catering and conferences were

FIGURE 6-2. BUSINESS MODEL AND STRATEGY.

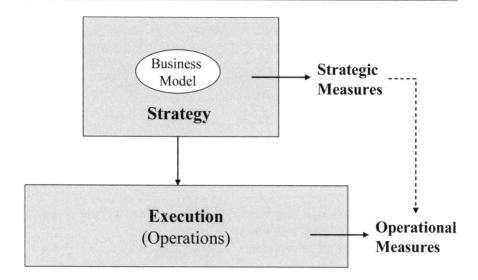

to the economics of its business model. It focused too much on room occupancy and not enough on booking meetings and on catering. As a result, although it achieved very high room occupancy rates, it ended up destroying value for its shareholders, because it didn't understand the essential synergy between the three components of its business model—rooms, meetings, and catering.

While there are generic business models (Adrian Slywotsky's work on "profit models" identifies about twenty of them),[9] don't be misled that you can win today with a generic business model alone—or with generic business "metrics."

Furthermore, the selection of the right performance measures with the business model and strategic priorities is not a one-shot activity, but must be done consistently, especially as priorities change during the lifecycle of a business. For example, at one company, when the business basics had been mastered, the focus of measurement shifted from critical operational measures to measuring brand building. At another company, which was moving into a slower growth phase, the priority measures shifted from customer acquisition to retention.

Successful companies are learning that ongoing enhancements of their business models is an essential step for sustaining competitive advantage. These new and enhanced business models won't come off-the-shelf from a consultant. Companies have to invent them *themselves*, although consultants can help.

## Measuring What Matters Most

In order to thrive—not just survive—and move to a higher level of performance, organizations need to focus on one or more *critical measures* that
matter most, and companies need to focus *everybody's* attention on those
measures. Goldratt insists that "a fraction (0.1 percent) of the variables
determine 99.9 percent of the result."[10] Although this assertion is likely an
exaggeration, it is still something that anyone who wants to create value and
not destroy it should take seriously. Resources, both human and otherwise,
are too valuable to waste, but our current measurement systems are inadequate to manage our most valuable sources of value.

Not only must the right measures exist, but they must be communicated
and "socialized" properly throughout the organization so that people can
use them. Remember that measurement is a very social process of identifying, developing, understanding, refining, dialoguing, etc. It is not primarily
about collecting, analyzing, and reporting on data.

As you will see in the next chapter, value creation (and the avoidance of
value destruction) occurs when everybody is aligned and operating according to an integrated set of measures.

The search for the perfect measures has too often encouraged procrasti-
nation or avoidance. The challenge is not one of finding the "magic metric,"
but measuring most appropriately. However, some measures are much better than others at revealing the highest leverage factors in value creation.
Let's look at a few examples of organizations that have done just that.

### Measuring What Mattered Most at Southwest Airlines

Southwest Airlines' business model was designed to operate an airline more
like a bus company, *but better*—getting people quickly and reliably from
point A to point B on a limited number of high-demand routes on-time at a
minimum cost. The assumptions upon which the business model was based
was that there were many passengers who weren't being well-served by traditional airlines and that these passengers would be willing to endure some
inconveniences (like multiple stops en-route, no meals, no reserved seats,
no first-class, no use of travel agents, or operation out of secondary air-
ports) to reduce complexity of route and fare structures. Although *all* businesses ultimately measure their success by some variant of profit, the drivers
of profitability are often very different, depending on the business model.

The Southwest Airlines business model focused on keeping costs low
and filling up its airplanes, while charging everyday low fares to customers
who might have otherwise traveled by bus or some other form of ground
transportation. By purchasing all the same airplanes (Boeing 737s) to facilitate maintenance, servicing, and interchangeability of crews, Southwest
could reduce turnaround time to between fifteen and twenty minutes, com-

pared to one hour or more for traditional airlines. Together with well-selected short-haul routes, this enabled Southwest to dramatically increase aircraft utilization. While many of the traditional routine airline measures might be valid for Southwest, the key driver of its business model was low "cost-per-passenger" and the primary driver of low cost-per-passenger was high "aircraft utilization," and the primary driver of high aircraft utilization was quick "turnaround time." No company has leveraged the strategic importance of time as well as Southwest Airlines.

"Turnaround time" became Southwest's most transformational measure—the fulcrum that leveraged its business model. More than any other measure, it has enabled Southwest Airlines to make its unique "airline as bus company" business model work—allowing Southwest to maintain the best on-time performance in the industry and reduce costs by 25 percent compared to traditional airlines. They realized that "fast" is not just quicker and cheaper; it is also better!

Another extraordinary result of the "turnaround time" measure was that for the measure to work, everyone (flight crews, ramp agents, operational agents, baggage handlers, cleaners, fuelers) had to work together collaboratively. Like many other high-leverage and transformational measures, "turnaround time" proved to be a cross-functional one.

## Measuring What Mattered Most at Dell Computer Corporation

Dell Computer Corporation founder and CEO Michael Dell explains that "very early on, Dell made the connection between its business model and its performance measures."[11] The success of the "Dell direct" business model, based on building computers "to order" and selling them direct to customers, depended on simplifying its supply chain. Dell began to measure "touches" (how many times a component was touched by a worker), and set out to reduce that number. More touches meant longer cycle time, increased costs, and more opportunities for defects. Like Southwest Airlines, Dell was able to achieve considerable leverage from focusing on one key measure until significant improvement was achieved.

Necessity is often the mother of invention—in measurement, as well as in many other areas—and Dell's most innovative measure resulted from a very painful *near-death* experience. Michael Dell noted that at first the priorities at Dell was "growth, growth, and growth." But the company was learning the hard way that "cash is king." As Dell recounts the situation: "We were consuming huge amounts of cash, while our profitability began to deteriorate, and both our inventory and our accounts receivable were piling up."[12] Dell needed to find a measure that would help correct this situation and provide the company with a way to significantly improve its cash position on a continuing basis. To respond to this challenge, Dell focused on a measure that ran counter to traditional manufacturing thinking. Rather than focus on a traditional measure like "manufacturing cycle time," Dell targeted a new measure: "cash conversion cycle time" (or cash-to-cash cycle time)—the time from the outlay of cash for parts to the receipt of payment from customers. This measure helped Dell change its priorities from "growth, growth, and growth" to "liquidity, profitability, and growth." Dell took cash conversion cycle time from 70 days to *less than zero*—which means it now collects cash before paying for inventory!

But this extraordinary achievement didn't just improve Dell's cash position. In order to achieve it, Dell had to do a lot of other things well (including sales, purchasing, and inventory management). By using this measure, Dell was able to transform its business from one that was on the brink of disaster to a company that is cash rich, and able to operate profitably in almost any business condition. Such is the power of the right focal measure, and is a prime example of how a single measure can have a transformational impact on an entire company. However, as powerful as individual measures can be, companies cannot stick doggedly to them. Effective management depends on a constellation of measures, not just a single one. In fact, Dell Computer is now faced with a new challenge that their old transformational measure won't help them solve: how to turn all its idle cash into shareholder value!

## Measuring Intangible Assets

Value creation, business models, and strategy can be quite abstract until they are operationalized through measurement. Only when you are able to measure the key drivers of value creation will you be able to take appropriate actions to truly leverage the business model and strategy. Measurement can also expose hidden assets and other resources that are crucial to the value creation process. But without good measurement much of any pool of assets—tangible or intangible—can be largely wasted.

Tangible assets tend to be more readily measured and managed because it is easier to put a financial value on them and most of them appear on a company's balance sheet. But tangible assets are increasingly becoming commoditized, and therefore are rarely a major source of competitive advantage anymore.

The most important drivers of value in today's organizations are mostly intangible. As researcher Debra Amidon has aptly articulated the imperative of intangible value measurement: "The unmeasured must be measured. If it cannot be measured, it isn't considered of value."[13]

While intangible assets account for as much as 80 percent of some companies' market value, almost no intangibles ever appear in a company's financial reports—at least not as anything other than an expense. As a result, it has been found that, in both the private and public sectors, existing measurement systems are tracking *less than half* of organizational value. Assets such as talent, leadership, knowledge, motivation, employee relations, customer relationships, culture, brands, innovativeness, speed, flexibility, responsiveness, agility, resilience, alliances, knowledge-sharing, ethics, sustainability—and the list could go on and on—are hardly measured at all, and therefore hardly managed at all. Not only that, but in services the operational processes and measures are also mostly intangible. So, if you are in services (especially complex services) and you can't measure and manage intangibles, you're really in trouble! And, because of poor measurement, nobody really knows how much of this crucial intangible value is being wasted, underdeveloped, and mismanaged.

While most companies are aware of the importance of developing new intangible sources of competitive advantage, few know what to do about them, because most of this value is packaged in vague concepts. This sense of helplessness is exemplified by Boulton, Libert, and Samek's finding, in their book *Cracking the Value Code*, that "some 85 percent of these executives [surveyed] reported that they recognized the importance of investments in intangible assets like employees and customers. However, less than 35 percent said that they acted accordingly."[14] An Institute for Management Accountants survey reported that fewer than 10 percent of respondents rated performance measures for intangible assets as either "very good" or "excellent." As a result of this measurement gap, much of the potential value of these invisible sources of competitive advantage is being wasted—and, to make matters worse, no one really knows how much waste there is. Clearly a lot of potential value is being overlooked, or otherwise underutilized!

Admittedly intangible measurement is not perfect—far from it—but one of the key ideas presented in this book is that "everything that should be measured can be measured in a way that is superior to not measuring them at all." Without a doubt, high-leverage intangible assets should be better measured, so that they can be better managed.

## High-Leverage Measuring

Leverage is one of the most important concepts that was ever discovered. The concept was most famously expressed by ancient Greek mathematician Archimedes when he said, "Give me a lever and a place to stand, and I will move the world." Today, the major object of leverage, in business at least, is not the entire world, but about competitive advantage. It's about find the measurable "points of leverage" that will leverage your business model and strategy the way that Southwest Airlines and Dell Computer have done.

The key to high-leverage measurement is finding the most crucial few measures that provide the organization with the greatest insight into competitive advantage. It measures factors that clearly relate to how value is created through the organization's business model. There are some very small changes that can be made that will make major differences in the outcomes achieved. That could be the fulcrum of your entire business strategy! When you do find potential high-leverage measures, you might ask questions like, "What would a change—say 5 percent—mean in terms of a valued outcome, like revenue or profitability?"

But where this focus should be, and where the leverage is, is not always obvious. That's why only the most innovative organizations, and those with a positive context of measurement, even try to deviate from routine measurement.

But in those organizations that have caught the vision of what high-leverage transformational measurement can do, there is ongoing commitment to diligently measuring only what is most important, not everything or what is easiest to measure. They are continually searching for more relevant, informative, and innovative measures.

To a large extent, what we measure defines how we see the world. As we observed in Chapter 1, throughout history, measurement has been a force that has enabled society to progress. When measurement does operationalize new paradigms, or mental models, they provide a *new lens* through which people can view the world, or a part of it. To change our perspective, we must change our measures. If you continue to view the world with old lenses, you will never be able to see the new. One well-known example of this is that the natives couldn't "see" Columbus' ships because they didn't have the "measurement lens" that enabled them to recognize ships.

As David Meador has articulated it: "Changing the way we measure changes everything."[15] But in order for this to happen, organizations must be willing to take the risk of using new measures and new measurement instruments—and, as you will see, that is no small challenge in the overwhelming majority of organizations that tend to resist change.

There is certainly no lack of powerful concepts for transforming business and government. Nothing is more exemplary of transformational measurement than the breakthroughs in quality measurement. Most readers are, no doubt, familiar with the enormous paradigm shift that occurred from the focus on "removing product defects through after-the-fact inspections" to "solving product defect problem their source (high process variation)." This breakthrough was enabled by a measurement innovation—process measurement control charts—which Frederick Reichheld called the measurement innovation that "unlocked the door to the quality revolution."[16]

As we have seen, the use of the "turnaround time" measure at Southwest Airlines enabled people to see something that was formerly invisible (because it wasn't being measured) so that it could be managed to create value and achieve competitive advantage. And the use of "cash conversion cycle time" at Dell Computer helped the company conquer its cash flow problems, and also provided the mechanism to make its innovative business model work in practice, not just in theory.

At both Southwest and Dell, the measures we discussed above were not just abstract "metrics" or numbers in reports or on ledgers understood only by functional or technical specialists, they were pivotal to the initial success of those companies—and they yielded impressive results for each organization. That is why it is not surprising that other organizations are prone to copy the transformational measurement successes of others. As a result of Southwest's breakthrough, many other airlines have significantly reduced their own turnaround times. At health sciences firm Perkin-Elmer, more than 10,000 employees have received training in "compressing the cash cycle" to improve their own cash conversion cycle. But it is important to remember that, because transformational measurement is business-model specific, what might be transformational in one organization might *not* be transformational in another. This is another good reason not just to use industry standard measures—even if they were once considered "transformational."

## Emergent Measures

Most transformational measures start off as what I call "emergent measures"—measures that *emerge* through increased understanding of the major drivers of business success. They rarely come from a textbook, off a menu, or are provided by a vendor. Many of the emergent measures will be measures of difficult-to-measure intangibles, because transforming organizations are realizing that many of their key value drivers are intangible. But don't let anyone tell you that something isn't measurable. *Everything* is measurable in some way that is superior to not measuring it at all.

However, such new measures are not likely to emerge in an organization that doesn't like or *trust* measurement—that is, in a "negative context of measurement." Despite their potential to revolutionize a business, emergent and transformational measures are often resisted or not used because of fear of change, perceived measurement difficulty, and the prevailing negative attitudes toward measurement that still exist in many, if not most, organizations. Thomas Kuhn informed us, in his classic *The Structure of Scientific Revolutions,* that virtually every major change in perspective (paradigm shift) is initially rejected—often vehemently—before it gains widespread acceptance and use.[17] But whether resisted or not, in an emergent world measurement needs to be emergent as well. Information technology thought leader Marilyn Parker's advice is: "We must prepare for both thinking about and implementing new ways to measure and be measured."[18]

Even though everything can be measured, it sometimes takes a quite a bit of creativity, persistence, and even courage, to do so. Some of the most important insight-generating measures are rarely the obvious ones. Furthermore, many transformational measures probably wouldn't have even received cursory attention in the past because they appear "too soft" to merit serious attention and because they are "too difficult to define." Even today, as emergent measures begin to become accepted, their diffusion throughout organizations is hampered by poor communication, including unclear and inconsistent definitions.

When emergent measures are validated to achieve high-leverage outcomes in actual use, they become "transformational measures." An *emergent measure* becomes a *transformational measure* when it contributes to significant improvements in organizational practice.

These new measures can be used to improve almost anything in an organization. As soon as someone, or some organization, figures out how to measure particular transformational concepts, we can then start using them, measuring their effectiveness, and drive continued improvement. It is my contention that there are virtually unlimited opportunities to discover emergent business measures that can have a transformational impact on the way people in organizations view the work they do, their products, and their customers. These new measures will transform business thinking by helping progressive business leaders view aspects of companies differently, or to "see" formerly invisible assets and phenomena (like intangible assets and process capability) that were invisible in the past because of the lack of an appropriate way of measuring them. But when we finally are able to "see" these things, we will probably wonder why we had previously been blind to something that was "so obvious."

Although some of these measures will be catalogued in Chapter 14, I do want to provide the following example to show how transformational measurement has had a dramatic impact on progressive organizations in one particular area.

## New Customer Measures

Nothing illustrates the power of transformational measures more clearly than new customer measures. One of the most profound measurement-driven shifts in thinking is in the area of *"customer profitability."* Until recently, most companies established marketing goals to attract as many customers as possible—*any customers*. It used to be thought that "all customers are good customers," and unbridled customer acquisition was encouraged. Many companies had an idea that some of their customers were more desirable than others, but they based this belief on amount of revenue they generated, not on profits obtained. This turned out to be a serious oversight, because many of these companies found out, to their consterna-tion, that many of their "best" customers were actually losing them money!

It is interesting to note that the measurement innovation that has changed the "rules of the game" in marketing actually derived from ac-counting—but from non-traditional accountants! *Activity-Based Costing (ABC)* has sent shock waves through the business world that still reverber-ate! ABC has enabled some pioneering companies to make the true and full costs of serving individual customers visible. The results have been astonish-ing! It has surprised almost everyone that, in most companies, between 30 and 80 percent of all customers are unprofitable—and some are *extremely* unprofitable. This new measurement revealed that the "hidden costs of sales" for some customers are significantly higher than for others.

Because of traditional accounting rules, most companies had buried cus-tomer expenses in company overhead and could never link them with spe-cific customers. Companies knew the profitability of products, but didn't have a clue as to the profitability of customers. Most companies didn't even keep track of customer-related activities, much less differentiate between customers in terms of how much was being spent to serve them. As a result, there was little or no way to determine the appropriateness of discounting and promotions, and service levels were being provided to customers that many of them didn't value and couldn't afford. Salespeople didn't care, because they weren't being penalized for unprofitable customers.

Transformational measurement of customer profitability has led some companies to start calculating the *real costs* of activities involved in serving customers, and, from that, are determining "customer profitability" for each major customer and customer segments. Now knowing who their "best cus-tomers" *really* are, these companies are discovering how to dramatically increase their overall profitability by making unprofitable customer profit-able, "firing" unprofitable customers who cannot be made profitable, as well as doing a better job of targeting new customers who have the "right stuff" (profit potential).

A related transformational measure, *"customer lifetime value,"* has helped companies realize, and better manage, the *full potential* of some of their best customers. For example, automakers project a top customer's lifetime value at $200,000, and so do supermarkets. Therefore, learning about, and nurturing, relationships with the most profitable customers has taken on a much greater sense of importance and urgency. That is why one of the most important intangible assets today is *"customer relationship"*—and it is measurable!

Another transformational customer measure is *"customer experience,"* which is creating a paradigm shift in the way companies are viewing their interactions with their customers. This has moved the focus from the tradi-tional "transactional" product or service model to viewing the overall end-to-end customer experience—from initial contact throughout the entire relationship—extending even to how the relationship is terminated, if necessary. Furthermore, this is the kind of transformational measurement breakthrough that will have profound effects on how organizations must work together—rather than in traditional silos—since virtually everyone in the company has some impact on customer experience. The concept of integrated measurement is the subject of the next chapter.

The new, transformational customer measures cited above stand in stark contrast to the more traditional measures, like "customer satisfaction," which, although still important, have deceived many companies into thinking that they were competitive while driving some of them into bankruptcy. For example, it has been shown that as many as 90 percent of departing customers said that they were "satisfied" immediately prior to their attrition! Contrary to long-held misconceptions, "customer satisfaction" is actually a good measure of "customers' rationalizations of their past buying decisions," but not highly predictive of future buying decisions.[19]

This new thinking about the customer has radically changed the focus of sales and marketing organizations in enlightened companies, and it couldn't have been done without the new emergent measures, where true data-based knowledge has now replaced faulty intuition.

## Don't Expect Perfection

If we demand that measures be immediately objective, quantifiable, and statistically reliable, then we are ruling out most emergent and potentially transformational measures. Increased accuracy will come over time, but increased relevance must be made to happen, or nothing else will. People must be empowered to find and use temporary and tentative indicators, while better measures are being sought. Even if a new measure isn't totally accurate, it may still be a step in the right direction and may provide a rough way of gauging progress—which is certainly better than no gauge at all.

Precision has to do with how many numbers after the decimal place— who cares? Lack of precision is only a problem if your decision involves precision. Too many organizations prefer to select measures that are "precisely wrong" over those that are imprecise, but reveal exciting new insight. Organizations should be seeking truth, not necessarily accuracy. It might not require a thermometer to tell you what to wear. However, you can't be sure about whether to bring an umbrella if you don't have access to a weather forecast. So, the type of measurement you need depends on the circumstances and the risk of making a wrong decision. Does it matter if your thermometer is a few degrees off? It depends on how it is being used. The key to creativity in measurement is to never lose sight of the goal, why you are measuring.

It is important to measure directly what you can, and what you can't measure directly, *estimate.* Don't expect perfection. There are no perfect measures or perfect measurement systems. Good measurement—especially emergent measurement—is a process of discovery. Just remember the wise words of Hap Klopp, founder and former president of The North Face, ". . . an open mind can measure *anything.* You may not be able to quantify it, but you *can* measure it."[20]

In this emergent world, more measures will be qualitative and even quite subjective. For example, well-designed rating scales can often be worthwhile measurement tools for many intangibles that cannot yet be measured in a more objective way. But emergent measures have to be taken seriously. When companies experiment with new measures but don't take the time to collect data, nothing changes. It's like buying a new pair of glasses, but never wearing them—your sight won't improve very much!

Nothing will create change in organizations more quickly than when the performance measurement lens is changed. But there is still considerable resistance about trying to measure the "difficult-to-measure things." Fortunately, there are some innovative organizations that realize that it is often futile to try to measure intangibles with traditional quantitative measures, so they are willing to embrace "the brave new world" of qualitative measures, especially in the early stages of measuring a construct.

My best advice at this point is to diligently measure what is most important, It is an ongoing quest, and one of the most important that your organization can commit itself to. Nobody in any organization should be afraid to try out new measures—and, as long as there is a positive context of measurement that doesn't encourage gaming, or self-serving measurement, or condemnation—this will happen more frequently.

Don't let the industry or any other external forces determine your organization's measurement priorities.

## The Next Step

As measures become more focused—and more innovative—it is even more essential that they be integrated into the overall framework and structure of your organization. Focus is necessary, but it alone isn't sufficient. Measurement also must reflect the performance goals of the organization *as a whole.* One of the major problems in most organizations today is the poor integration or alignment of the organization's measurement system. In fact, most organizations don't have a single measurement system, but rather many functional measurement systems that frequently work at cross-purposes.

In the next chapter, the social, organizational, and political issues related to information ownership, sharing, and collaborative decision making will be discussed, along with recommended tools for promoting *integration and acceptance* across the organization.

# CHAPTER 7

# The Integration of Measurement

In Chapter 6, I emphasized the importance of measuring what is most important. Yet this is only a piece of the "big picture." The key message of this chapter is that an organization cannot just focus on isolated measures—at least not for long. Here the emphasis shifts from focus to integration—the relationships among measures. Depending on one or two measures to drive organizational success is rather like "calling the play" in a football game versus having an overall strategy for winning the game, or depending on one investment to achieve wealth instead of managing the full portfolio. Both focus and integration are essential to organizational performance measurement success.

As powerful as *individual* transformational measures can be to create value, they can also become ineffective if they are not integrated into a framework that shows how they are related to other measures. It is the relationship that will yield consistent, ongoing value creation over the long haul. The bottom line message of this chapter is: If it is going to have a truly *transformational* long-term impact, performance measurement must reflect the interconnectedness and holism of the total system—and integration across the organization.

## The Importance of Measurement Integration

There are actually two types of measurement integration: vertical and horizontal. *Vertical* integration involves the connection between strategy and measures up and down through the organization. *Horizontal* integration is the connection of measures across organizational functions and processes. Both of these forms of measurement integration are depicted in Figure 7-1.

Achieving any worthwhile goal requires coordination in order to make sure the parts are working together. As performance measurement expert Bob Phelps has described the challenge of integration: "The problem of

## FIGURE 7-1. VERTICAL AND HORIZONTAL INTEGRATION.

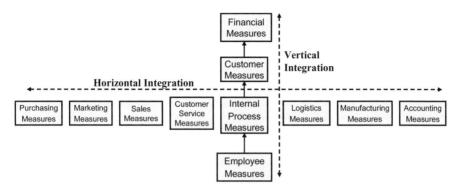

organization is how to ensure that a large body of people of disparate skills and backgrounds all put the maximum effort into attaining the goals of the organization."[1]

Without integration of measures, the organization will inevitably be operating at cross-purposes, often imperceptibly, wasting resources that could be focused on mutually creating real value. For example, organizations today tend to have scorecards all over the place that are disconnected from each other. Worse still, many of these functional scorecards have nothing whatsoever to do with a larger organizational measurement system. Individuals and functions might be achieving "good scores"—but nobody really understands what these scores mean in terms of the success of the organization as a whole.

## The Dis-Integrated Organization

Most organizations are composed of functional silos. They typically evolve from small simple ones to large complex ones. As separate functions emerge, each function wants to own its share of resources. Functional boundaries become strong and more entrenched. Traditional disciplinary thinking creates and reinforces individual departmental factions, commonly referred to as "silos." People tend to "see" the world through their own functions, roles, and measures, i.e., by their job descriptions and what they need to do to achieve success. As Dan Burke explains, "We view the world and make decisions from an extremely disjointed and myopic perspective."[2]

Much of what passes for management today, by necessity, involves trying to get the isolated pieces of work done—turning the *dis-integration* of our organizations into something that is reasonably integrated. But it is an uphill struggle. As Benko and McFarland report, "Today, nearly every large organization across the globe is feeling the impact of its internal misalignment."[3] One organization I know of has 1,400 initiatives going at the same time!

Individual functions see the world through their own functional lenses, and the more they do so, the more deeply entrenched they becomes in their own positions. According to management professor Leonard Sayles, "there is an almost built-in centrifugal tendency in organizations that causes departments to become less and less coordinated (or in sync) with each other over time."[4] The fundamental characteristic of a poorly integrated organization is WASTE! Sadly, it also fails to make use of the valuable synergies that are any organization's greatest resource.

Why does the silo phenomenon arise? The major culprits are social and cultural factors. People from different disciplines have different educational backgrounds, training, language, mental models, experience, career path, aspirations, etc. This makes it very difficult to communicate, much less have a common perspective.

Everyone, it seems, has horror stories to tell about siloed behavior. For example, Shapiro, Rangan, and Sviokla in an aptly titled *Harvard Business Review* article, "Staple Yourself to an Order," recount the antagonistic battles between engineers, accountants, and field sales force related to cost estimating and pricing. Not only do they ultimately reach suboptimal outcomes, but, in the process, each group questions the motives, competence, and goals of the others. Meanwhile the customer waits unattended for the bid or quote, unaware of the *battle royal* that is causing the delay![5]

Most companies are composed of pieces vying for scarce resources—operating more like competitors than cooperators—acting individually, without regard to systemic interdependencies. People don't act this way because they are obstinate or nasty. They do it because the organizational systems condition them to do so. People are simply following the traditional, if flawed, logic, which is: "If every function meets its goals . . . if every function hits its budget . . . if every project is completed on time and on budget . . . then the organization will win." However, it should be clear that such thinking no longer works, if it ever did. Organizations should be focused on the performance of the whole, not the independent performance of the parts.

Unfortunately, it is very difficult to manage an entire organization in an integrated manner—especially without a very well-integrated measurement system. It is far easier just to hold the parts accountable for independent results. Chances are that your organization is not well-integrated either, and the primary reason is likely to be the fragmented measurement system! Coordinating an organization and keeping it coordinated requires a framework that is aligned with the business model and its strategy, and which can be modified systemically on an ongoing basis. A good measurement system is the best coordinating mechanism there is.

## Dis-Integrated Measurement

The following dis-integrated measurement scenario should be all-too-familiar to readers: Sales is focused on revenue, by territory and product line, and the sales people have a laser focus on meeting their individual sales quota targets. Marketing is focused on market share, brand image, and customer satisfaction. Manufacturing is focused on productivity, meeting forecast, and quality. Logistics is focused on delivery. Project managers are focused on individual project time and budget milestones. Human Resources is focused on HR program deployment, participation, and employee satisfaction. Information Technology is focused on IT project funding and on technology availability. Finance is focused on controlling costs.

As Hackett Benchmarking & Research reports, the typical company has twenty-nine different financial systems for each billion dollars in revenue![6] According to Rummler and Brache, "The result is a collection of largely unrelated and unmanageable measures, leading in many cases to 'measurement gridlock'—managers in a state of paralysis because they can't move performance affecting one measure in a positive direction without (seemingly) moving two other measures in a negative direction."[7] No wonder there is a big problem with everyone pulling in different directions.

In some organizations, functions and processes operate so independently that there is virtually no connection between them at all. In a fairly common scenario, managers at one financial services company were tracking 142 different departmental performance measures that were totally uncoordinated. No two managers could agree on which measures were most strategically important. And, before long, every function seemed to have its own idiosyncratic measures, and every employee or role had its own personal scorecard or instrument panel. Poorly integrated measures allow managers to pursue their own or departmental interests ahead of those of the company or its shareholders.

Can you imagine flying on a jumbo jet where all the crew members are trying to control the aircraft from their own functional perspectives using their own instrument panels, without an integrated set of measures established on a common flight plan? Or how successful would a team be in sports if the players were all just trying to maximize their individual statistics? The individual players on a sports team, no matter how spectacular their performance, cannot win a championship by themselves. They need the others on the team to do their parts. Just as *real teams* are the ones that succeed best in sports, so also are *well-integrated organizations* the winners in business and in the public sector.

But in the business world, it isn't enough to just align an isolated team. In business, the *whole organization* must be aligned, and it takes real leadership to integrate an organization. In order to achieve integration, most people advocate the use of aligned compensation arrangements and cross-functional incentives so that *self-interest* will more readily coincide with *organizational interest*. However, relying on external incentives alone is dangerous because rewards tend to reinforce individual efforts and they are so resistant to change in response to changing circumstances.

People in different functions and units must be continually reminded to look beyond their silos. Cross-functional communication will help. But whatever steps are taken, none of them will be truly effective—at least not for long—unless the organizational measurement system is integrated. Organizational integration is impossible without measurement integration! And most organizations have a long way to go in this respect.

## Dis-Integrated Data

Data quality is also a major issue that impedes integrative performance measurement. The raw material of measurement is data. Gartner Group estimates that the average company collects 120 terabytes (a unit of computer memory equal to 1,024 gigabytes, or 1 trillion bytes) of customer data alone.[8] Organizations today store a lot of data because IT systems *allow* them to do so. But data storage capabilities have far exceeded the other capabilities needed to effectively *use* all the data. Furthermore, the data that most organizations have in storage is of questionable quality. By and large, people input data into information systems, blindly accepting that everything they input is true—that all data is of equal and high quality.

Not true! Despite huge advances in Enterprise Resource Planning (ERP) and other cross-enterprise integration technologies, many organizations still fail to adequately connect disparate data repositories. Much of available data remains disconnected, inconsistent, and inaccessible. This all-too-common problem has been variously described as data scatter, data disorder, data fragmentation, data hoarding, dormant data (data that has never been accessed, and probably never will), legacy data (data gathered because at one time management asked for it, but now might be obsolete), or database fiefdoms.

It has been estimated that data quality problems cost U.S. business $1.5 trillion per year, or 8-12 percent of revenue! Much of this data quality conundrum is also due to functions that aren't very well *coordinated*. And like most functional problems, much of this is due to politics—in this case, the politics of data ownership. That's why data dis-integration is, at its root, a social and organizational problem.

## Strategic Measurement

As explained in Chapter 6, strategy should be the major integrating force of any organization. But as we all know, it is one thing to come up with an organization-wide strategic plan, and it is quite another to execute it well organization-wide. There tend to be huge "dis-connects" between strategy, strategic measures, and operations. That is why so much is being written today about "strategy execution," which has become a number one management priority. And strategic *measurement* has become a central enabler of effective strategy execution.

As Samuel DiPiazza, Jr., CEO of accounting giant PriceWaterhouse-Coopers, and performance measurement guru Robert Eccles have said, "Measurement plays a dual role: It focuses attention on what is important, as determined by the company's strategy, and it monitors the level of performance along those dimensions in the effort to turn strategy into results."[9]

Unfortunately, strategy tends to be too abstract for most people in the organization to follow, and not readily measurable. For example, let's say the strategy calls for "customer-centricity," "high quality," and "timeliness"—what do those strategic assertions really mean in practice? Most executive strategy pronouncements are vague and rarely measurable. Such strategic "platitudes" need to be made more concrete through the right performance measures if strategy is going to be effectively executed and if this execution is going to be verifiable.

## The Balanced Scorecard

In order to make strategy more readily executable through the use of performance measurement, Robert Kaplan and David Norton developed the concept of a "balanced scorecard," an organizational scorecard that would facilitate the integration of functional measures and enable better organization-wide strategy execution. The basic idea of the scorecard is to describe the essential ingredients of business success.

There is nothing magical about a balanced scorecard. In fact, the idea of a multi-dimensional scorecard had been proposed numerous times previously. However, it was Kaplan and Norton's seminal 1992 *Harvard Business Review* article, "The Balanced Scorecard: Measures That Drive Performance"[10] that launched the concept into respectability and helped it achieve widespread acceptance. A balanced scorecard is really nothing more than a set of organizational measures that is *balanced* by having multiple "perspectives" or dimensions, including both financial and nonfinancial measures. It balances the Financial perspective with Customer, Internal, and Learning and Growth perspectives. Many readers might be familiar with its most common depiction as a "scorecard" divided into four quadrants, each representing one of the four perspectives.

The popularity of the balanced scorecard is attributable to the following three innovative principles:

1. It is a management system, not just a measurement system. The intent is that the scorecard be used to manage the communication and deployment of the strategy, not just to measure it after-the-fact.

2. The four perspectives of the scorecard are supposed to be causally related. The Financial and Customer perspectives describe the outcomes the organization wants to achieve; the Internal and Learning and Growth perspectives describe how the organization intends to achieve these outcomes. While financial "outcomes" measure the desired "final score," the key is to use the "drivers" in the other perspectives to move the financials in the right direction.

3. The scorecard is supposed to focus attention on creating "capability in the present" (through customer value propositions and outstanding internal processes) and "future value" (through developing the intangibles in the Learning and Growth perspective). Also, because it addresses nonfinancial measures, it is more relevant than previous financial-only scorecards to those in the organization without bottom-line P&L responsibility.

The balanced scorecard has been heralded as a breakthrough for strategy execution, because it helps to translate strategic concepts into practice. The idea is that the relevant measures from the "strategy scorecard" get cascaded downward through the organization to achieve greater clarity of strategic intent to those who need to execute on those measures.

Today, a majority of companies probably have some form of balanced scorecard, and an entire industry has been created around it, including abundant technology "solutions." There is no doubt that balanced scorecards have *the potential* to increase the clarity of business strategy and enhance the organization's ability to communicate (cascade) the strategic direction to others. But while balance is important, it is *only one* of many characteristics of a good measurement system. Ultimately, scorecards succeed or fail based on the quality of their measures, how they are implemented, and how well people use them. As Nils-Goran Olve explains it, "Just putting a number of measures down on paper will not give us a balanced scorecard. The essence of the scorecard is the process and the discussion relating to the measures—beforehand, during, and afterwards."[11]

I believe that the primary problem with balanced scorecards today is that they have become viewed as a "panacea" and are often used as a "quick fix." This is not the fault of the concept but rather that many companies that adopt balanced scorecards do not adequately understand the underlying principles and are not implementing the concept properly. The balanced scorecard is not just a four-quadrant template for categorizing existing measures—although that might be beneficial if the right measures are already in place. But a balanced scorecard will not make the wrong measures right.

## The Value of Measurement Frameworks

One of the most important assumptions encapsulated in the balanced score-card is that strategy is composed of a set of hypotheses of cause-and-effect relationships. After initially releasing the balanced scorecard, Kaplan and Norton began to realize that it was not enough to imply that the measures in the scorecard perspectives should be causally linked; it was also necessary to explicitly link measures both within and between perspectives. This gave rise to their concept of "strategy maps."[12]

A strategy map is a visual representation of the organization's strategy, which provides a discipline for linking objectives in the four perspectives (from the balanced scorecard) to promote greater understanding of the strategy, and hopefully greater commitment to executing it. Once created, the strategy map becomes, in concept at least, a powerful communication and strategy execution tool. It also visualizes at least part of the organization's value creation process.

Strategy maps are a specific application of a broader area I call "mea-surement frameworks." Measurement frameworks communicate the logic of the business, or a segment of the business. Strategy maps, measurement frameworks, cause-and-effect models, causal maps, causal chains, and the like—terms you are likely to be familiar with—are all pretty much variations of the same theme. An example of a measurement framework using the balanced scorecard/strategy map perspectives is depicted in Figure 7-2.

FIGURE 7-2. MEASUREMENT FRAMEWORK: STRATEGY MAP FORMAT.

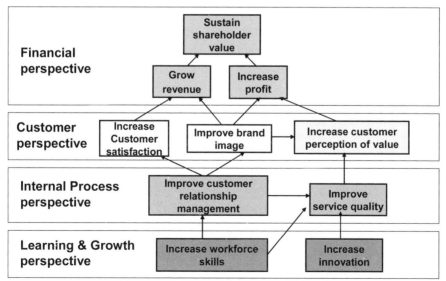

## It's About Relationships

The key to successful integrated measurement is not to connect what people are currently doing, but what they should be doing—*executing the strategy*. What is so important to consider about this approach is that the *relationships among the measures* are as important as the measures themselves. The weakness of most implementations of the balanced scorecard and strategy maps is that the measures are rarely codified into a comprehensive model. A measurement framework is a more comprehensive hierarchical organization of measures that fit together according to a logical structure. The key is to first determine the desired *"outcomes"* of the organization and then determine the *"drivers"* of these outcomes, and show how they are related.

## Understanding and Visibility

In organizational performance measurement, there are usually *many* right answers. The key is to achieve continuously better (and deeper) understanding of how the organization's strategy translates into outcomes and drivers of success, and then to find the best mix of measures that conveys strategic intent and integrates the organization to execute that strategy. *Understand* first; *measure* second. Performance measurement is not about filling out "templated" scorecards, it is obtaining *increasingly* deeper understanding that leads to *progressively* better actions that drive desired results, and then communicating that understanding throughout the organization through integrated measures so that everyone can execute in an integrated manner across the entire organization.

One of the most important things you can do is to get senior managers to agree on the value creation process in the organization: What are the organization's performance objectives, the performance drivers of those goals, and how do they relate together. Create a simple model of how the organization "works." This is not a one-shot discussion, but an ongoing journey of discovery.

A good measurement framework also provides managers and employees with visibility into how their "local" measures fit with the organization's "global" measures. Employees are constantly wondering (whether or not they overtly express it): "Why in the heck are you making me take all these measurements that aren't important?" Employees need measures that are meaningful to them, which provide a "line of sight" that enables them to appreciate the linkages between what they are doing and what is important to the organization as a whole. "If I do this, this will result?" "What is the relationship between my behavior and organizational performance?"

That is one reason why the quality movement had such a profound impact—performance measurement was relevant to employees doing the work, and they could also predict the impact that their local quality measurements would have on the organization's success.

## Improving Decision Making

Too often we encounter the situation that Michael Hammer describes in the following: "The measurement system did not connect the numbers to each other in a meaningful way or provide executives with any guidance as to how to improve them."[13] As a result, managers had no idea how they could affect any of the measures. And so, the measurement system reverted to being just a *reporting system* instead of a decision-guiding system.

The most crucial role of managers is to ensure that the right integrated decisions are made across the organization. For example, if a manager wants to change X, he or she should start by measuring and managing the drivers of X. These decisions need to be based on common understanding of the basic assumptions—and all strategies contain implicit assumptions about factors that drive performance and create value. As Peter Senge said, "We can argue like cats and dogs about the strategy, but without any way of getting at the assumptions behind the strategy the argument is virtually pointless, because we have no way of achieving a deeper, shared understanding."[14] There is little doubt that, if done well, measurement frameworks will increase the likelihood that all functions and all levels in the organization are pulling together—*both vertically and horizontally*. I can quickly gauge how integrated an organization is by looking at its measurement system—especially its measurement frameworks—*if any exist*.

## Managing the Future

Another great benefit of measurement frameworks is to help predict future performance, so that better organizational decisions can be made. It doesn't accomplish much to only measure the past. The performance we should care most about is in the future. Lebas and Euske define performance as "doing today what will lead to measured valued outcomes tomorrow."[15] It isn't the final score that is important; what is most important is to understand what happened to produce that score, and therefore what can be improved next time. Furthermore, it is important that employees don't feel that measurement is being used to just monitor their past and present performance. They will respond much more positively when measurement is being used to improve future performance.

Measurement frameworks are catching on, and their value is being widely acknowledged. DiPiazza and Eccles found that 69 percent of executives said that they had attempted to demonstrate empirical cause-and-effect relationships between different categories of value drivers and future financial results. "Without question, companies that have grasped how to measure and manage their value drivers do a better job of delivering top-line revenue growth."[16] According to Ittner and Larcker's research, companies that used measurement models that linked nonfinancial drivers to financial outcomes produced significantly higher returns on assets and equity over a five-year period than those that did not.[17] Much of this business value is due to the increased integrative understanding that comes from developing and using measurement frameworks.

## Measurement Frameworks and Trade-Offs

Once you start thinking seriously about measures, and relationships among measures, you inevitably need to consider trade-offs. Virtually every decision involves trade-offs. One of the most important aspects of organizational management and measurement is to make the best trade-off decisions. In Chapter 2, we saw the kind of dysfunction caused by suboptimization, which is making trade-off decisions to benefit a particular function. In contrast, "optimization" is about making trade-off decisions for the benefit of the overall organization. Measurement frameworks increase our ability to make more optimal organizational decisions—that is if we take the time to develop them and use them well.

Measurement frameworks visually depict the *interdependencies* between measures. In any interdependent system, you can't change one measure without affecting the others. With an overall framework that shows the relationships between measures, it is easier to make the proper trade-off decisions, so more optimal decisions can be made.

The major trade-off in an organization is ultimately between performance (including quality and timeliness) and cost. Nobel Laureate Herbert Simon framed the issue of performance versus cost trade-offs pretty compellingly when he said: "Oh, you can make zero-defect products. The question is, can you do it profitably?"[18] His implied answer, of course, to his rhetorical question is: "No, you can't!" Remember: Whenever a decision is made to focus on a particular measure, trade-offs must be considered.

Consider the following trade-off questions:

"How much am I willing to pay for a certain level of quality?"

"How much are we willing to pay for faster delivery?"

"How much inventory should we hold in order to reduce the possibility of stock-outs?"

"How much emphasis should we put on profits versus customer satisfaction?"

"How much should we reduce cycle time at the expense of flexibility?"

These are relatively simple *two-factor* trade-off questions; it gets even more difficult when considering three or more factors in making trade-off decisions. None of these questions are easy to answer, especially not in dis-integrated, highly-political systems.

## Developing Measurement Frameworks

In any organization, there are an infinite number of potential measures, relationships, and connections. Developing measurement frameworks is directly related to developing a deeper understanding of the value creation process. Most people really don't understand what they are trying to measure until they see a measurement framework, and then it all starts to make sense.

A measurement framework is a model. Although no model is perfect, to the extent possible, measurement frameworks should reflect the organization's strategy and the interconnectedness of the total system. But it doesn't have to be totally comprehensive. Focus on the measures that are most important. Don't try to measure everything. One of the most challenging aspects of developing measurement frameworks is to decide where to start and when to stop.

Measurement frameworks often start with hypotheses. For example:

"We believe that more satisfied customers are more loyal . . . but we don't know for sure."

"We believe that making these improvements in our delivery model will increase customer satisfaction, loyalty, and profitability."

Don't be afraid to test hypotheses. But if a relationship is hypothesized, it is important to be honest that it is an assumption and not a fact. One of the purposes of measurement frameworks is to foster new understandings through hypothesizing and testing hypotheses, not just to describe what is already proven.

A measurement framework doesn't have to cover the entire organization. (It can describe a component, as long as it is a complete component and separating it won't cause the kind of dis-integration that we discussed earlier in this chapter.) The challenge is to create a systemic view with simplicity, so that it is understandable and usable.

Deciding on the right things to measure is not primarily a measurement decision; it is a business decision. It requires business acumen and holistic thinking—so don't delegate it to a "measurement person!" Furthermore, you don't have to get it right the first time. Don't try to create the perfect measurement framework or you'll fall prey to analysis paralysis. Developing a measurement framework is only a starting point for understanding relationships among key performance measures.

In developing measurement frameworks, you should heed Albert Einstein's admonition, "Everything should be as simple as possible . . . *but no simpler!*" Building simple, but not simplistic, models and identifying the key drivers is rarely easy. I call the type of cause-and-effect embodied in a measurement framework "contributory causality," because there is usually more than a single driver for each higher-level driver or outcome. Some cause-and-effect linkages are often difficult to discern and, until proven, are always questionable. But don't feel that you need rigorous proof before hypothesizing that a causal relationship might exist. As T.S. Eliot said: "Between the idea and the reality. . . . between the conception and the creation . . . falls the shadow." Accept the fact that there is almost always the shadow of uncertainty between causes and effects.

There is no one right way to create a measurement framework. You can use the "strategy map" approach, and use the four perspectives (Financial, Customer, Internal, Learning and Growth) of the balanced scorecard. Although the approach I advocate is similar to a strategy map, it doesn't necessarily need to be depicted according to "perspective." However, it does need to reflect credible cause-and-effect logic. This alternative approach is depicted in Figure 7-3.

Certainly it is generally appropriate to start with the desired financial results at the top of a measurement framework. Then, the major drivers of

FIGURE 7-3. SAMPLE MEASUREMENT FRAMEWORK.

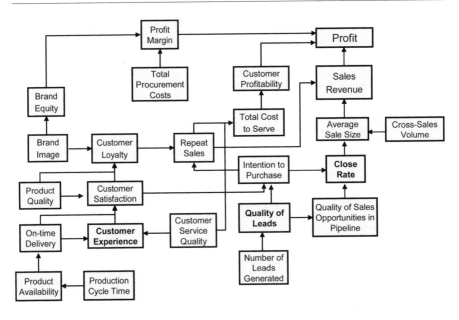

those financial results should be identified. Since customers are the major source of revenue and profits, it does make sense to include the major customer measures next. These measures can then be connected with the financial outcomes. And then, in the same way, key customer outcome measures can be identified and linked with relevant process (internal) and intangible (learning and growth) drivers.

One of the areas that needs a lot more emphasis in measurement frameworks are intangibles like innovation, reputation, and collaboration. Kaplan and Norton have given these measures little attention in the Learning and Growth perspective of their balanced scorecards and strategy maps. The future competitiveness of our organizations and our entire society will depend on our ability to more effectively measure and manage the intangibles that have been long considered the "softer side" of performance measurement and are now becoming the essence of competitive advantage. You will find much more on this subject in Chapters 13 and 14.

## Cross-Functional Integration

One of the key concepts in this chapter is the desirability of breaking down the traditional functional silos, and driving more cross-functional integration, and consequently more collaboration. You will notice that in the measurement framework depicted in Figure 7-3, there are measures that relate to a number of different functional areas. There are measures for *sales* (e.g., sales revenue, average sale size, cross-sales volume, close rate, repeat sales, quality of sales in the pipeline), *marketing* (e.g., number of leads generated, quality of leads, intention to purchase, brand image, customer satisfaction, customer loyalty, customer profitability), *production* (e.g., product quality, product availability), *logistics* (e.g., on-time delivery), and *procurement* (e.g., total procurement costs). Typically each function would focus only on its own measures, and would be oblivious to the measures of other functions and what the trade-offs among the measures might be.

One of the great benefits of measurement frameworks is that they can stimulate positive dialogue across functions about some of the crucial integrative issues that will make the difference between success and failure in the new economy. Silo-based organizations are increasingly becoming an anachronism. By discussing the implications and trade-offs of the measurement framework, barriers can be removed and more cross-functional collaboration can be instigated. This can be truly transformational!

One of the keys to doing this is the identification of cross-functional or "integrating measures." Candidates for integrating measures are highlighted on a revised version of the measurement framework example, as illustrated in Figure 7-4. The highlighted measures are profit, quality of opportunities in the pipeline, customer profitability, total cost to serve, customer experience, and on-time delivery.

FIGURE 7-4. MEASUREMENT FRAMEWORK: ALTERNATIVE FORMAT.

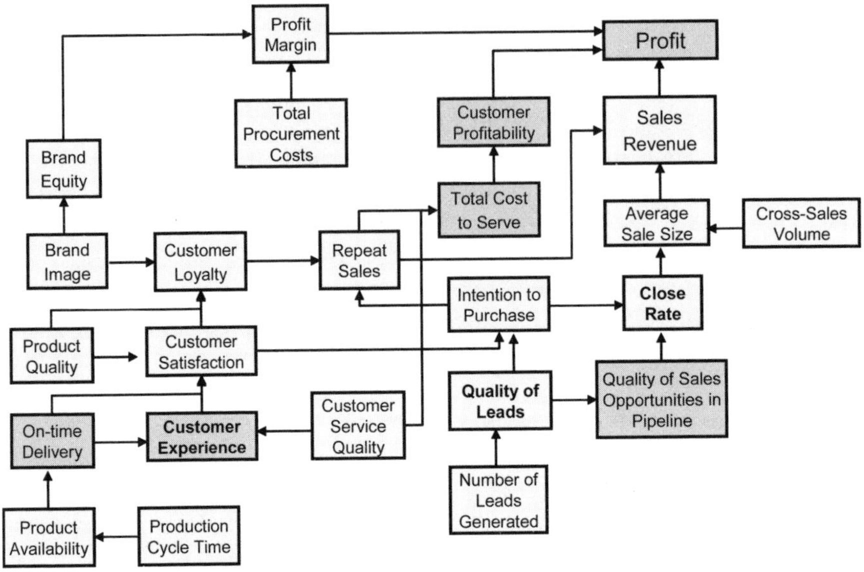

Let me explain briefly. It is increasingly important today to get everyone focused on profit, not just sales revenue. As discussed in Chapter 6, customer profitability is a potentially transformational measure that can change the way people in an organization view customers. Cross-functional discussions about customer profitability, and how to optimize it, can have a significant impact on how different functions like Finance, Marketing, Sales, Purchasing, Manufacturing, and Customer Service can work together.

For example, a measure that can have integrative impact is on-time delivery. After all, there are many functions that need to work together to make sure that products are delivered on-time. Again, there are trade-offs. If on-time delivery is too important, then logistics or customer service might intervene in a late order and expedite it to a customer at huge expense, which might seriously affect customer profitability—and even company profitability if this pattern repeats itself too many times.

There are virtually an infinite number of potentially transformational measures that can lead to extremely valuable integrative opportunities. What is important is that these measures and key issues be made visible through measurement frameworks, or else new transformational measures will never be adopted and the critical issues related to them will never addressed.

## Measurement Innovation Must Be Encouraged

However they are created, measurement frameworks are initially composed of *hypotheses* (assumptions) of the key measures and their causal relationships. These hypotheses are then tested with actual data, and can be confirmed, disconfirmed, or modified. That is what the measurement framework examples in Figures 7-3 and 7-4 show. The arrows between the measures are hypotheses of the relationships.

Measurement frameworks should not just be viewed as a way of depicting the way an organization currently measures itself, but how it can measure itself to become more effective. That is what transformational performance measurement is all about—*using new and innovative measures to drive significantly higher levels of performance across organizations.* However, even when these causal hypotheses are validated, they still might not remain valid forever, so you must remain vigilant about the continuing validity of the framework.

Whatever you do, don't fall for the easy way out, which is to just use standard industry frameworks or scorecards. There is no harm in adapting an existing measurement framework, as long as you are willing to challenge it mercilessly. Gartner's guideline is a good one: Frameworks can consist of 70 to 80 percent standardized measures, but should include 20 to 30 percent that are company specific.[19]

## An Iterative Approach

Again, it bears repeating that creating and refining a measurement framework must be viewed as an *iterative process*. Like Shewhart's[20] and Deming's[21] Plan-Do-Check-Act cycle, the process of creating and refining measurement frameworks is circular. First, you need to understand the organization as a system and identify the key measures, both the outcomes and the drivers, and their relationships (Plan). Once the initial measurement framework has been created, you can start using it to make decisions (Do). Then, collect data and use that data to test the hypotheses reflected in the measurement framework (Check). Then, modify the measurement framework (Act) based on new data. This is the kind of approach I will stress in Chapter 8 in order to iteratively turn data into knowledge and wisdom through data-based interactive dialogue.

In creating measurement frameworks you will be working with abstract concepts and often new and emerging measures in an area of considerable uncertainty, where many do not feel very comfortable. There might also be impatience and conservatism. You are likely to face some "context of measurement" challenges. For example:

How much support can you expect for developing measurement models?

How well will efforts at developing a measurement framework be accepted by stakeholders in your organization?

How much credibility will it have?

These are just a few of the social issues that must be considered in taking an integrative approach to performance measurement.

## The Need for a CMO

One final element that needs to be mentioned (and I will cover it at more length in Chapter 9) is the need to establish a new management position, a CMO—a Chief Measurement Officer.

How are all the issues in this book—especially those requiring the integration of performance measurement—going to be addressed, and coordinated, given the way most organizations are currently structured? How is the huge potential for performance measurement and performance measurement technologies going to be realized? Whether people are part of a business, government agency, a sports team, or any other organization, common measurements will help to get people aligned around a common purpose and common goals. But if everyone and every function is trying to maximize the numbers on their own scorecard, and is working to achieve functional optimization, then someone has to orchestrate all the individual scorecards and functional agendas to make sure that the *organizational scorecard* is also optimized. Who is going to encourage the development of transformational, emergent, and cross-functional measures? Someone has to coordinate the development and use of cross-functional measurement frameworks. Unfortunately, I don't know of anyone today who has that job!

One could say that the CEO is really the person who should be doing this. But who is going to advise the CEO on these matters? What about the CIO? Perhaps, but I don't think so, because too many of the issues have little or nothing to do with technology. It does not appear to me that any existing C-level executive can provide the kind of objective, integrative measurement leadership that is so desperately needed. Whether or not he or she has the title of CMO, somebody must assume this role, or else dis-integration, not integration, will continue its insidious influence on organizations everywhere.

## The Next Step

Keeping the organization focused on the right targets and moving *together* in the right direction is no easy job. Technical people would love for you to believe that they have the solution in the form of an electronic scorecard or dashboard, but don't believe them. No scorecard or dashboard is going to overcome this challenge without a lot of work on the social and organizational side of the equation—and without a lot of improvement in communication and *interactivity*.

# CHAPTER 8

# The Interactivity of Measurement

It is the key thesis of this book that without the inclusion of a strong social component, performance measurement will *never* be transformational. Very few organizations have established a *social or organizational context* that is sufficiently supportive of their technical measurement system components. In fact, to dramatize this, just compare the investment in the technical versus the social aspects of the measurement system in your organization. Chances are, you won't be able to find much of a social investment at all.

Everywhere we look, it is hard to miss the fact that the real solutions to organizational problems are predominantly social, not technical. There is no denying that the technical components are important, but it is the context of measurement that will determine the ultimate effectiveness of any measurement system *in use*. The technical aspects of measurement will only take performance measurement to a minimal level of effectiveness. True transformational performance measurement requires extensive social *interactivity.*

One of the reasons why it is so important to establish a positive context for measurement is that the context will either encourage or discourage interactivity around measurement. If people in an organization view measurement as just routine "numerical transactions," they will be missing the most important parts of measurement—which are the "social interactions"—the communication, insight, and learning that should occur throughout the measurement process.

Performance measurement should include highly interactive and iterative (ongoing) discussions, or *dialogues*, which are the most important aspects of measurement. When these dialogues are built on the foundation of a positive context of measurement, focus, and integration, then performance measurement will likely be transformational.

## The Importance of Interactivity

Effective integration and interactivity of measurement will do more than anything else to break down the silos that are keeping organizations from realizing measurement's transformational potential. In the previous chapter, we saw how individuals (predominantly operating within specific functions) bring only their own perspective on an issue. In order to obtain an integrated (and a richer) picture of any subject, it is essentially to get people with different perspectives (and with different versions of "the truth") interacting—both within functions and across functions.

The importance of interactivity is receiving increasing attention in management circles. Even the literature on performance measurement is beginning to acknowledge the importance of the communicative aspects, but not nearly to an adequate extent. For instance, Robert Kaplan and David Norton state in *The Strategy-Focused Organization*, "Understanding the strategy, through extensive and innovative communication processes, is the initial building block for creating strategic awareness. . . . Open communication of performance information provides the opportunity for a new kind of infrastructure." One of the reasons for this increased emphasis is their finding that "85 percent of management teams spend less than one hour per month discussing strategy."[1]

In their best-selling book *Execution: The Discipline of Getting Things Done*, Larry Bossidy and Ram Charan also emphasize the importance of the interactive aspects of management. They describe "dialogue" as "the core of culture and the basic unit of work." They go on to say, "How people talk to each other absolutely determines how well the organization will function."[2] Pretty strong stuff!

When Total Quality Management (TQM) has been really successful, it has been largely because of the way it was socially and organizationally implemented. When Six Sigma has really yielded powerful results, it has been because of the social and organizational context that surrounded it, more than the technical aspects of the methodology itself. Why was Comp-Stat so powerful in reducing the crime rate in New York City? Again, it was the social and organizational context—including Rudolph Giuliani's leadership of the measurement effort. Although the data collection and analysis was important, the transformation was due more to how that data was "socialized" and used.

One of the most valuable assets of an organization is the synergy that diverse resources and capabilities provide. It is crucial to appreciate how important it is for "the pieces" of an organization to interact. Unfortunately, few organizations are able to take advantage of much of the synergistic potential at their disposal. Without a systemic, holistic approach, great opportunities for synergy are missed. Because organizations need to become more integrated, functions and people within organizations need be become more interactive. You can't just change the organizational chart or produce and communicate a measurement framework; the interaction around them is what will turn the plan into a changed reality.

As I have emphasized, the most important aspect of measurement is the dialogues that should occur at every stage in the measurement process. This is where the otherwise lifeless data and information is infused with meaning, and transformed into knowledge, insight, and wisdom through ongoing, interactive learning. These are aspects of measurement that require a high level of attention and engagement from business leaders, and intensive and extensive communication throughout the organization. They should not be delegated to specialists! The fact that these crucial social aspects of performance measurement are ignored or given cursory attention is one of the major reasons why performance measurement is so rarely effective, let alone transformational.

Although almost all organizations have a long way to go on the performance measurement transformation journey, some companies have been identified as being more effective than most in using performance measurement. They have been dubbed "measurement-managed organizations"[3]— and have enviable records of both financial and nonfinancial performance. These companies are not more successful because they *take* isolated measurements, but because of how much more effectively they *use* measurement data as a critical part of managing and doing work on a continuing basis.

## Data, Information, Knowledge, and Wisdom

*Data* is essentially just isolated facts *out of context*. Most numbers are data. Data is acquired from surveys, logs, and reports. Data is the raw materials from which information, knowledge, and wisdom can ultimately be created, but it won't get you very far until you do something with it.

*Information* is an organized selection of data presented in such a way that its meaning can be recognized by a user. It is the first step on the way from data to wisdom. Information often describes, defines, or provides perspective, and is usually created from data by such means as organizing (e.g., sorting, combining), comparing, analyzing, and visualizing. Information is commonly used to support what we already know and to justify decisions; this is okay, but this won't create any new insight, knowledge, or wisdom. One of the easiest ways to convert data into information is to add some historical perspective. For example, depicting a relevant trend in numbers in a table or on a graph is information ("Our sales forecast is . . ."). It is also helpful to have some basis for comparison—a target, a baseline, a benchmark—something that will enable you to add a meaningful context to the data. A valuable rule of thumb for information presentation is to always focus on the meaning, when others might be focused on calculations.

When information is combined internally with other information and personal experience into a form that can be useful it becomes *knowledge*. Knowledge is personally relevant information you can take action on. Action-oriented insights gleaned from deeper analysis of charts or graphs can become knowledge. "Know-how" is knowledge. For example, "We can attain our sales forecast by . . ." Personally appreciating the implications of the trade-offs between measures in a measurement framework is knowledge. The ability to make credible predictions and forecasts requires knowledge.

As additional knowledge and experience is accumulated, the base and level of knowledge available should increase. When we achieve real knowledge about some subject, our reaction is "Aha, now I get it!" Knowledge can be individual or organizational; it can be explicit (documented) or tacit (include one's head or in corporate memory). The more effectively knowledge is managed, the more readily it will grow as knowledge, rather than just as additional data or information.

*Wisdom* is deep, rich understanding and insight that usually develops through a combination of extensive knowledge (knowing) and personal experience (doing) over time. Wisdom cannot be seen directly, but can be inferred from a track record of consistently good decisions. Wisdom grows through the interplay of existing knowledge, new knowledge (extracted from new information) acquired through study and communication with other knowledgeable people, practical experiences, reflection, etc.

Figure 8-1 shows that as data gets converted into information, then into knowledge, and finally into wisdom, there is a progressively greater increase

FIGURE 8-1. PROGRESSION FROM DATA TO WISDOM.

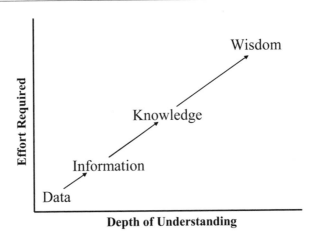

in understanding. However, it also entails a progressively greater amount of effort.

Data contributes very little to our understanding, but generating it is very easy. In contrast, wisdom contributes maximally to our understanding, but it requires considerable effort to achieve. Data is freely available everywhere. But there is no such thing as "instant wisdom" and it can't be purchased from a consultant. Every organization (and every person) must develop its own wisdom. Performance measurement done right, in the right context, is a powerful vehicle for developing organizational, as well as individual, wisdom. And wisdom, when it is acquired, usually looks simple—"Why didn't I realize that before?"—although the process of acquiring it certainly isn't. In fact, very few organizations are willing to invest much effort in driving performance measurement from data into wisdom!

Clifford Stoll has said it well: "Our networks are awash in data. A little of it is information. A smidgeon of this shows up as knowledge. Combined with ideas, some of that is actually useful. Mix in experience, context, compassion, discipline, humor, tolerance, and humility, and perhaps knowledge becomes wisdom."[4]

The real value of measurement is realized when we use it to optimize our circumstances—to manage complex affairs to an optimal outcome—individually or corporately. One of the keys to success is identifying the most important things to measure and using that measurement to take the most appropriate actions. For example, when the stock market went into its downturn after 9-11, those who were able to use the readily available measurement indicators to manage their portfolios were likely to fare pretty well, while those of us (like me), who just let the business cycle run its course, lost great opportunities to minimize investment losses and maximize gains. One of the most serious mistakes I made—that is clear in retrospect—was not *discussing* the readily available data with those who had wisdom about it.

In fact, one of the biggest obstacles to individual measurement is that our personal emotions and naïve intuition tend to get in the way of truly wise decisions. Furthermore, most people tend to assume the numbers are factual and true, and that they tell the whole story. When most people see numbers, they don't ask how they were arrived at; they could be entirely contrived. Rarely does anyone question them. It's so easy to be impressed by numbers. Bottom-line: Measurements can be very enlightening, or very deceptive. Most people have very poor "measurement literacy."

Whether it is managing personal health, wealth, athletic performance, a business, or almost anything else, those who use measurement best tend to fare best. But, unless we *interact* with others, we are very unlikely to pool our knowledge with others into wisdom, maintain the discipline that measurement requires, be able to recognize the right signals, and take advantage of them when we do. Wisdom comes from continuous learning, and continuous learning comes, to a large extent, through interactivity.

## The Data-to-Wisdom Conversion Process

The data-to-knowledge-to-wisdom conversion process reflects one of the great positives of transformational measurement. Although it is possible for individuals to do this alone, the most effective way to create knowledge and wisdom from measurement is through frequent and high-quality interactions between people with complementary knowledge. Ask anybody (including yourself): "Do you learn more from data or from interacting with other people who have a like-minded mission?" I have asked this question of hundreds of leaders in all sectors of the economy and in government, and the resounding answer is unequivocally: "From our interactions with others." It is ultimately the *social things* that will help convert measurement from information into knowledge and wisdom and, in the process, positively transform the context of measurement.

Figure 8-2 depicts the data-to-wisdom transformation process.

You will notice the feedback loops that are so crucial to the process. Figure 8-2 shows how interactive *and* iterative the process is, sometimes requiring several or more iterations of feedback. That is what happens during social interactions as the data is presented, information is displayed (sometimes in multiple forms), knowledge is created through progressively increasing insight, knowledge is acted upon, and knowledge is gradually transformed into greater and greater wisdom. This rarely occurs as a straight-shot up the middle of the diagram. More likely, the process at each

FIGURE 8-2. DATA-TO-WISDOM TRANSFORMATION PROCESS.

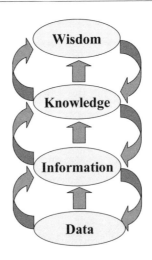

stage loops down and up again, sometimes many times. As you will see, that's what "dialogue" is all about.

According to Jim Collins, co-author of *Built to Last*, "Turning mountains of data into useful concepts is an iterative process of looping back and forth, developing ideas and testing them against the data, revising the ideas, building a framework, seeing it break under the weight of evidence, and rebuilding it yet again. That process is repeated over and over, until everything hangs together in a coherent framework of concepts."[5] Gee, I couldn't have said that any better!

## Examples of Interactivity to Generate Wisdom

Let's take a look at a few examples of how interactivity can benefit performance measurement in the data-to-wisdom conversion process.

Consider a company that wants to reduce waste in a critical process in a manufacturing plant. First, *data* is collected on the "start time" and the "end time" of the process, and the total process time is calculated. This current process cycle time is then compared with several benchmark comparatives to determine whether there is a discrepancy (*information*). Once the problem has been confirmed, structured observation reveals *knowledge* on all the wasteful activities in the process (those that add no value to the customer or to the process). Then, generalized principles (*wisdom*) are derived from the performance measurement effort and applied to other waste reduction efforts in the plant. This project—if done well—involves a lot of interpersonal interaction, and therefore a lot of learning. It is not just a matter of taking measurements, calculating, and analyzing data. The most valuable parts of the effort are the opportunities for interactivity that lead to a deeper understanding of the processes involved.

In a second example, a government agency was concerned about the high cost of information technology. Cost *data* was collected on all aspects of computer workstation acquisition and use (including initial acquisition, software, upgrades, maintenance, etc.). This data was summarized in a table (*information*) that showed the costs for each stage of the computer's lifecycle. This is an interesting example, because it shows how important it is to "look beyond" the obvious cost data to identify the costs at each of the lifecycle stages. This is something that might have been missed if this had been viewed as a purely technical measurement exercise. In such a case, there might have been no dialogue around the "equipment's lifecycle" and all the associated costs, and an enormous amount of information would have been missed and knowledge lost. On the other hand, in this case, the information generated enormous *insight* into the "total cost of ownership" (*knowledge*), and enabled this organization to derive guidelines (*wisdom*) for reducing the total cost of ownership by millions of dollars by actually increasing the initial acquisition costs through pre-sale service and software agreements and outsourcing some services.

In a third case, a company wondered why it was losing so many customers who had responded on customer satisfaction surveys that they were "happy." The company compared customer satisfaction with customer attrition *data*, and used that data to identify *information* on the more egregious instances of high reported satisfaction and attrition. Interviews with these "satisfied" ex-customers indicated that the customer satisfaction survey had not been asking the kinds of questions that would enable the company to predict attrition potential (*knowledge*). Based on this knowledge, a new customer satisfaction survey was developed, incorporating all that had been learned during the performance measurement study (*wisdom*).

In all three cases, there were extensive internal and external interactions around the data that facilitated the data-to-wisdom conversion process. Without that human interaction, there would have been much less yield of knowledge and wisdom.

## The Performance Measurement Cycle

In order for the full power of performance measurement to be realized, there must be considerable interaction at each phase of the process leading to new insights about what to measure and how to measure it. Figure 8-3 shows what I call "The Performance Measurement Cycle." This cycle shows many, if not all, of the activities that are part of the *expanded view* of performance measurement.

FIGURE 8-3. THE PERFORMANCE MEASUREMENT CYCLE.

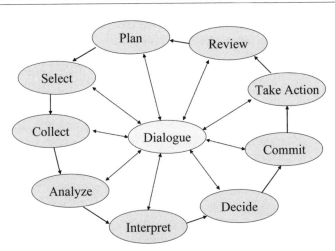

## Plan

The cycle begins with *Plan*. The most important aspect of planning is to frame the right measurement questions. Knowing what questions to ask entails careful consideration of the organization's vision, mission, and values. Those often-elusive factors must be translated into concrete inquiries that speak to the aims and objectives of the organization—or it is very likely that the entire performance measurement process will break down before it even gets going! Mark Twain said it well: "Data is a lot like garbage; you need to know what you are going to do with it *before* you start collecting it." That is why it is so crucial to involve the right people in these initial discussions, which are almost entirely business (not technical) in nature. It is truly sad to see how often even this phase of performance measurement is delegated to measurement specialists—and, then, measurement instruments are prepared and people just go out and collect data and more data.

Planning is really the business engine that drives performance measurement. If the right questions aren't asked, then most of the performance measurement process will be a waste. As James Thurber said, "It is better to know some of the questions than all of the answers." Here are the two basic measurement questions I always recommend that an organization begin with:

1. "How should we measure success as an organization?"
2. "How can we maximize the likelihood, on a continuing basis, that everyone in the organization is working together most synergistically to realize the most important common measures of success?"

Here are some other "magic questions" that will unleash more of the power of performance measurement at this early phase:

"What does success look like?"
"How will we know that we have achieved success?"
"How will we know we are making progress?"

## Select

The *Select* phase involves the identification of what to measure. Obviously in this book we are most concerned with focusing on the critical few high-leverage measures, especially those that will be transformational to the organization, and considering emergent measures as well as those that are established ones. This kind of selection (and definition) of measures requires iterative dialogue, and sometimes debate. People in the organization should also be empowered to question existing measures and to try out emergent measures. Remember that transformational measurement is, above all, a process of discovery. Measures must also be operationally defined, because most business concepts are quite abstract. "Quality," "Productivity," even "Profit" are all open to different definitions. How you measure something is your real definition of the concept. Until this is done, the measure can't really be understood.

Also, at this phase, measurement frameworks should be used, and developed if need be, so that the interrelationships (and trade-offs) among measures can be understood and managed. The Select phase is key and provides much of the foundation for everything else that follows.

## Collect

Once relevant measures are selected, the *Collect* phase (the data collection phase) can begin. This is when data collection instruments are developed, based on each measure's operational definition. A data collection plan (including a sampling plan) is developed, and the data can be collected. (Because there is so much existing literature on this and the other more technical aspects of performance measurement I will not go into the subject in much depth. Furthermore, if the Select phase has been well-implemented, the Collect phase should be relatively straight-forward, and is typically handled by technically competent measurement personnel anyway.)

## Analyze

The next phase is *Analyze.* Data analysis is often rather technical, and like the Collect phase, this one is also typically the province of highly trained technical professionals. Although it is a good idea to have some leadership and key employee engagement, these parts of the process can confidently be delegated, outsourced, or insourced. Some analysis is so sophisticated that it is very difficult for a non-technical person to understand it. Furthermore, analysis is not something that usually happens once and for all. Like so many other aspects of performance measurement, it should be iterative and highly interactive. When the data reveals something interesting, it is often important to go back use different analytical methods to expose additional insights. Too often in the traditional measurement model, the cycle breaks here. Data is collected and analyzed. Then, it goes into some database somewhere and is forgotten.

Part of the problem is that this is where the hand-off between the measurement specialist and the business sponsor doesn't usually happen. This is one of the reasons why it is so dangerous to entirely delegate any aspect of performance measurement. Collaborative and iterative analysis is vital to get from information to knowledge. In addition, the information that is produced is often so technical that very few in the organization can use it. Without an adequately high degree of engagement and a socialization process in place, the cycle will break down, and this happens more often than organizations would like to admit.

## Interpret

Once the data has been analyzed, it must be interpreted. *Interpret* is a crucial phase of performance measurement that is often ignored, because people often consider it to be too self-evident: "Of course we have to interpret the data." Others assume that the analysis will be "self-interpretable." But it is vital that this is not considered merely a routine and automatic activity. DiPiazza and Eccles remind us that, "Stakeholders are not data miners. They require and deserve clear, logically presented information."[6]

Intepretation is about *really understanding* 'the story' that the performance measurements are attempting to convey. Nothing is more important in the interpretation of data than the questions that are asked that deliver deeper and deeper levels of understanding. If there aren't compelling enough questions driving the interpretation, the likely response is: "This is interesting, but I must get back to my office and do some real work"! This is particularly true when findings reveal counterintuitive insights, and managers don't know how to deal with them. Often you must loop back to analysis to further expose deeper and deeper insights. Andy Grove, former CEO of Intel Corporation, expressed it this way, "You have to be able to argue *with* the data . . ."[7] Questions can be asked to stimulate interpretive understanding, such as: "How much could this customer spend with our company?" "How profitable is our relationship?" and "How can the profit be increased?"

Interpretation of data is enriched when it is done interactively with others. To get the most out of measurement information, take a complete "value chain" perspective rather than just look at the individual pieces in isolation. Furthermore, because today there is a strong natural tendency for individuals and functions to act on their own agendas, cross-functional interactivity is critical in producing an integrated (whole-systems) view of what is best for the organization.

## Decide

Next, you need to *Decide* what to do, if anything, about the measurement. Don't bother measuring unless you are prepared to take action on the data you collect. UK-based consulting firm, Customer Champions, found that, while 95 percent of all firms surveyed collected customer feedback, only 30 percent used the data to make decisions about service levels, and only 10 percent actually deployed the data to the front lines.

But this phase is fraught with peril. Many people don't even know what the numbers really mean, but if they are below target, action is automatically taken. In other situations the measures indicate action, but when appropriate action is *not* taken, then the primary benefit of measuring is lost. One of the great forms of waste in organizations is useless and unused measurement data. You can weigh yourself twenty times a day, but you won't lose an ounce unless you take action. However, the flip side is to be sure not to decide on inappropriate action. Taking premature action is what quality guru W. Edwards Deming has referred to as "tampering," calling it a "deadly disease" of management.

## Commit

Once the action has been decided upon, the next thing to consider is the whether it is important to get buy-in from others in the *Commit* phase, which very likely involves some dialogue with key stakeholders. It is vital that stakeholders commit to action based on real knowledge, not just reacting to data. This is your opportunity to educate them.

## Take Action

Then there is the *Take Action* phase when action (if any) is implemented. Of course the readiness for, and effectiveness of, any action taken will depend on what has been done in the previous phases of the performance measurement cycle. Here's the key point: Don't take action on data without adequate understanding. Unfortunately, too many people are told to take action on a red or yellow light that pops up on a dashboard without any real understanding of what led to that signal. No wonder people are confused or reluctant to act.

## Review

And, finally, there is the *Review* phase. This is when the action—in fact, the entire process—should be reviewed. Everything that is important should be subject to this kind of continuous improvement feedback loop. This phase, then, as you can see, feeds back into the Select phase. Empower people to question any measure Too often dysfunctional measures are "institutionalized," because no one felt empowered enough to question them. This is one reason why I only use the term "metric" when the measure has been validated for organization-wide use.

Whatever you do, don't miss this opportunity to close the loop, and consider the implications for the next iteration of performance measurement! Learning and reflecting on measurement can lead to dramatic improvements in all kinds of measurement-related abilities, such as increasing the accuracy of estimates and forecasts, and deeper understanding of variation. If people are forced to think about, and discuss, trade-offs and other critical measurement issues, these discussions can result in considerable new insight.

How will you know if you are using the right mental model, and are viewing the world through the right measurement lens? Remember that measurement is just a proxy for reality. We have already seen the dysfunctions that can occur if the wrong measures are selected and are poorly defined. However, we have also seen that a more positive context of measurement (including appropriate interactivity) can go a long way toward ameliorating any temporary technical deficiencies in the measurement system. The good news is that the interactive and iterative nature of the Performance Measurement Cycle enables the continual *reassessment* of measure selection and definition throughout the end-to-end performance measurement process.

You will notice that *Dialogue* is at the very center of the Performance Measurement Cycle in Figure 8-3. Dialogue, which is what enables this continual reassessment, is the subject of the next section.

## Dialogue: The Key to Measurement Interactivity

The word "dialogue" means "sharing collective meaning." Those who are most knowledgeable about dialogue differentiate it strongly from "discussion." It is interesting that the word "discussion" comes from the same root word as percussion and concussion and has to do with beating one thing against another. The word "communication" is a more general term meaning "to make something common." So, communication can be done by discussion or dialogue. When information is made common through discussion, it is often two monologues—an attempt to convey your opinion to another person, and nothing more.

In contrast, a dialogue is a *mutual* search for shared meaning or understanding. In order to take advantage of this opportunity to dialogue, we all need to consider ourselves as equals, each having valuable *insights* to share on the subject being considered. The belief that some are more "expert" than others and that some are "subordinate" to others will undermine dialogue. It will cause some to defer to the others who may have a superior knowledge, or a superior position. How often is this true of your performance measurement conversations? Unfortunately, very few people are skilled at dialogue, and very few organizations currently have a strong capacity for dialogue. In fact, most organizations suppress dialogue. And note also that debate is a more formal and adversarial process that is antithetical to dialogue, because the purpose is for one person to win an argument. And that's why a positive "context of measurement" is so important.

Dialogue thrives on openness, candor, and inviting multiple viewpoints. In dialogue, *diversity* of perspective is almost always good—whether it be functional, cross-functional, local, global, systemic, or whatever. The more perspectives involved, in theory at least, the richer the dialogue can be. The kind of insight that comes from different perspectives reminds me of the well known story about the blind men and the elephant. Each was only able to gain a very limited perspective, depending on the part of the elephant that each touched. But together they were able to synthesize a very rich "picture" indeed.

Dialogue as interactivity should incorporate learning, understanding, defining, listening, modeling, hypothesizing, balancing, linking, integrating, etc. It is an important part of the total transformation of measurement package. Transformational and emergent measures, especially, require the synergy and support that interactivity around measurement provides.

A facilitator can be an asset toward creating the discipline of real dialogue in an organization, or to maintain a flow of dialogue, since otherwise it is too easy for interaction to degenerate into discussion, debate, or worse.

Bossidy and Charan, in their book *Execution,* describe dialogue as "the core of culture and the basic unit of work. How people talk to each other absolutely determines how well the organization will function." They lament that, rather than engaging in dialogues, in most meetings people sit passively watching PowerPoint presentations. They don't engage in dialogue; they don't question; and they tend to leave with no commitments to action. Bossidy and Charan state further that "the reason most companies don't face reality very well is that the dialogues are ineffective."[8] As a colleague told me recently, knowledge organizations are really little more than the sum total of their conversations.

Real performance measurement dialogues can be instrumental in generating much higher levels of knowledge, insight, and wisdom—even with the same data, the same computer systems, and the same people. Upgrading the technical performance measurement capabilities will also help, but don't do it without upgrading the social capabilities.

## Assessing an Organization's Measurement Capabilities

In *Execution,* Bossidy and Charan say that "You measure your organizational capability by asking the right questions."[9] The same is true for assessing performance measurement capabilities. It is most interesting to look at the Performance Measurement Cycle in terms of *your* organization's relative capabilities for performing each phase. There is a tendency to view performance measurement as a single capability. That is a serious error. If you do that, you will tend to stock your organization with a lot of technical measurement people and a lot of analyzed data—but data just the same!

To better understand this more fully, take a look at Figure 8-4. In this version of the Performance Measurement Cycle, you can see the percent-

FIGURE 8-4. SAMPLE PERFORMANCE MEASUREMENT CAPABILITY ASSESSMENT.

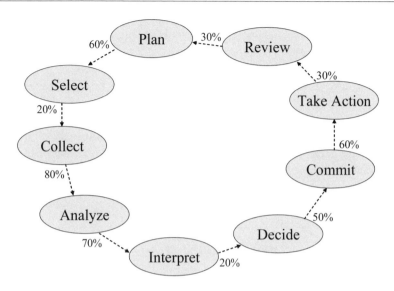

ages at each phase indicating the extent of *capability* of this hypothetical organization in implementing each phase of the process—from 0 percent (no capability) to 100 percent (outstanding capability). Reviewing this organization's capability profile is quite revealing. This organization is quite strong in the Collect phase (has strong data collection capabilities), but is quite weak in the very important Select and Interpret phases.

Pause for a moment and mentally use this as a quick organizational "self-check." How well does your organization stack up in each phase? Doing this will give you some indication of the problems your organization might face in using performance measurement.

Interestingly, the organization whose profile is depicted in Figure 8-4 might ordinarily be viewed as very strong in performance measurement—at least in the traditional areas of data collection and analysis. It is also likely that this organization has a good IT infrastructure and probably people with strong traditional technical measurement skills. But, of course, that doesn't tell the whole story—not by a long-shot! If you look closely, you will see that this is really an organization that is in deep trouble with respect to its overall performance measurement capabilities.

The extent of the problem can be more fully understood if you consider that because the Performance Measurement Cycle represents a progressive sequence of phases in which each phase is dependent upon the previous one, the cycle can break down—or at least seriously weaken—at any point. Any of these links can be deficient and can cause the overall measurement system to malfunction. For instance, if the wrong measures are selected (because of the 20 percent capability for the Select phase), it might even be a waste to continue to invest much effort in performance measurement at all. One could, in fact, argue that the entire process is no better than the weakest phase in the cycle—in this case, 20 percent capability—which would probably translate into 20 percent overall effectiveness.

Also, you might want to rate your organization in terms of the quality of dialogue, because dialogue supports and enables every phase in the Performance Measurement Cycle. This type of simple self-assessment, if honestly done, can serve as a valuable tool for promoting dialogue in an organization around performance measurement. When people feel that they don't have to *promote themselves,* and that the environment will support their candor, such subjective assessments can be of enormous value to promote learning and improvement.

## The Challenge of Interactivity Today

One of the major challenges of transformational measurement is to create an environment in which performance measurement data can be efficiently and effectively converted into useful information, this information can be transformed into knowledge, and this knowledge can be the basis for real wisdom. This kind of environment is very rare, because most of the time measurement is not dealt with interactively or iteratively. Data is generated and it goes into databases, somewhere. There is little or no interaction about the data, or the information produced from the data. Without interaction, if any data-to-wisdom conversion does occur, it will be more haphazard than systematic—and it will not occur consistently.

In most organizations today, very few employees understand the meaning of most performance measures that are used. There is rarely any meaningful discussion or education on performance measures. Most organizations are performing a lot of measuring, but not learning from their measurements. To most people, measurement remains "just numbers," and few people understand the "the big picture" of measurement. As a result, the easy-to-measure things tend to get measured, and there is little interest in using the real power of performance measurement.

Most communication about measurement, when it happens, occurs within a particular function, like sales or manufacturing. The failure to appropriately socialize measurement across the organizational continues to reinforce the silo mentality. Embracing interactivity outside of our own roles and functions—about anything, but especially about measurement—is an "unnatural act" in most organizations. Worse still, according to human relations consultant Doug Finton's experience, "95 percent of all the problems in organizations are due to performance conversations that never even occurred."[10] Of course this needs to change. And it will.

The key to interactivity around measurement is performance conversations that start with an invitation to dialogue:

"Let's look at the measures and see how we're doing?"

"What does this data say tell us about (customer satisfaction, profitability, quality)?"

"Let's discuss why we are starting to see some improvement in this area, but not there."

Collegial functional and cross-functional performance conversations about measurement will become a fundamental part of new knowledge work in organizations.

Many organizations have leaders who disagree on the most important measures, and this is not bad, unless this disagreement is suppressed—which it too often is. Disagreement is actually an invaluable opportunity for synergy through dialogue about the business strategy and the execution imperatives. Social interaction through dialogue is crucial for determining the right measures, for the critical trade-offs, for making the right cross-functional decisions on an ongoing basis, and—most importantly—for the alignment of leaders and functions across the organization. Unfortunately, today there is more "spin" than real "dialogue" about measurement in most organizations.

## The Tendency to View Technology as the Panacea

The biggest danger in organizations today is the "dumbing down" of work—*especially management work*! It is certainly safer to follow the blinking lights than to make decisions based on real knowledge and wisdom. Technology seems to make this all so easy: "Let's let the software do the thinking."

This delegation to technology, which too often abdicates the responsibility for thinking and understanding, tends to deceive people into believing that the time-consuming and initially uncomfortable hands-on involvement with performance measurement, and the intensive social interaction around it, are not needed. Not only that, but there is often a focus on one particular type of tool or technique (like Business Performance Management, Customer Relationship Management, Scorecards, Dashboards) that reflects the biases of those who are leading the effort. And, unfortunately, one of the most difficult things to do in an organization is to challenge long-standing assumptions. It is important to go into this with your eyes open about the tendencies that can easily, and often unintentionally, skew your well-meaning efforts in the wrong directions.

There are so many issues in business and government that require interpersonal deliberation, including the selection of the right technology. As surprising as it might seem, the growth of technology has actually increased the demand for knowledge about "softer" issues. Furthermore, if people understand what the numbers mean and how they relate to each other, then measurement is no long a mystery; if mistakes are made or missteps are taken, they can be detected and the issues resolved. Transparency is not just valuable for external reporting; it is essential for internal visibility. No technology will be able to direct a vessel on the right path in uncharted waters.

One of the keys to success for organizations in the future will be recognizing when to rely on technology, and when to recognize and work around its limitations. It is not a matter of choosing between technology and people; it is a matter to using each appropriately. This is the subject of Chapter 11.

## Making Progress

As you have learned, transformational measurement is a journey, not a destination, and it operates on a continuum. You will know that you are making progress on the journey when people in your organization stop mindlessly collecting data and start asking the right questions, and are engaging in dialogue rather than independent technical measurement projects.

Look for a more questioning organization, a more dialoguing organization, an organization more focused on learning. Look for more cross-functional interactivity around measurement. Look for people who are actually measuring the effectiveness of what the are doing. Look for measured experiments and pilot projects before people jump on the bandwagon of the latest and greatest idea. Look for people talking about what they are learning as they are measuring and reviewing measurement information. Look for the kinds of interactions that tell you people are seeking knowledge in pursuit of wisdom, not data in the pursuit of information. Look for increased trust—and, without trust, there won't be much sharing.

You will know things are *really improving* when people in your organization stop asking, "What do I do when I see a yellow or red light?" or "How do we keep the numbers up?" and start saying instead, "Oops, we're veering in this direction and it's adversely affecting this initiative. It's time to *talk* about a course correction!"

The next chapters will guide you through some topics vital for implementing and sustaining transformational performance measurement in your organization.

# CHAPTER 9

# Measurement Leadership

E mbarking upon the kind of transformation of performance measurement presented in this book—much less completing it—is no small
undertaking. Therefore, it should come as no surprise that the single most
important aspect of transforming organizational performance measurement
is leadership. I cannot emphasize too strongly the crucial role of organizational leaders, whether you are leading a project, department, or an entire
organization, or whether your organization is a business, government
agency, hospital, school, religious institution, or any other type of organization. In this chapter I will explain the challenges of "measurement leadership" and provide recommendations for implementing and sustaining the
kind of transformational measurement being advocated in this book.

## The Importance of Measurement Leadership

Leadership sets the tone for everything that happens in an organization,
and measurement is no exception. Unfortunately, today almost nobody sees
performance measurement as something that requires leadership *in its own
right*. Measurement is typically not viewed as something that specifically
requires leadership. The prevailing attitude is that if any leadership is
needed, department managers are the default "measurement leaders."

However, we have already seen the problems that this current lack of
concentrated leadership causes, such as disparate measurement systems,
measurement silos, dis-integrated data, and lack of vertical and horizontal
alignment across the organization. And without specific measurement leadership, measurement in organizations will continue to become even more
*dis-integrated*, *sub-optimizing*, and *non-transformational*. At the root of the
problem are two misconceptions: 1) that measurement is primarily a technical activity, and 2) that no one individual has *overall* responsibility.

## Why Measurement Leadership Doesn't Happen

While most managers publicly extol the value of measurement, few actually *use* it systematically and well. In addition, because of the pervasiveness of measurement and the role it plays in so many activities ("Of course we measure!"), it often blends into the background or is considered "just another tool set"—too basic for *serious* leadership consideration. Furthermore, most managers, who are not in "measurement jobs," don't see it as a significant part of their responsibilities. If they do, it is as part of their financial measurement tasks, not in non-financial areas that are the real drivers of value creation today. In addition, very few executives have advanced within organizations—or received significant recognition—for anything they have done relative to measurement.

That is why organizational leaders are more than happy to delegate measurement to accountants and "measurement specialists." They don't realize how strategic measurement is, and how much management attention it requires to do it right. As such, measurement is one of the most *underappreciated* organizational activities, and measurement leadership is one of the *least appreciated* leadership roles. In fact, there is currently no established role of "measurement leader."

## The Tension between Intuition and Measurement

Another reason for the slow acceptance of performance measurement as a critical aspect of organizational leadership is that most leaders rely on intuition more than measurement in their own decision making. Intuition, also referred to more colloquially as "gut feelings" or a "sixth sense," is typically based on "pattern recognition"—recognizing patterns in new experiences that lead us to respond as we did to past situations with similar patterns.

There are many reasons why intuition is often preferred to measurement. It is seen as more exciting. Intuition is easy; it requires virtually no time or effort—it is, by definition, instantaneous. It is also easily reinforced, because people tend to remember their correct intuitions and forget their incorrect ones. Intuition is also typically viewed as creative; in fact, most people think that measurement will constrain their intuition and creativity. Although these are misconceptions, they are still widely and strongly held.

There is no doubt that when used appropriately, intuition is an incredibly valuable tool. Unfortunately, too often it is used inappropriately—as a *replacement* for measurement, rather than a complement to it. This is unfortunate, because both are actually more powerful when used together. Measurement can enhance intuition, and intuition can enhance measurement. Barbara Dockar-Drysdale expressed it well: "Intuition informed is an essential tool; intuition uninformed can be a dangerous weapon."[1]

## The Myth of the Intuitive Leader

The myth of the "intuitive leader" is a powerful and persistent one. Many executives are hired and reinforced for their intuition. Although we are all familiar with the names of legendary "intuitive leaders," too often the legend comes from misconceptions about their actual performance. Remember that all ships rise with the tide. And many legends are based on a single success in a particular situation. In fact, those who do an *honest* audit of their overall intuition batting average are usually shocked at how low it is. Many intuitive leaders might actually have a .200 intuition batting average, but think that they are batting .500 or better. Furthermore, as Robert Mittlestaedt has explained, "Business mistakes, except for the largest, are hidden from view."[2] So, without good *measurement,* it is easy for intuitive leaders to avoid blame for many errors.

One of the most dangerous pitfalls that is common to intuitive leaders is over-confidence. As Bossidy and Charan say, "Too many leaders fool themselves into thinking their companies are well run."[3] In addition, leaders who view themselves as particularly smart tend to believe that their expertise is a license to make intuitive decisions. Unfortunately, even the smartest people often make the wrong decisions—sometimes *really wrong* ones.

An even a greater threat than an intuitive leader is an "intuitive organization." Even if a leader has extraordinary intuition, that is no reason to encourage others, who might *not* be so gifted, to rely on intuition as well. Unfortunately, the examples of intuitive leaders often sends a powerful message to others. As other managers decide to *follow the leader,* a few mistakes can easily turn into hundreds.

One of the great challenges involved in transforming performance measurement is to create an environment in which performance measurement is valued, at all levels of the organization, *at least* as highly as intuition.

## What Happens in the Absence of Measurement Leadership?

A large part of leadership is about identifying and taking advantage of the best opportunities—leveraging those that create value and avoiding those that destroy value. There is no doubt that measurement—especially transformational performance—can help leaders and their organizations achieve more of their potential. Opportunities are virtually everywhere. But as Gerald Kraines reveals, as much as 60 to 70 percent of any organization's potential effectiveness goes unrealized.[4] If there are so many unexploited opportunities to create value, why are so many organizations missing them?

### Missed Opportunities

So much of what is both right and wrong in organizations is *invisible.* Without good measurement, most of the opportunities can't be seen, properly assessed, or leveraged. How do you know who your best customers are? How do you know which products and services are most profitable? How do you know which investments and projects are paying off? What are the best opportunities for synergies within your own organization and with your extended value net? Measurement will provide *facts,* while your intuition is very likely to be wrong.

## Value Destruction

When the right measurements and measurement frameworks are devised, value creation and destruction can quite readily be seen. Without the right measurement tools and attitudes, it is quite easy for organizations to leak significant value to the detriment of all.

As with an automobile fluid hose with pinhole leaks, without good measurement, one cannot detect that the hose is even leaking, until it is too late. In a like manner, organizations try to compensate for value destruction by adding resources, which only perpetuates the problem. But applying the right measures to a situation can reveal a great deal of otherwise hidden truths. This can increase knowledge, wisdom, and the ability to manage phenomena that are invisible to those who fail to effectively measure them.

In addition, the capital allocation process in most large companies doesn't discriminate between value creating and value destroying units. Many companies end up investing in unprofitable units and thus accelerate value destruction. What makes this so insidious is that no one sees this happening, as value tends to imperceptibly leak out of most organizations due to all kinds of waste and misalignment.

Although value destruction (leakage, evaporation, dissipation) occurs in all organizations, well-measured organizations do a much better job of identifying the sources of value leakage and taking action to reduce its otherwise inexorable entropic tendencies. Because performance measurement is the key to exposing value creation and destruction, measurement leadership must become a fundamental part of the job of any organizational leader.

## The Epidemic of Waste

One of the major reasons why organizations are creating disappointing value today is the enormous waste that exists in most organizations. Most organizations don't realize how wasteful many activities are. Cyril Northcote Parkinson, who deduced Parkinson's Law, describes what happened in the British Air Force when his superiors went on leave: "The work lessened as each of my superiors had disappeared [and] by the time it came to me, there was nothing to do at all. There never had been anything to do. We'd been making work for each other."[5] Although one might be tempted to snicker at this and perhaps dismiss it as an aberration of government bureaucracy, I daresay this situation is not terribly unusual in most businesses.

A sampling of the types of waste that exist in most organization include: missed due dates, hand-off delays, excess handling, long lead times, defects, returns, rework, warranty claims, scrap, incomplete shipments requiring expedited handling, skill loss, unused skills, high inventory levels, overproduction, over-processing, excessive service levels, unused ideas, redundant development efforts, excess features and functions, unutilized assets and resources, wasted time looking for information, absenteeism, accidents. The list could go on and on. What is so sad is that all of these examples of waste could easily be detected by measuring the right things—and being open to what measurement is saying.

John Whitney observed that 50 percent of corporate activities are waste.[6] Accountemps found that executives waste 20 percent of their time dealing with company politics. For organizations in general, Dow and Cook maintain that paperwork and meetings consume 70 percent of the typical organization's time,[7] while Hronec has posited that more than 50 percent of the activities within a typical process do not add value.[8]

Measurement is the only way we can see most waste. Without effective measurement, no one really knows what's happening—and the waste goes on.

## Fads and Quick Fixes Are Allowed to Proliferate

Nothing is more wasteful than fads, quick fixes, and supposed panaceas. Everyone seems to be looking for the "holy grail" prescription for organizational success. There are so many apparently effective approaches—from Autonomous Teams to Zero Based Budgeting. Too many leaders feel pressured to do something—*anything*: "Let's just find the magic formula and everything will be fine." We are so pressed by the need to "do something" that we settle for quick fixes and stop-gap measures, leaving the basic problems undisturbed.

One of the most egregious sources of waste is all the "programs" and "improvement initiatives" that organizations get involved in but never measure. One executive pointed out that the "overabundance of on-off initiatives" led to "execution attention deficit disorder," and, once launched, the initiatives weren't even measured. Christopher Hart cites research concluding that *over half* of the quality improvement programs undertaken by companies in recent years have been abandoned or scaled back.[9] I frequently hear managers and employees say things like, "Sure, we're making good progress . . . *I think*." Most people in most organizations do what they hope is right, but they have no way of knowing—often until it is too late.

What works? You really don't know unless you measure. As Peter Senge explains, "In complex human systems, there are always many ways to make things look better in the short-run."[10] But eventually people realize that they were fooled, and morale inevitably plummets.

One of the best ways to avoid that problem is to *measure,* and to *dialogue* about the data. Lest you and your organization fall prey to the flavor of the month, program du jour, or the "next big thing," I suggest you *lead* with measurement. I believe that the major reason why quick fixes and panaceas have been allowed to drain organizational resources is the reluctance to measure them. Many fads wreak havoc on organizations because management can't tell that they aren't working, and they don't discontinue them quickly enough.

A smart leader will always perform a measured pilot before buying into any program—no matter how compelling it seems. If you measure your own experience during a pilot, you will see whether the method stands any real chance of success. As Stanford professor Jeffrey Pfeffer has explained, "No matter how smart you are, you can't preplan everything and then roll out your program. What you want to do is to try some stuff and see what happens."[11] That's why using measurement is so smart. It can help you identify waste before it becomes a crisis.

### Important Problems Are Not Solved

Most organizations muddle along for long periods of time with serious problems which are often hidden well beneath the surface and are rarely known until a great deal of damage has been done. Without good measurement, how do you know you have a problem, or that it's worth solving? Furthermore, most of what we "see" are symptoms, not problems, and symptoms can't be solved. Because of time delays, it often takes a long time for the symptoms to manifest themselves. Measurement provides proactive information on incipient problems.

## Routine vs. Transformational Measurement

Unfortunately, many senior leaders wake up one day and find they have a serious problem, or that they missed some great opportunity which was not on their radar screen until it was too late, because they weren't measuring it. To make matters worse, as we have already established, most measurement systems are already inefficient and ineffective, having evolved piecemeal by different people at different times for different purposes.

However, the biggest problem with the acceptance of measurement as a transformational discipline is that so few leaders have experienced it as such. It is a *vicious cycle.* Experiencing measurement as mundane leads to further routine use of measurement, which leads to low impact, which leads to subsequent mundane measurement, and so on.

Despite the mundane way measurement is treated in most organizations, Frederick Reichheld insists that "measurement lies at the heart of both vision and strategy. It's hard to overestimate its importance in determining the future course of the business. . . . It is measurement that allows managers to harness vision to the earthly realities of daily business practice. Measurement turns vision into strategy and strategy into fact."[12] This doesn't sound mundane to me!

## The Challenges of Changing Measurement

In organizations, most change occurs when people start looking at the same things differently. Nothing will create change in organizations quicker than when the lens of performance measurement is changed. But, not only is measurement a crucial enabler of change, but changing measurement *itself* represents perhaps the most important change of all.

Most organizations suffer from inertia. Whether an organization is at rest or in motion, it takes a concerted effort to change. As Machiavelli famously stated: "There is nothing more difficult to take in hand, more perilous to conduct, or more uncertain in its success, than to take the lead in the introduction of a new order of things."[13] The significance of changing measurement was well articulated by David Meador when he said, "Changing the way we measure changes everything."[14] Thus, aside from the normal resistance to change, changing measurement systems carries additional sources of resistance.

Measurement is particularly resistant to change because it is so closely related to security and rewards. Even if the reward system is somewhat dysfunctional, there are still many people—especially those in leadership—who are benefiting from it. Better the devil you know! In addition, since people are aware that measurement triggers almost everything else, changing *any* aspect of the measurement system can have significant implications for one or more other management systems. And because people already feel uncomfortable about measurement, adding change to the agenda will inevitably increase that discomfort.

Transformational performance measurement requires specific leadership because it goes beyond the traditional expectations of simply administering existing measures. It requires people to do things that are significantly different from their existing routines. We often don't realize how deeply entrenched existing measures and measurement practices are. For example, consider the difficulty that would be required in your organization to successfully achieve a measurement change in Marketing from customer satisfaction to customer loyalty; in Sales from traditional revenue and pipeline measures to customer profitability; in Accounting from traditional cost accounting to Activity-Based Costing (ABC); in Human Resources from employee satisfaction to employee engagement; and in Training from tracking numbers trained to training's contributions to organizational results. Then, there are the even bigger changes required for the adoption of integrated measurement frameworks, and moving away from functional "silo" measures to truly cross-functional ones.

Unfortunately, many leaders don't realize that one of their responsibilities is to "create an environment conducive to measurement change," not just to "get the measurement work done." Most organizations have very competent people crunching and keeping track of numbers—but that's not the real challenge. You can find someone who can take measurements and analyze data, but only you—as a *measurement leader*—can create the right environment for making sure that the right questions get asked, that the right information gets generated, and to use that measurement information to progressively generate more and more knowledge and wisdom.

## Leading Transformational Performance Measurement

Leaders have a profound personal impact on the climate of the organization or organizational area they lead. To a large extent, employees judge an initiative by the person who's leading it. A lot of things are said, but it is ultimately what leaders *do* that makes the difference. According to Larry Bossidy and Ram Charan, "You change the culture of a company by changing the behavior of its leaders."[15]

The only real answer to the challenges cited earlier—for maximizing value creation, stemming the tide of value destruction, and ending the epidemic of waste—is to *exercise leadership* to transform performance measurement in your organization. According to Noel Tichy, leaders do two things differently from others. They "see reality"—that is, they perceive the need for change when others don't—and then they "mobilize the appropriate responses" to respond effectively.[16]

It is unlikely that any significant aspects of performance measurement can be transformed without an effective leader leading the transformation. Just implementing the status quo is not real leadership; it's management. That is why leadership requires courage, and measurement leadership is no exception.

## Establishing an Environment Conducive to Change

The first thing that any measurement leader must realize is how important it is to establish the right environment for new measurement behaviors. In order for this change to occur, an environment that is conducive to these behaviors must be established. While the performance measurement "system" includes the *technical* aspects, the most important aspect is the *con-*

*text*—the social and organizational environment in which the technical measurement system is embedded.

The sections that follow list some of the ways measurement leaders can create an *environment* in their organization that is most conducive to implementing transforming performance measurement.

## Create a Leadership Coalition

This kind of measurement leadership requires leaders who are willing to "sign up" to lead the transformation. Ideally this begins at the top. The most successful changes, including Balanced Scorecard and Six Sigma, are led actively from the top of the organization. Although it is great when organizations can create positive change top-down throughout the entire organization, it is not always possible from the start. Even when it is not, you can still have a significant influence on the context of measurement in your particular area of responsibility. And, at the very least, I would suggest finding one or more senior-level leaders to "share the vision" and team with you to exert active measurement leadership.

## Recognize the Difficulty

Transforming performance measurement requires a very significant paradigm shift from the way things are currently done in most organizations. For others than those who specialize in it, performance measurement is not something that most people want to do or feel that they do well. Performance measurement is a habit that must be developed.

You might want to consider assessing existing attitudes in your organization toward measurement in order to gauge how difficult the journey might be. This will also help you to determine areas within the organization that might be more receptive during the early stages of the transformation, and to identify individuals who might be "early adopters." Leaders must head into this challenge with their eyes wide open, and not perceive it as "just another program"—which brings us to the next point.

## Avoid the "Measurement Program" Mentality

Given the popularity and perceived successes of particular measurement approaches, such as the Balanced Scorecard or Six Sigma, it is tempting to latch on to one of them and then delegate measurement to "implementers." In such cases, all too frequently the measurement "project" is declared completed and the report is filed!

Transformational performance measurement should not be viewed as "just another project"—or, even worse, "just another IT project." In fact, when they have been successful, both Balanced Score and Six Sigma have been treated as *systemic* changes.

## Demonstrate Visible Commitment to Measurement

Transforming performance measurement will require more than lip-service compliance to a corporate directive. It must be valued by those who lead it, or others will detect the lack of integrity. Unless it is truly and authentically valued by leaders, it won't be used well. That is why it is so vital for leaders to lead *visibly.*

It is important for the leaders driving the transformation to become educated in the principles and practices of transformational performance measurement. It sends a very powerful message when leaders are visible role models in the *use* of data-based leadership, decision making, and improvement. One of the most important and viable things a leader can do is to include specific performance measurement tasks and competencies in staff job descriptions, and to discuss them in providing feedback on their performance.

## Provide Support for Measurement

David Bain provides an interesting example of how little support there is in most organizations for performance measurement. He explains that in American football there is a specialized crew ("the chain gang") whose only job is to measure the progress of the ball toward a first down (ten yards). And yet he is amazed that "in business and service organizations there is often resistance to adding measurement resources to gauge progress in that more important game of reaching the organization's objectives."[17]

Although measurement has a cost associated with it, if done right, it delivers enormous value. Don't starve the transformation before it has the opportunity to take root. Allocate the resources, including education and personnel resources, necessary for making transformational performance improvement happen.

## Be Sensitive to the "Measurement Experience"

How we experience performance measurement is the product of the environment that our leaders create. Unfortunately, many executives are oblivious to the serious problems of measurement abuse and dysfunction. Most of the time in organizations, bad things don't happen on purpose, but they are *allowed* to happen, generally because these things were never identified and the problems never addressed. It is particularly important to expose and openly discuss the measurement dysfunctions (including both unintentional and intentional "gaming") that probably exist in your and virtually every organization, and are due to the past lack of effective measurement leadership. Then, both the opportunity and, more importantly, the motive can be addressed.

## Emphasize the "Improvement Purpose" of Measurement

Nothing speaks more loudly of the commitment of leaders to really transforming performance measurement than to see the *focus* of measurement changing. Is it being used to provide real understanding and helpful feedback, and to foster learning and improvement—or is it perceived as just being used for justification, reporting, judgment, and control? Of course, performance measurement will always be used to monitor and control, but when managers and employees alike see that it is being used much more often for the purpose of improvement, then everyone will know that a change is truly taking place!

Another powerful message will come when there is more openness to failure, and learning from it. Very few organizations place as much emphasis on learning from mistakes as they do on congratulating themselves for success. As we will see in the next chapter, learning from measurement is one of the most important organizational capabilities, not just performance measurement capabilities.

## Insist on the Truth

It seems that "trust in measurement" is an oxymoron today. Unfortunately, the truth often hurts, and it is especially dangerous in organizations where the employees know that one of the primary "rules of the game" is to tell their leaders what they think they want to hear. This is a great disservice, and it will only retard the organization's development.

If you want truthful results, make sure that those doing the measuring don't have a "vested interest" in the outcome. Because of the negative context of measurement in most organizations, I see too many cases of selective, biased measurement for the purpose of promoting a favorite program or other investment. Without good measurement, it is amazing how much of the "truth" remains hidden. Organizations that hide the truth rarely learn, and almost always destroy value and underperform those that do. Whatever you do, never, never, never punish people for telling the truth, and never condone fudging the numbers—for any purpose.

## Separate Measurement from Judgment and Rewards

We have discussed at length the importance of separating measurement, evaluation, and rewards. As powerful as measurement is, strong rewards can be much more powerful, and people will tend to use the measurement system to obtain rewards, rather than to be guided by the information. Alignment between measures and rewards is good, but linking them *too closely* ("If you attain this level of performance on this measure, you will get this reward") will almost always have dysfunctional effects. Furthermore, if you want honesty, openness to the informational value of measurement, and a desire for *real* improvement, try not to use performance measurement for disciplinary or punitive purposes. Once you link measurement closely with discipline, the context of measurement will almost instantaneously become negative.

## Emphasize the Importance of Learning About and from Measurement

Learning from measurement should be considered one of the key outcomes of performance measurement, which can accrue enormous organizational benefits, such as greater desire to use measurement properly, continuous improvement of performance measurement capabilities, and increased accuracy of all forms of measurement (including estimating, forecasting, and other forms of "predictive measurement").This topic will be discussed in greater detail in Chapter 10.

## Making the Transformation Happen

The topics discussed above are recommended for the purpose of establishing the *right environment* for transformational performance measurement. Here are some things you, and others in the organization who are committed to measurement leadership, can do to motivate, implement, and sustain the transformation.

• *Gain Active Involvement.* Although it would be nice if everyone could "catch the vision" of transformational performance measurement right from the start, it is probably not feasible. But it is not important that everybody be involved in the early stages. It is better to initially involve those who *want* to be involved—those commonly referred to as "innovators" and "early adopters." Change has to start somewhere. If it is done right, the influence will quickly spread, and eventually a critical mass will be involved.

• *Measure What Matters Most.* Effective measurement leaders are relentless about determining what performance matters most, and making sure that people can clearly "see" their impact on that performance. If employees at all levels understand and have access to the right measures, they can be quite effective at self-managing the value creation process.

• *Establish Clear Line of Sight.* "Line of sight" is one of the most important concepts in performance measurement. It refers to the ability of employees, at all levels, to "see" how their work and performance measures relate to the work and performance measures of others, and ultimately to the measures of organizational success. If you want to determine the extent to which line of sight exists in your organization, ask employees to make the connection between what they are measuring, and organizational results.

• *Encourage Measurement Conversations.* To repeat, because the most important aspects of performance measurement are social, it is important to encourage open dialogue about measurement—"measurement conversations." Examples of key questions you can ask to stimulate these discussions include: "From your perspective, are we measuring what matters most?" "What do you do that most directly affects organizational results?" "How does your work affect the work of others?" "What do you think is most important to measure about your work?"

Challenge managers and employees to ask probing measurement questions, and then to initiate efforts to answer them. But don't stop there! Challenge them to create knowledge and wisdom from the data.

Very few leaders ask the "right" questions about measurements—or even know what the "right" questions are. I see so many examples of leaders depending on others for their understanding, or being satisfied to rely on the standard data and interpretations. The measurement conversations in virtually all organizations need to be significantly upgraded. And, I daresay, that the higher up the executives, the more they need to question the measurement data and interpretations that are being fed to them.

• *Challenge People to "Measure It."* Organizations are full of opinions. Opinions are fine, but they can make leadership quite difficult if they impede communication, collaboration, and progress. As former Intel CEO Andy Grove puts it, "Altogether too often, people substitute opinion for fact and emotions for analysis."[18] When in doubt, challenge people to "measure it." Measurement substitutes facts for opinion. It will resolve many conflicts, and it will encourage managers and employees to do less by the "seat of their pants" and rely less on intuition alone, which, as we saw earlier in this chapter, is so prone to error.

• *Challenge People to "Make It Measurable."* The mere act of making something "measurable," even if you don't actually measure it, can serve as a powerful communication tool. Performance measures provide a tool for clarifying expectations, problem solving, understanding, and all kinds of work discussions. Data tends to ground discussions in reality. Most executive strategy pronouncements are vague and rarely measurable. When something remains vague, it seems remote, an abstract idea and not a reality." As Kaplan and Norton proclaim, "The use of measurement as a language helps translate complex and frequently nebulous concepts into a more precise form that can gain consensus among senior executives."[19]

Nothing creates clarity like agreeing on how to measure something. If you find that people are talking at cross-purposes in a meeting, simply ask: "How do we measure that?" Forcing measurability reduces the ambiguity and conflict that so often surround concepts.

• *Encourage Integration.* In the absence of a system-wide view, each function contends for investment that optimizes its function, and therefore suboptimizes the whole. Measuring has too often been prone (and still is to a great extent) to assess one process, one person, or one product, out of context—thus perpetuating the silo-mentality—which is one of the reasons why many people don't see much organizational value in it. Holistic measurement is what is needed. Using common measurement frameworks and cross-functional measures can help break down those barriers—but not without strong measurement leadership.

• *Encourage Measurement Innovation.* Some of the most important levers of competitive advantage are either newly discovered or yet undiscovered. We are learning more every day about how much potential organizational value is currently not being measured, and therefore not being effectively managed. If you want your organization to experience the real transformational power of performance measurement, you will have to help people move away from measuring just the routine things and using standard "metric." Encourage your workforce to be innovative about measurement and direct those who know the most about key areas of your organization to figure out new ways of measuring internal and external sources of value.

Even if you don't change your measurement system right away, these new measurement suggestions, by their very existence, will get people thinking in different ways. Eventually, these embryonic innovative approaches might lead to the discovery of transformational measures that will transform your function, your business, and maybe even your industry!

• *Measure and Recognize Transformational Performance Measurement Accomplishments.* If you want transformational performance measurement to be sustained, measure that it is happening! Measure that emergent measures are being developed and tested. Measure that learning is taking place. Measure that measurement conversations are occurring. Measure that data is being converted into information, knowledge, and wisdom. Use all kinds of measures of progress and learning!

## Measurement Leaders

"Measurement leaders" are not measurement specialists, but real organizational leaders in functional areas as well as in senior positions with important measurement roles and responsibilities. To a large extent, measurement leadership determines whether performance measurement remains "just data" or creates information, knowledge, and wisdom for others in the organization.

There are many people today who exemplify at least some of the values and aspirations of transformational performance measurement. In the following pages, I will profile a small number of "measurement leaders," who are being recognized for their contributions to transforming performance measurement. Note that not one of them is "a measurement person"—they are all organizational leaders. The one thing they all have in common is that they have recognized the transformational power of performance measurement, and they realize that it is not the act of measurement itself, but what you *do* with measurement that counts. I would like to apologize to the many others whom I have missed. This is intended to be a "starter list," which will be added to from time to time.

### Michael J. Critelli, Chairman and CEO, Pitney Bowes

Critelli has used performance measurement to focus on new avenues for growth at Pitney Bowes. He is asking the right questions, and views measurement as an iterative and interactive process. He has said: "If I can bring in different frameworks, new lenses, and fresh vocabulary to help spring people from their entrenched mental models, that may help us to innovate in strategically creative ways."[20] Pitney Bowes has reinforced this new perspective on growth with new performance metrics. Where the organization used to ask, "How many meters did we place, and how many customers do we have?" now it asks, "How many pieces of mail are we participating in and how many pennies do we get per piece?" Sounds like Pitney Bowes has discovered transformational measurement!

### Bob Galvin, Former CEO, Motorola

Bob Galvin might not have invented Six Sigma, but he understood the potential and championed it at Motorola. (Dr. Mikel Harry and Bill Smith created the concept of Six Sigma at Motorola and developed it into the unique blend of change management and measurement it is today.) Through Galvin's leadership, the paradigm of quality measurement was fundamentally changed at Motorola. Clearly Galvin has long understood the positive power of measurement and the "improvement purpose." My favorite Galvin quote is: "Anything can and should be measured if you want to improve it."[21]

### Jack Welch, Former CEO, General Electric Company (GE)

Jack Welch is well-known for his accomplishment in driving Motorola's Six Sigma methodology through GE. To him, it was a major business initiative that permeated all of GE, and it was the centerpiece of his effort to continuously improve operational excellence and instill deep discipline into the GE culture. He also successfully applied and popularized it as a major part of leadership development. At GE, leaders are expected to lead measurement initiatives. They can delegate the details, but not the leadership. A favorite Jack Welch quote is the following: "Only integrity can keep measurement systems from being exercises in paper-pushing."[22] How true!

### Larry Bossidy, CEO, Honeywell International

Larry Bossidy learned Six Sigma when he was a direct-report to Jack Welch at GE. When he left GE, he used it to drive improvement at Allied Signal and then at Honeywell International, which was formed through the merger of Allied Signal and Honeywell. In addition to his leadership in promoting

Six Sigma, Bossidy has been cited many times in this book, and is especially recognized for his concept of the "social engine" (the conversational process around strategy execution) which became the hallmark of his personal leadership philosophy. Bossidy is a major champion of the fact that effective measurement is the fundamental key to effective strategy execution.

### Jack Stack, President, Springfield Remanufacturing Company

Jack Stack is the originator of "Open Book Management." He came up with the ideas when he was faced with transforming a dying division of International Harvester into Springfield Remanufacturing Company, which became one of America's most successful small companies. Much of the new emphasis on "financial literacy" is a result of Stack's pioneering efforts. In a company fully employing Open Book Management employees tend to become very knowledgeable about how their job fits into the company's financial plan.

### Josh Weston, Former Chairman and CEO, Automatic Data Processing (ADP)

When Josh Weston assumed leadership at ADP, he assumed the self-appointed role of the "chief measurement officer as well." As he explained it: "When I became COO, I decided it was my job to become involved in guiding the design of our reporting and measurement systems. . . . I wanted to shape metrics for managers—numbers that would help us design, reinforce, and evaluate business strategies and motivate employees to implement them effectively." Weston also appreciated the social and interactive nature of performance measurement and understood the transformational power of emergent measures. He explained that in less than a year, ADP had developed a dozen high-leverage measures. And he boasts, "Now we have fifty."[23]

### Carlos Ghosn, CEO, Nissan

Carlos Ghosn was responsible for the turnaround of Nissan Motor Co., Ltd. from a Japanese also-ran to one of the most successful and innovative companies in the world. In 2005 he was named President and Chief Executive Officer of Renault S.A. as well, and has done a similar turnaround there. He also has understood the importance of measuring and managing in tough times. As he explains: "My goal was to find existing assets in the culture that I could use to leverage change."[24] While Ghosn appreciated the Japanese's thoroughness at problem-solving, he was not a fan of the slow speed with which they did it. An example of a transformational measure he came up with is "problem-solving cycle time"—the elapsed time between the time a problem is detected and the time at which its resolved.

### Steve Bennett, CEO of Intuit

Steve Bennett is another graduate of the "Jack Welch School" at GE. Since he took over as Intuit's CEO in 2000, revenue growth has surged and operating profits have soared—even in the middle of the technology recession. Bennett is known inside Intuit for the measurement-based, performance-driven culture he has created. He is known for continually asking executives questions like: "What are the critical few drivers of revenue growth and how can we measure them?"[25] He takes a very social and high-leverage approach to performance measurement by focusing on key drivers, measuring the critical few, and asking the right questions.

## Leo Pujals, Founder of Telepizza (Spain)

Leo Pujals left a comfortable career with Johnson & Johnson to start a pizza restaurant that became a chain, growing from one restaurant to 1,000 in less than ten years. He began by stuffing neighborhood mailboxes with promotional fliers. Keeping an accurate count of the number of fliers delivered and the number of orders received, within months Pujals knew precisely how many fliers had to be delivered each day in order to receive the desired number of telephone orders. As profits began to mount, he had a replicable "blueprint for success."[26] Pujals also realized that by measuring the orders received, he always knew the response rate from his advertising, and how much he needed to invest in order to keep his restaurants buzzing and telephone ringing.

## Rudolph Giuliani, Former Mayor, New York City

Everybody knows of Rudy Giuliani's leadership after 9/11, but few know that his success as mayor of New York City was more due to his leadership of the CompStat program that was responsible for dramatically reducing the city's crime rate. CompStat is a computer software program that predictively measures crime by generating electronic "pin maps" of crime locations citywide based on initial reports, rather than waiting for fully verified incidents. The idea was to take the biggest dot on the CompStat map and "make it go away." The most important component of the CompStat process was the social interaction around the data. It was during regular meetings that the trends were discussed and commanders were held accountable for solving problems. Giuliani attributed the success of the process to the CompStat *meetings*, rather than the measurement software. As he said, "After eight years, I remain electrified by how effective those CompStat meetings could be."[27]

## Glen Renwick, CEO, Progressive Insurance Company

Glen Renwick is a great example of a leader who really "gets it." He believes in open and honest measurement to an extent rarely seen. As Renwick says, "When you have information, you should disclose it, good or bad, exactly as it is." Renwick views his job primarily as a "strategist." He says, "I should be evaluated long term on a body of work and collection of results, rather than a quarter by quarter estimate."[28] He is the antithesis of so many leaders today who are in bondage to Wall Street analysts. Renwick is adamant that "the numbers" are what they are, so he feels no need to manipulate them, and he and his organization have found that being open pays off, because it builds trust and higher performance.

### Brian Pitman, CEO, Lloyd's Bank

When Brian Pitman became chief executive of Lloyd's Bank in 1983, he found a company that was confused and faltering. One of his first acts was to convince his board, and subsequently the management team, that they should decide on a single performance measure to assess overall performance. After some discussion, return on equity (ROE) was selected as the key measure. However, the key point here is not what measure was selected, but rather how Pitman socialized the new measurement within the bank. Pitman realized the power of a single transformational measure to focus a disparate organization. "For people to be truly committed to a strategy of shareholder value creation," says Pitman, "they have to believe in it . . . If they adopt such convictions—and don't simply pay lip service to them—it will change the way they run their operations."[29]

### Gary Loveman, CEO of Harrah's Entertainment

Gary Loveman started as Harrah's COO in 1998 and became its CEO in 2003. As CEO, Loveman is leading Harrah's Entertainment to success using the power of measurement. Loveman admitted that before he discovered how to measure, "My ability to manage our performance was undermined by my inability to measure it." Loveman is one of the pioneers in both customer profitability and business intelligence. His major weapons have been a business intelligence initiative, and Harrah's Total Rewards loyalty program. In order to achieve outstanding loyalty, each aspect of a property's service delivery is measured. Actions are taken to optimize service and revenue from the "best customers." The success of this approach helped Harrah's debunk an industry myth that customers are loyal to a location (such as Las Vegas or Atlantic City), not to a casino or a brand.

### Billy Beane, General Manager, Oakland Athletics Baseball Club

Michael M. Lewis made a celebrity of Billy Beane, general manager of the Major League Baseball team Oakland Athletics, in his best-selling book *Moneyball: The Art of Winning an Unfair Game*.[30] By changing the strategies that produce wins on the field, the Athletics became competitive with the New York Yankees and others who spend millions more annually on their players. The combination of his counter-intuitive based thinking and his data-based system for finding value has proven itself extremely effective, and has ensured Billy Beane a place in the performance measurement Hall of Fame (if not the baseball one)! Now other teams, like the Boston Red Sox, are using this measurement-based approach to talent selection, and it has even begun to permeate other professional sports.

### Frederick W. Smith, Chairman and President, FedEx Corporation

Founder and CEO of FedEx, the world's largest express transportation company, Fred Smith really understands how to leverage the power of technology-enabled measurement. He is a firm believer in that "You can't manage what you can't measure." FedEx replaced its single measure of quality performance (percent of on-time deliveries) with a 12-component index, Service Quality Indicator (SQI), which *every day* provides a mathematical measurement of FedEx service levels. The company also has a well-developed, thoroughly deployed management assessment system called Survey/Feedback/Action (SFA), which enables managers to develop written action plans for improvement and greater efficiency. At least in part because of the positive use of this data, over the last five years, 91 percent of employees responded that they were "proud to work for FedEx."

## Needed: The Role of Chief Measurement Officer (CMO)

As strong as each of these leaders have been, several times in this book I have alluded to the need for someone at the "C-level" who can be responsible for the overall transformation and leadership of an organization's total measurement system. Think about who is responsible for measurement in your organization. Probably, there are several people. Now think about who is responsible for the *transformation* of performance measurement. Probably, no one. And there is probably no one in the position to even acknowledge the need.

Who owns performance measurement in general? Probably, each function. In fact, it is my guess that there is no unified performance measurement system in your organization to be owned. Who owns the forecast? It probably depends on which forecast. Who is responsible for learning about measurement? Probably, no one. And the list of questions, and unsatisfactory answers, could go on and on.

When we view performance measurement as an *organization-wide* management system, and not as a financial or technical measurement one, it becomes clear that we must look outside of the traditional leadership structure. In that regard, we can all take our cue from the examples provided by the measurement leaders discussed above. All of them were recognized for their historical contributions to an emerging field. As the concepts and principles in this book become more widespread, I fully expect that future lists will become larger and larger, eventually including measurement leaders in your organization—perhaps even you!

# CHAPTER 10

# Learning About and from Measurement

Nothing is more important for transforming performance measurement than learning. Learning about and from performance measurement can make a huge difference in how people relate and respond to it—and to each other. In this chapter we discuss the importance of learning *about* using measurement transformationally and learning *from* measurement.

## Transformational Learning

Most learning is informational, not transformational. Transformation is about trans-form-ation, a *"change in form."* Learning aimed at increasing our store of knowledge or existing repertoire of skills is valuable, but it doesn't promote change of form. Organizational learning expert Jack Mezirow believes that transformational learning (or "transformative learning," as he refers to it) must not only change "what" we learn, but "how" we learn.[1] It isn't just about quantity or quality of knowledge, but also the "ways of knowing." As such, transformational learning involves "learning about learning" (or what some might call "meta-learning"). So the process of learning through *changing* the way learning takes place in our organizations is transformational learning!

It is vital that we transform what is measured, how it is measured, and what is done with the measurement. Transformational performance measurement is performance measurement that is constantly learning about itself, and improving itself.

## The Process of Learning

Learning is how we acquire knowledge—our "know what," "know why," and "know how" about the world. Our "know what" gives us our basic information about what exists; our "know why" tells us why things happen; and our "know how" tells us "how to do" things (our skills). All of us are products of our learning, or lack of learning. Truly successful people are not only those who possess greater knowledge, but are also the most adept at the process of learning.

In school, the test is the primary measure of success, and it creates expectations for what should be learned and what should be taught. Most traditional learning involves the transfer of "content" from a teacher to students, who are rewarded for passively absorbing content and then repeating it back on a test. The test tends to measure information *acquisition* more often than true knowledge and understanding. What is "on the test" is what directs learning, and most teachers "teach to the test."

This kind of testing also reveals much about the dangers inherent in the basic principle of measurement ("you get what you measure"), because learning is typically deemed to be "successful" when the student can pass a test—whether anything useful has been learned or not.

In the workplace, it is much the same. Workplace "students" also tend to learn what is measured, whether by a test, by completing a class, or demonstrating on-the-job what was learned in class. Sometimes they aren't measured at all—which is why organizations tend to get "the learning they measure"—or, more aptly, the lack of learning they don't measure.

Just as in school, this leads to conformity to an established body of knowledge. People learn to do their jobs according to expectations and are tested on the "scores" they attain on *their performance measures*, which are rarely linked to any meaningful learning. The routine things are measured in other organizational areas as well, such as the project manager who gets credit for a project that, though worthless, was completed!

When we think of the "curriculum" in the workplace, we tend to think of "subjects" like standard operating procedures, rules, enforcement, monitoring, and compliance. Employees learn that they are "strongly encouraged" to learn and comply with the "the way we do things around here."

Actually, traditional learning and performance measurement are at the very heart of why it is so difficult to change organizations. Because people *do* what they are measured on, it is critical that we measure the right things. But rarely is this the case.

When people become creative, it is usually *in spite of* the formal education or workplace performance measures. Creative answers lie *outside* of the traditional curriculum. Measuring the amount of content absorbed does not measure innovation or the capacity for it.

For successful people, the key to their success does not lie as much with the content they have assimilated as with their ability to be creative *beyond* the standard curriculum.

## The Learning Loop

All learning occurs through a kind of iterative loop. The learning process depicted in the diagram below shows that, as a first step, people engage in some learning "experience," such as attending a lecture, reading a book, or just doing some work. The second step is "observation"—something is observed or gleaned from that experience. The third step is "internal change"—something happens in the brain if learning has occurred. Then, there is another experience, which might be an opportunity to apply the internal change (which is really the "learning"). So, the loop is:

Experience ➡ Observation ➡ Internal Change ➡
Experience, and so on

The internal changes can take many different forms. Knowledge can be acquired and simply added to memory; it can become "know-how" that is eventually turned into skill; or it can progressively alter the store of internal knowledge to make our knowledge base increasingly richer.

Internally, learning occurs through assimilation and accommodation. *Assimilation* is absorbing what we are told, while *accommodation* is the "struggle" to try to fit what we are told, or what we have learned through experience, into our existing store of knowledge. Good learning isn't necessarily easy. Actually, the more struggle we experience in learning, the deeper the learning becomes.

This is similar to the process of converting data into information, knowledge, and wisdom. For the most part, what is taught or learned is data or information. In formal learning, it is mostly information, since the instructor has already converted the raw data into informational content. However, in informal learning we are often confronted with new data, and therefore have to start at the beginning. This can be an advantage, since it gives us the opportunity to perform our own data-into-information conversion, rather than relying on someone else to do it. And when we convert data into information, it can actually enhance the quality of knowledge we acquire since "we did it ourselves." It is also likely to be more meaningful to us.

When we really understand the information, it becomes *knowledge*. That knowledge can be used together with other knowledge and experience to eventually produce *wisdom*. That's why people with a certain level of experience tend to be wiser than those who might have a lot of education but lack experience. The better organized our internal knowledge is and the better our learning tools are, the more effective and efficient we will be in converting information into wisdom.

Contrary to what we may think, most learning does not occur in formal settings. Most of what we learn, we learn through experience and experimentation in everyday life. Some estimates are that as much as 90 percent of lifelong learning occurs informally. This kind of informal learning is pervasive, continuous, and *profoundly social* in organizations. It happens wherever people do their work: on a shop floor, around a conference table, onsite with customers, or in a laboratory. Most people are continuously learning.

## Single-Loop and Double-Loop Learning

There are two types of learning: single-loop and double-loop.[2] Single-loop learning occurs when there is a single feedback loop, with individuals modifying their actions according to the difference between expected and obtained outcomes. This is an ongoing *error-correction* process that continues until an acceptable level of knowledge or action is achieved. The most common example of single-loop learning is a thermostat set on a particular temperature. The heating system then attempts to find that set-point temperature. When it does, it stops "learning." Single-loop learning is also exemplified by increasing competence in an already-acquired skill, until a satisfactory level of competence is attained. With single-loop learning, practice, feedback, error correction, and repetition will improve your ability at whatever you are currently doing. Becoming more adept at using the same measure is a good measurement example of single-loop learning.

In *double-loop learning*, individuals question the very content of the learning, test those beliefs they have taken for granted, and challenge the expectations, values, and assumptions that led them to adopt the knowledge or engage in the actions in the first place! If they are able to modify expectations, then a second-order, or double-loop, of learning has occurred. If the thermostat could ask questions about why it is doing what it is doing, that would be a case of double-loop learning.

As such, double-loop learning can be thought of as "learning *about* single-loop learning." Double-loop learning is important if people want to achieve *more than* increased efficiency in doing the same things. As people experiment with new and different approaches, double-loop learning is taking place. Innovation and transformation are double-loop processes. Wal-Mart and Amazon.com are great examples of companies that learn through experimentation. Both companies are not reluctant to try something new, but they don't deploy innovation without testing it first. They are committed to learning from measurement.

In performance measurement, questioning existing measures and adopting new ones (transformational and emergent measures) are examples of double-loop learning. After double-loop learning has occurred, then single-loop learning can take over again, and we can improve the use of the new method or measure. At its best, performance measurement should be a continual interplay of double-loop and single-loop learning—double-loop to question existing measures and experiment with new ones, followed by single-loop to fine-tune the new measures.

The nature and relationship of single- and double-loop learning are depicted in Figure 10-1.

Most learning is the single-loop variety, because the objective is to become more knowledgeable or more skilled in a particular area. For example, an accountant learning the standard method for computing profits and a supervisor improving her performance appraisal skills are examples of single-loop learning. In contrast, an accountant questioning the validity of the standard method for computing profits and a supervisor deciding to adapt a new performance appraisal method might be considered examples of double-loop learning. In each case, rather than just getting better at the same approach, the validity of the very approach that was previously learned is challenged.

The more deeply rooted an existing approach, the more difficult double-loop learning is. That is why people who are particularly good at doing something are often the most resistant to learning something new. This is particularly true in traditional disciplines and functions. Performance measurement, for example, is deeply entrenched in the functional psyche and is extremely resistant to double-loop learning. That's why people in organizations tend to use the same "metrics" over and over again.

## Transformational Measurement and Double-Loop Learning

The distinction between single-loop and double-loop learning is particularly important for transforming performance measurement. Increasing proficiency with existing performance measurement methods is single-loop learning; questioning and changing existing methods is double-loop learning. Single-loop learning is great for traditional mass-production manufacturing. The single-loop mindset created mass production, and it drives it to new levels of increased efficiency. It is also great for practicing existing skills. For example, practicing estimating, based on existing principles, is

FIGURE 10-1. SINGLE VS. DOUBLE-LOOP LEARNING.

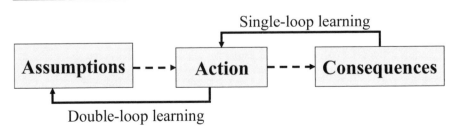

single-loop learning. However, single-loop learning doesn't challenge what is being done. So, if the parameters for estimating need to be challenged to increase accuracy, don't rely exclusively on single-loop learning.

By contrast, double-loop learning is looking at things through a new lens, which helps us to see the same things in a new way, but also to see new things. In the traditional mass-production manufacturing world, there are limited new things to see. However, in the new world of services and intangibles, there is an enormous amount of value that is not being seen, or not being seen clearly enough to manage effectively. That's why organizations everywhere are wasting some of their most important sources of value creation—customer relationships, supply chain partners, employees, and knowledge and intellectual capital that is not captured, enhanced, or exploited. All the Six Sigma projects in the world won't help organizations see things with a new lens, because, as valuable as they are for driving efficiency, they all use standard, single-loop "metrics."

As Michael Hammer explained, "Six Sigma can ensure that a process is performing as it was designed to . . . but it is powerless to create an alternative framework." This is where Six Sigma and transformational measurement could work hand-in hand, with double-loop learning enhancing single-loop learning, which, in turn, can enhance double-loop learnings.

Chances are, the performance measurement system in your organization is predominantly single-loop—concerned with doing the same things better. However, unless performance measurement is double-loop, many of the measures you are using might very well be obsolete. Double-loop learning is about continually challenging what is taken for granted, and seeking whether there might be a better way. The single-loops are *always* being challenged—not for the purpose of destroying them, but for the purpose of continually improving the effectiveness of the total system.

Although all individuals and organizations are constantly learning, almost all of the learning is single-loop learning, as people become better at doing the same things. This is not necessarily bad, but it won't *transform* anything. An organization that uses the same KPIs (key performance indicators) over and over again is destined to get the same results—no matter how well they are measured. Today's competitive pressures require not only more skilled players, but also better *strategies* for winning the game. Single-loop learning alone is no longer sufficient. In fact, it can be a hindrance. Organizations that are *too good* at single-loop learning can actually be at a disadvantage!

## Organizational Learning

While individual learning is concerned with improving individual capacity, organizational learning is focused on enhancing organizational systems and the organization's capacity for performance. Transformational performance measurement is just that—using performance measurement in new ways to enhance organizational systems and the organization's capacity for performance. When an organization "systematizes" organizational learning (makes it happen routinely), it is said to be a "learning organization." Peter Senge describes a learning organization as a place where people are continually discovering how they create their reality—and how they can change it.[3]

Organizational learning is learning that involves an entire organization or organizational entity. It almost never takes place in a classroom, nor does it use a standard curriculum. It is not about a particular content or set of methods. Organizational learning is *action learning* that is accomplished in the work environment and is usually integrated with work.

Transformational measurement is a great way of facilitating organizational learning, and organizational learning, in turn, is a great way of fostering transformational measurement. Remember the measurement scenarios and snapshots in Chapters 4 and 5? The people described in them are excited about measurement and how it can help them to learn and improve. For them performance measurement is not boring or threatening, it is positive and motivating. *It is organizational learning in action.* The reason for this is that this kind of measurement can provide the kind of visibility, clarity, and interactivity needed for practical learning at work. When you are sitting in a classroom, you are probably passively listening to a lecture. When you are measuring or dialoging about measurement, you are learning *by doing*.

It is vital that organizations empower people to transform the work they do, not just learn how to do the same work better. This kind of learning can lead to a much deeper understanding than could ever occur through a traditional learning activity. The questions and patterns of interaction in transformational performance measurement are clearly those of a healthy *double-loop* learning system. But this involves risk, and it's risk that most people don't want to take. "Why should we look at things differently?" "We don't need new measures—our metrics are just fine—we're just not doing as well as we would like on them." "If the measure isn't 100 percent valid and reliable, we don't even consider it." If these kind of comments don't sound familiar to you, then your organization is already more advanced than most.

Occasionally I see some examples of organizational learning, such as asking questions, engaging in dialogue, cross-functionally interacting, proactively measuring value and effectiveness, implementing measured experiments and pilot projects, talking about what is being learned through measuring, and so on. But rarely. One of the most remarkable organizational learning activities we will hopefully see increasingly occur in the future is the effort of a cross-functional team attempting to measure a difficult-to-measure construct. This is real organizational learning in *action*. This is the kind of double-loop learning with respect to measurement that needs to be commonplace in organizations that want to win in the twenty-first century.

## Why Smart People Do Dumb Things

So, why isn't this kind of active learning the norm in most organizations today? Organizational psychologist Chris Argyris presents the basic problem of learning for both individuals and organizations.[4] Even when we engage in learning, there are individual *and* organizational "learning disabilities" that not only prevent optimal learning, but also prevent effective performance. Argyris notes that most people are quite smart, but that to succeed, they've learned to find "correct" answers (even if they are the *wrong* answers), and they tend to ignore or cover up the "incorrect" ones (even if they are actually *right*). This happens because of "blind spots" in what people see. These tendencies are exacerbated in organizations, and are often reinforced by existing measurement systems.

When smart people with learning disabilities are put together in groups, "reverse synergy" occurs, and the whole actually becomes significantly less than the individuals. That's why organizational learning guru Peter Senge rhetorically asks, "How can a team of committed managers with individual IQs above 120 have a collective IQ of 63?"[5] Below are a few examples of learning disabilities that may shed some light on this issue:

• *Labeling.* There are all kinds of habits of thought, perceptions, and emotions that can cause our minds to distort reality. Our thinking tends to be subjective and self-serving, and we often tend to "label" things the way we want to see them, rather than the way they really are.

• *Fixed Mindsets.* Much of our idiosyncratic view of things is caused by our "mindsets" or "mental models." According to Peter Schwartz, fixed mindsets are attitudes about every situation in our lives and every person we come across. "In many cases, our mindsets have been built up, slowly, from childhood and may not have much to do with actual reality."[6]

• *Filtering.* All people tend to unconsciously filter information, preferring good news, or information that confirms our preconceptions and self-image.

• *Tunnel Vision.* This is the tendency to focus on one thing at a time, to take things out of context ("fragmentation"), or to pay attention only to the most recent, the most familiar, the traditional, or the short-term.

• *Justification.* We all have a tendency to seek out information that confirms that we did indeed make the right decision. But if perchance we didn't make the right decision, our minds are very adept at dealing with the result-ing "cognitive dissonance" through denial, defensiveness, or rationalization.

• *Habit*. All human beings are creatures of the past, and of habit. A lead-ership survey of executives who were asked to name "the things that get in the way of effectively executing business strategy" found the highest rated responses were "the past, and habits."

• *Target Fixation*. Slywotsky and Morrison specifically warn executives to avoid an extremely dangerous "relative" of tunnel vision. As they explain, "One of the biggest risks to a dive-bombing aviator was called 'target fixa-tion.' The pilot could get so focused on keeping the sight on the target, to ensure an accurate drop that he or she forgot the altitude and flew the plane right into the ground—excellent micromanagement of the current measurement ('Are we on target?'), but no connection to the broader real-ity."[7] The authors blame this bias for such organizational leadership errors of judgment as: fixating on increasing the market share of yesterday's prod-ucts and on the revenue growth of commoditized products, focusing exces-sively on reducing manufacturing unit costs when value is created elsewhere in the value chain, being the first to market with the wrong product, and defining quality by internal statistics that don't reflect quality in terms of the customer.

• *Conformity*. Another source of bias is associated with group dynamics, especially the pressures toward conformity to the will of the group. As we all know, there are literally thousands of examples of this!

Unfortunately, smart people do dumb things all the time in organiza-tions. As renowned psychologist William James summed it up: "A great many people think they are thinking when they are merely rearranging their prejudices."[8] That is why many individuals, functions, disciplines, and orga-nizations hold on doggedly to existing measures—even when they are shown to be inadequate and lead to sub-optimization and other dysfunc-tional negative consequences.

## How Performance Measurement Can Help

Probably the best way to reduce biased thinking and flawed habits is through the effective use of performance measurement. Without good measurement, bias will almost always win, and performance will lose. To slightly rephrase what I said in Chapter 1, "In the absence of data, anyone's *biased* opinion is as good as anyone else's." Although we can never eliminate our personal biases, we can reduce their negative impacts by becoming more aware of them.

But even when people become aware of their biases, the habits still re-main. To replace a habit often requires a disciplined approach that most people (especially people who pride themselves on their intuition) resist.

That is one reason why disciplined *measurement* can be so effective. Measurement provides a new, more objective lens for confronting reality— seeing it for what it really is. It can help check our biases and prevent costly errors in judgment, which otherwise we might not even "see," especially in the "heat of battle." Measurement can help make decisions more objective, disciplined, and less political. This is one of the things that has made Six Sigma so successful.

But it will only work if done well and with wisdom. That's why I urge you to consider reviewing some of the books on measurement literacy and on logical thinking included in the notes for this chapter.[9] There is a wealth of knowledge that can be learned from these discussions of how easily our thinking is distorted by numbers.

Also consider two of the Transformational Measurement Action Plans in Chapter 14: Section 32, Information Orientation, and Section 33, Information Proficiency. Information Orientation is a measure of how well an organization uses information and Information Proficiency is about measuring how well individuals use it. In this day of enormous progress in Information Technology, it sometimes seems as if the richer we are in data and information, the poorer we are getting at making good decisions.

## Learning New Ways of Thinking About Performance Measurement

As devastating as making wrong decisions can be, it is even more damaging if nothing is learned from the mistake. In organizations today, most people are not able to learn from their experiences. The most transformational individuals and organizations are those that openly confront the reality of mistakes, and spend the time to learn from them.

Unfortunately, most individuals and organizations spend a disproportionate amount of time recounting their successes and glossing over their failures. This is a surefire recipe for mediocrity. While success is great, we don't tend to learn very much from it. Most people feel much more comfortable sharing their "best practices" (which tend to come from reflection on successes) than their "lessons learned" (which are derived from failures and mistakes). I have seen so many "lessons learned" meetings in which team members try their hardest to come up with mistakes that don't reflect too badly on them, rather than being brutally honest about what happened and what should be learned. It is much like a person answering a job interview question, "What is your greatest weakness?" by saying, "I work too hard."

Honest acknowledgment of failure is an invitation to learn. Denying failure or discounting it is antithetical to a learning organization. Properly used, measurement is one of the most powerful learning tools there is. Improperly used, it can serve to reinforce biases and perpetuate ignorance. Consider an interactive meeting during which everyone describes the five or six biggest mistakes they've made during the year—and how they have *learned* from them! Can you imagine the positive, transforming impact *that* discussion would have on future organizational decisions?

## The Keys to Transformational Learning

The kind of learning described above requires a context that is open enough to support it. As you know, the keys to transformational measurement are context, focus, integration, and interactivity. The same is true for transformational learning. Is there an environment in your organization that is conducive to measuring the truth? Is your organization focusing on measures that are the most important for creating value? Does your measurement approach foster organizational integration and alignment? Is the measurement being done interactively and iteratively? All of these reflect learning—and not just any type of learning, but a lot of *double-loop* and *active* organizational learning.

If the context is trending in a positive direction, you should be seeing organizational learning increasing as evidence of that. If there is an effort being made to continuously find the right transformational measures, there will be double-loop learning occurring. If a high degree of interactivity is occurring, then it is virtually guaranteed that organizational learning is occurring.

The following sections include some topics in what I would call an "Action Learning Curriculum" for a new kind of measurement literacy.

### Inquiry vs. Advocacy

In most organizations, people rise to the top through successfully advocating their own opinions, ideas, and agendas. The relative importance of advocacy is probably inevitable. However, the key to both transformational learning and transformational measurement is *inquiry.* Inquiry is the ability to ask a question that hasn't been asked before—the ability to inquire, not just dictate or advocate. According to Peter Senge, "Genuine inquiry starts when people ask questions to which they do not have an answer." However, he adds, "That is rare in organizations."[10]

### Permission to Question

In a double-loop learning environment, people must be willing to openly share and test their perceptions, intentions, and theories with reality and learn from the discrepancies. "What do these measurements really mean?" "Where did these numbers come from?" "Who did the measuring?" "Do they have any ulterior motives?" In a double-loop learning environment, people are not afraid to question the numbers, or the theories that gave rise to the numbers.

## Permission to Experiment

Few managers realize how powerful the mere act of trying to make something "measurable" can be—even if they never actually collect data. Just discussing the definition of new measures can be a transformational learning opportunity. In fact, that's how most transformational measures begin—as a hypothesis by someone who dares to put forward an idea that challenges the conventional wisdom.

And this is exactly how some of the intangibles that currently defy measurement (and therefore are poorly managed) will someday be routinely measured! Someone simply needs to step forward and begin the discussion by asking: "How do we measure that?" without being afraid to suggest that it be measured in a qualitative or even subjective way. But this isn't going to happen in an organization with a negative context of measurement, or where people don't feel empowered to do so.

One of the key concepts in this book is that emergent measures are almost never able to be measured in the traditional purely objective, quantitative ways, and when we try to do so, we often devalue or trivialize them. People need to be educated in the new rules of transformational measurement. Some new measures will require people to make "educated guesses." If so, then organizations had better start educating the guessers!

Furthermore, enormous learning occurs through the use of subjective assessments and self-assessments. However, most people are unprepared to take advantage of the challenge, because they are accustomed to be defensive. That is only natural, but for performance measurement to be transformed, it is vital that the climate for learning from measurement be transformed.

## Supporting Measurement Conversations

Most people in organizations are accustomed to being told what to do. As such, measurement becomes little more than an accountability mechanism. No wonder people don't feel much ownership in current measures—they have had no active involvement in them. Few people will be very excited about being told to "measure this."

In addition, almost all of this traditional learning about measurement is single-loop learning, and certainly much of this can be delivered through presentations, either live or recorded. But true double-loop learning cannot occur through one-way presentations, or even question-and-answer sessions. This kind of learning will only happen interactively!

These measurement discussions can become true learning situations in which participants can examine and modify their existing measures, as long as managers and employees are given the opportunity to converse about, and *question,* the current approach.

### Facilitating Conversations Around Measurement Frameworks.

As discussed at length in Chapter 8, measurement frameworks are invaluable for helping people see and understand the "big picture" view of the organization, and to make the connections between elements that are not apparent in everyday work. This is a great opportunity to discuss "line of sight" connections between what employees are doing and measuring, and organizational *results.* Nothing is a more powerful stimulus to learning than conversations around measurement frameworks. As Michael Hammer said, the most important thing you can do for your company is to help everyone understand the business in the same terms as the CEO.

It is important to discuss what the measures mean, how they are related, and, most importantly, to compare the *theory* of the business with the operational *reality*—to make explicit observations about how employees connect with customers, and how they connect with the business plan and the budget process. So far so good, but too often measurement frameworks are treated as if they were hard-wired. Measurement frameworks are not irrefutable fact. Most of the time, people tend to just seek confirmation of the existing frameworks, rather than really test or try to improve them.

Some of the measurement framework conversations can revolve around questions such as: "What does the evidence (data) say?" "Is this logic correct?" "Why were the measures selected?" "What is most important to customers?" "Are these priorities reflected in the measurement framework?" or "Is there anything else that should be measured?"

Just think how much employees can learn by considering the conflicts and trade-offs between operational performance measurements and customer-focused measures for both external and internal customers. In many cases, operational measures are in diametrical opposition to positive customer- and user experiences. For a learning organization, of course, this is not a problem, but a wonderful opportunity to find an optimal trade-off.

### Generating Greater Understanding of Value Creation and Destruction.

If your organization has a strong "theory" of the purpose and direction of the business, then you particularly want measurement that gives visibility to the factors you consider important to success. Visibility in itself becomes a powerful tool to influence effort. The fact that you bother to measure something draws people's attention to it. Unfortunately, value creation (and destruction) are rarely overtly *visible*. Most managers and employees don't really know if they are creating or destroying value by their actions.

People should be actively involved in discussions about how more value can be created, and less value can be destroyed—whether through egregious waste, minor leakage, or just evaporation. Just think how many instances there are of people *inadvertently* destroying value in almost every area of every organization around the globe. Consider how many organizations still hold on to antiquated assumptions about customers ("All customers are profitable" and "All customer churn is bad"), about employees ("All employee turnover is bad"), about market share ("All market share is good"), and about revenue ("All revenue is good"). Only increased double-loop learning will stop the bleeding!

## Interpreting Numbers and Statistics

It isn't important that *everyone* in an organization be able to interpret sophisticated statistics as they apply to individual function and responsibility. But in order to transform performance measurement, people have to be willing to discuss and challenge "the numbers."

Organizations are very quick to adopt new quantitative measures, and those numbers are often blindly accepted as reality. Because numbers have the appearance of credibility, it is often difficult for most people to challenge, or even question, them. Most people accept the numbers, but don't really understand or *learn* from them. That is why it is important that people in your organization not be intimidated or deceived by *quantitative* measurements.

Many managers react to numbers the way they do to any elevator door opening; they take action without thinking about whether it is the right thing to do. W. Edwards Deming warned about the danger of reacting to isolated numbers. He always advised his clients not to look at isolated numbers, but to look at patterns.[11] Nothing is more revealing than to track the variance of a process using statistical process control charts. Nothing is as important to understand as variation. In fact, Deming called the failure to understand the nature and interpretation of variation the central problem of management. What is vitally important is what H.G. Wells called "statistical thinking" (not to be confused with calculating statistics). He predicted that statistical thinking will one day be as essential as the ability to read and write.

It is important that employees feel empowered to question the numbers—both financial and nonfinancial. For example, if someone says, "We're averaging 90 percent customer satisfaction," which sounds pretty good, I would immediately ask questions about the "range" of responses. It might turn out that everyone is about 90 percent satisfied, but we'd still need to know how large the sample was, what questions were asked, and how this average rating compared with the competition. However, the same average might also mean that there are quite a few customers who are less than 80 percent satisfied, while others are 99 percent satisfied. Depending on the competitive context, this could be a problem worth investigating. There are virtually an infinite number of questions that could be asked about statistics such as these!

Now let's say, in that same situation, it was found that "staff friendliness" and "satisfaction" were related. What does that really mean? How closely related are they? Is there a causal relationship?

One of the biggest problems of statistics is the lack of understanding of the difference between "correlation" and "causation." *Correlation* just means that two variables are related. *Causation* means that one causes the other—a much higher standard. Correlations are everywhere; causation is rare. Many correlations are really just coincidences. Also, the relationships (causal or otherwise) could be very weak or mediated by a large number of "extraneous" factors. I am always amazed at how often executives take credit for their poor decisions that end up with good outcomes because of fortuitous circumstances. As a consultant wisely observed, "A poor decision that leads to a successful result is still a poor decision!"

Can you imagine what kind of rich "measurement conversations" could occur if the managers and employees in your organization had a minimal level of statistical literacy? This could greatly increase their business insight and motivation—not to mention their ability to participate in transformational measurement discussion. I think that it is very desirable for those who are concerned about customer service to be knowledgeable and empowered enough to suggest how the situation could be improved. This level of knowledge is not difficult to attain, and could be achieved in a very short time—without ever having to make a single calculation!

## Learning to Predict

Prediction is essential for effective management. In fact, as Deming said, "Management *is* prediction."[12] One of the most important functions of measurement is to enable prediction.

Whether we are consciously aware of it, almost everything we do involves some form of prediction, according to some "theory" of action. A theory is nothing more than a cause-and-effect prediction about how planned actions lead to expected outcomes: If I do X, Y will be the result. Why is a particular practice linked to performance improvement—what is the logic? In a learning organization, theory-based predictions are systematically being tested and the theory is being revised—using both single-loop and double-loop learning. Without theory, we have nothing to revise, and nothing to learn. We learn by comparing predictions from the theory with actual data.

Theory-building, measurement frameworks, and organizational learning involve "system thinking." The behavior of a system is not a function of what each part is doing in isolation, but on how the parts interact. In order to understand a system, we need to understand how it fits into the larger system. As understanding increases, so does the ability of individuals—and the organization as a whole—to predict.

Unfortunately, most managers fail to develop even the most rudimentary theory that allows them to jointly, interactively predict cause-and-effect, and then improve their predictions. This predictive learning cycle is: predict, test, and learn.

When organizational leaders keep repeating their mistakes, it's because they almost never perform "measured improvement experiments" and consequently fail to learn about the system that they are managing. If you can't explain the underlying logic of why something should enhance performance, you are likely engaging in "superstitious learning" and may well be doing something that is irrelevant or even damaging.

The emphasis in most organizations on "doing" actually inhibits learning because managers and employees are not required to take the time to properly predict (develop a theory) and learn (systematically test that theory). As a result, every action or initiative is viewed as an independent activity, and whether it will succeed or fail depends more on chance. Without good theory-based predictive measurement and learning, it will be impossible to determine what is working, or not working, and why. Under such circumstances, experience and resources are often wasted.

## Increasing the Understanding of Measurement

There are a few simple, generic models that are very helpful for framing action learning and measurement conversation. The Input→Process→Output→Outcome model is very helpful in creating and testing measurement cause-and-effect theories, and in generating new measures.

According to this model, all organizations (and major parts thereof) involve the conversion of "inputs" (resources, such as people's time, capital, and raw material) that the organization expends through a "process" (the internal activities performed) to produce "outputs" (the consequences of actions taken within the process or what is produced by the process) to create "outcomes" (benefits or value provided by the outputs to customers and/or other stakeholders).

This model helps to identify key measures and make predictions about the efficiency and effectiveness of the system. It also puts the focus of performance measurement where it should be—on the customer and other stakeholders. Everything else in the organization should be done to support *the outcomes*. Certainly, it is important to have the right input measures, the right process measures, and the right output measures, but it is the outcome measures that ultimately determine the success of your organization, and whether your customers will keep coming back.

In addition, the model can help people realize how important it is for the organization to operate as integrated processes (not functions). The most powerful internal measures are *cross-functional* process measures. It is also great to discuss how different functions can produce "outputs" that are easiest to convert into customer value. Too often outputs are things that have no relevance to customers or any valuable outcome at all.

Feargal Quinn, founder and president of Superquinn, the Irish grocery chain, responded to measurement data that showed that 25 percent of Superquinn shoppers were not buying from the stores' bakeries. When he shared that data with bakery managers and employees, they realized that their internally focused activities were not producing the right outcomes. So, "they came up with scores of creative ideas to build traffic.[13] The Superquinn experience demonstrates that customer measurement provides employees with "the truth" about their performance relative to *customer outcomes*, compared with traditional performance appraisals that focus on individual performance relative to an internal standard (usually a subjective one), and which do nothing to inspire team or customer-focused performance.

Whatever the areas of performance measurement, the Input→Process-→Output→Outcome model will provide more opportunities for feedback and provide a powerful language for discussing performance.

### The Phases of Measurement

Another helpful model for increasing understanding of performance measurement describes the four phases of measurement.

* *Predictive measurement* is when you identify, develop, and/or refine your measurement theory of a situation (e.g., "Based on our measurement framework, when we do more of this, this will happen").
* *Baseline measurement* establishes the current (or beginning) value of a particular measure (before the action is taken).
* *In-process measurement* occurs while the change is being implemented ("what is happening as a result of the change").
* *Retrospective measurement* is the after-the-fact measurement at the end of a predetermined period, so that you can determine "what happened."

As you use this model and complete more and more measurement cycles, your predictions (predictive versus in-process measurements) should get increasingly accurate. Nothing will improve performance like timely measurement data that shows precisely how well you are performing over time in some area where you can actually change your behavior based on the feedback and see the impact. Measurement-based learning is extremely powerful.

Self-assessments are potentially powerful learning and performance improvement tools that are relevant to this model. People tend to have a "theory" about themselves or whatever they want to measure. Most of the time that theory (at least initially) is wrong. The baseline measure tells them just how wrong their theory was. So, they should be motivated to do something to make their behavior, for instance, more in line with their prediction. Over time, they should be able to see improvements, which should spur the desire to improve. At the end, they can bask in the glory of their accomplishment. That is the use of the model in a single-loop learning context.

Now let's suppose that when the baseline was measured, the person or team decided that they need to change their predictive model—let's say they found that their collaboration score was well below what they expected. However, instead of just using that information to incrementally improve their collaboration skills, they decided that they needed to adopt a different approach to collaborating, requiring an entirely different measurement instrument (and operational definition).

Some might criticize this example as trying to win by changing the score-keeping system. In a "negative context of measurement" that might be a temptation, but in a positive context (which was the case in this example), the team decided to develop a new measure, because the old one was reinforcing an old mental model of collaborative behavior that they knew needed to change. So, they worked with their internal clients to redefine "collaboration" in a way that was more consistent with the mental model that they wanted to adopt. The measurement process enabled this team to confront reality, not to deny it.

This is clearly an example of double-loop learning and transformational measurement. Without the predictive measurement (the theory, the existing framework) and without the baseline measurement (the test that they did poorly on), the learning and performance improvement would not have occurred. This is powerful stuff. Can you imagine what would happen if you could harness it on an organizational level? That is what a "learning organization" is all about!

## Incorporating Qualitative Measurement

Some insist that measurement is synonymous with numbers, and that "qualitative measurement" is an oxymoron! The emphasis on quantification sometimes discourages the consideration of a whole range of "softer" measures. Too often hard numbers drive out the soft ones, and important aspects of performance are missed. Some things are more difficult than others to translate into numbers. In fact, "soft data" can sometimes generate more insight and wisdom than "hard data." Measures only need to be accurate enough to serve the purpose for which they are intended.

Numbers are not always the best way to measure. For example, in the customer satisfaction example given it might have been useful to review selected open-ended responses to the survey. As valuable as a numerical Customer Satisfaction Index might be, it is no substitute for understanding customers *qualitatively*. That is why, at Marriott, the CEO reads every twentieth customer letter to get a better "feel" for what customers "really think" about the company— beyond the numbers.

In the retail world, observational studies reveal valuable insights that are crucial for driving more value. For example, retailers are redesigning stores based on observational studies on how customers navigate through a store to identify what causes them to become frustrated. Qualitative studies of customer shopping behavior has led to breakthrough store design ideas for increasing a key *quantitative* measure, "shopping time," which has been shown to increase another critical quantitative measure, "amount purchased per visit." Another important qualitative measurement methodology is *interviews*. One CEO explained, "Once we began talking to customers to understand what *they* cared about, everyone in our organization learned exactly what to concentrate on. Our measures took on a whole new look." When companies start seriously measuring what's really important to the customer, rather than just to them, a transformation occurs—and, at least initially, much of the data is qualitative.

## Practicing Subjective Measurements

Many intangibles cannot be easily measured in traditional ways, and doing so tends to trivialize them. Good subjective measures can be quite satisfactory surrogates for harder measures, especially during the exploratory phases of transformational performance measurement. As your organization encourages more measurement innovation, you will find that many of the emerging measures may begin as somewhat subjective *qualitative* concepts, which will gradually become more objective and quantitative over time. This is a natural part of double-loop learning and transformational measurement—and it is one of the reasons why a climate that promotes an active learning curriculum is so important.

In Chapters 13 and 14, there will be extensive discussions of qualitative emergent and transformational measures that can be used to increase measurement-based feedback to supplement or even replace some of the more traditional quantitative measures.

## How Well Does Your Organization Learn About and from Measurement?

As this chapter comes to an end, consider what kind of performance measurement-related learning is occurring in your organization: How much time is spent learning? What proportion of that time is single-loop learning and how much is double-loop learning? How much organizational action learning is occurring? How much learning about measurement exists? How about qualitative measurement? How much learning is devoted to helping employees think better and make better decisions?

Transformational learning is concerned with changing what and how we learn; transformational measurement is concerned with changing what and how we measure. The objective is not just to change a particular instance of learning or measurement, but to create an *ongoing capacity* for transforming both learning and measurement. In order to attain this capacity, an individual or organization must "internalize" the capability for continual transformation. Performance measurement can be incrementally improved, but it won't be *transformed* through the teaching and learning of more traditional measurement skills.

Positive, powerful performance measurement is not something that can be created once and for all—it is not a class you can take—it must be a continuous improvement process. That is where learning comes in.

But real learning isn't easy. In fact, double-loop learning tends to take people well out of their "comfort zones." But don't be reluctant to give your people the nudge they need. As Eliyahu Goldratt has cogently explained, "The minute you supply a person with answers, by that very action, you block them, once and for all, from the opportunity of inventing those same answers for themselves."[14] In other words, you rob them of the opportunity to really learn. Also, no matter how difficult, using measurement to foster learning feels a whole lot different, and better, than measurement used as a threat.

We have come a long way in this chapter toward realizing that, like the other aspects of transforming performance measurement, learning is a journey, and a process of discovery. It is important to remember that how well your organization *measures* depends, to a large extent, on how well it *learns*.

# The Uses and Abuses of Measurement Technology

As we saw in Chapter 10, learning is a fundamental process in any organization that hopes to be successful in the long-term. Without learning and the ongoing communication it entails, the greatest opportunities for using performance measurement effectively are lost. Technology can serve an important role in facilitating and sustaining individual and organizational learning and dialogue. In this chapter, we will discuss how to create a successful synergy between the social and technical aspects of transformational measurement.

While interest and investment in measurement-related technology is growing exponentially, technology is one of the most misunderstood, and poorly managed, areas of performance measurement. Is technology making measurement better, or just more automated? This chapter frames what I believe to be the most critical issues involved in the use of technology to support the transformation of performance measurement.

This chapter also addresses the unnecessary conflict between the use of technology and the social aspects of performance measurement.

Transformational performance measurement is about establishing a holistic measurement system that must exist within a positive context; it is unequivocally *not* primarily about technology. Technology should *support* the performance measurement system—it is *not* the system!

## In Search of a Quick Fix and a Technology Breakthrough

Organizations have gone fairly rapidly from having too little data to having *much too much*. Databases are now capable of retaining a virtually infinite amount of data. Furthermore, advances in data processing capacity and speed and analytical software have given rise to the spectacular growth of the data warehousing and data analytics industries.

Making business "sense" out of the mass of data is a challenge that few organizations understand or know how to resolve. Far from making our lives easier (both in our personal lives and at work), information technology has actually added complexity by providing so many more options and decisions to make.

Few business people fail to accept the importance of performance measurement, but few want to be actively involved in it. They know that it is vital to be compliant, but they also want to reduce unnecessary labor and drudgery. That's why automated systems sound like such a good idea. Too often leaders say: "Give me the answers." They don't want to take the time to struggle through turning data into knowledge, and knowledge into wisdom.

One of the greatest threats today is the "dumbing down" of work. It is certainly less risky to follow the blinking lights on a dashboard than to make personal decisions based on real knowledge. Technology *seems* to make this all so easy—"Let's let the software do the thinking."

There is a prevailing attitude among many of those accountable for performance measurement to try to extricate themselves from the responsibility. Because the level of commitment to measurement in most organizations is very low, it is very tempting to want to delegate it. When this is done, it too often leads to reliable and precise measurement of the *wrong* measures!

This attitude is also the perfect breeding ground for the adoption of yet another quick fix—any quick fix. And technology vendors always seem to have just the "solution"—some impressive technology that enshrines defective measurement systems, making managers look good—on the surface at least. That is why technology often attempts to replace human intelligence with "artificial intelligence." Although, in theory, there is probably no harm in trying to push the limits of technology, in practice, there is harm when these leading-edge technologies are inappropriately sold to unsuspecting consumers—especially without any objective consumer guidance about their potential pitfalls.

I believe that this is what is happening with many technology "solutions" that attempt to do too much interpretation. No doubt technology is impressive at data collection, data storage, and analysis, but it is not yet adept—and probably never will be—at interpretation. So, if decisions are being made today based on faulty interpretations by technical data crunching, the subsequent decisions and actions will likely be flawed. And in some cases technology is actually reducing the opportunity for human beings to do what they do best (interpretation) and to improve their capabilities further.

## Technology Infatuation

Unfortunately for those who are looking for a quick fix, technology does not make a bad measurement system good, and can even mask a bad one.

As former Marshall Industries CEO Robert Rodin said, "You can't expect technology to fix the flaws in your system. If you automate a broken process, you get an automated broken process."[1]

In recent years, there has been a tendency for organizations to become infatuated with impressive automated scorecards and dashboards, which are usually the visible front-end of performance measurement technology tools. Technical "solutions" can be quite impressive on the surface, but surprisingly misleading when one looks "behind the curtain." If you remember what happens in *The Wizard of Oz*, once the Wizard is "busted," he now has to tell the truth—that he really is a good man, but he's not a very good *wizard!* I like this analogy because it dramatizes the lack of substance that often exists "behind the curtain" of many technology implementations, especially in performance measurement.

Many organizations have impressive scorecards, dashboards, and mind-boggling analytics that provide them with little or no insight. As Tim Timmerman of USAA points out, "Technology will provide you tons and tons of data, but not a lot of useful information that helps you make good decisions about the products and services your customers want."[2] That's why dashboards and gauges, highlighted by fancy graphical indicators, often contribute to reaction based on isolated and superficial signals rather than on deep understanding of complex organizational systems.

Technology solutions also promise many impressive business benefits, but are they valid promises? The answer depends as much, or more, on the *human* factors as it does on the technical ones. As Davila, Epstein, and Shelton aptly say, "A common fallacy is that a 'perfect measurement system exists and can be designed' that leads to decision making being delegated to these analysis tools. This is potentially destructive. Every measurement system has limitations and nothing can replace good judgment."[3] It is the "human factor" that makes the difference.

## The Human Factor

Performance measurement systems, business intelligence systems, business performance management, scorecards, or dashboards are effective only when measurement data is being used and converted into insight, knowledge, and wisdom. No tools are better than the willingness of people to use them correctly and conscientiously. Today's workplace is a "mixed bag," with older workers and younger workers coexisting with very different experiences and attitudes toward both measurement and technology. In general, younger workers (especially knowledge workers) feel more comfortable with technology than their older peers, but they are more demanding. Knowledge workers insist on more knowledge, and they are not very enthusiastic about "idiot lights" or being told, "Here are your measures." They want to *understand;* they want more visibility into the system, and more transparency. For older workers, the technology is usually more threatening, so they don't mind the "dumbing down" as much.

Those considering measurement technology also must be sensitive to the roles of the people who will use the technology. Role and cultural compatibility are a key issue if measurement technology is going to be effectively and positively used, rather than just complied with in a defensive way. Unfortunately, for many people, technology plus measurement often means more *fear.* There is concern about technology being used to monitor performance (the "Big Brother" syndrome). This concern can easily turn into cynicism, and, for more tech-savvy knowledge workers, turn "measurement system gaming" into "computer gaming!" The point is that organizations need to be very sensitive to how their employees are going to respond to the technology. Any tools can be dangerous, especially tools that have particularly seductive features, and poor adoption of new performance measurement technology can actually impede the effectiveness of performance measurement. That is why, once the initial glow of the technology implementation wears off, many organizations are often left with a costly technological infrastructure, a big price tag, and a mad dash to do something about the *real enablers* of high performance that were never put in place. *The key thing to remember is that you can purchase a technical infrastructure, but you can't purchase a social one!*

## The Proper Role of Technology in Performance Measurement

Technology is helpful for enabling people to better deal with the complexity of organizations and the proliferation of data, and to *assist* in mining data for insights. Technology can assist in performing some tasks that people can't do effectively themselves, or do inefficiently. For instance, technology can measure *more,* more quickly; it can automate data collection; reduce data handling errors; perform intricate analytics (including modeling "what-if" scenarios); enable simulation and predictive modeling; present data in virtually any form, with impressive visualization capabilities, even customized for each stakeholder group; zoom in on detail, zoom out to see the big picture.

Technology can definitely reduce manual data handling, reduce human intervention where it does not add unique value, and prepare information so it is ready for the kind of interpretive activity that people can do best. Studies have shown that more than 80 percent of measurement time is spent on the administrative aspects, many of which should definitely be automated!

Let's take a look at Business Performance Management (BPM), of which performance measurement is the foundational component. It has been reported that 44 percent of companies with BPM systems test causal relationships in their measurement frameworks, compared with 24 percent of companies that don't. In addition, 73 percent of companies with BPM systems report using collecting data consistently across the organization, compared with 24 percent of the non-using group. However, in that same comprehensive study, titled *Business Performance Management*, the author Bernard Marr admits that most organizations spend the majority of their time collecting and reporting data and not enough on extracting valuable and actionable *insights* from their data. He adds, "The number of measures and the amount of performance data seem to grow constantly while the insights seem to decrease."[4]

Most analysts agree that organizations that are most successful in BPM and other performance measurement-related technologies do not view the data as the end result, but use it to establish *dialogue*. That is why it is so vital to understand the *proper role* of technology in performance measurement. One of the biggest errors made is confusing "the technology" with "the system." Make sure you understand that the technology should never *be* your organization's measurement system.

## Business and Social Architecture

If your organization doesn't have a sound "business architecture" (a coherent business strategy), or hasn't translated that strategy into a series of interrelated objectives and measures), a performance dashboard might help to drive your organization faster, but it will probably be in the wrong direction, leaving behind a trail of frustrated and demoralized employees. That is why executives must be willing to dig into the business and understand what drives internal company behavior and external customer behavior. It is shocking how many senior executives have erroneous assumptions about what drives the business and never test or validate assumptions. As a result, they make poor decisions that leave the business vulnerable to unseen market forces.

Organizations are also blindly adopting technology-enabled scorecards, dashboards, and entire measurement systems without creating the "social architecture" they need. Figure 11-1 presents a slightly altered version of the "Performance Measurement Cycle" (discussed in Chapter 8) showing that the primary impact of technology is in the "Collect" and "Analyze" phases. A "Store" phase has been added to acknowledge that one of the most powerful capabilities of technology is the enormous capacity for data storage. This diagram also shows that most of the cycle is still a predomi-

FIGURE 11-1. THE ROLE OF TECHNOLOGY IN THE PERFORMANCE MEASUREMENT CYCLE.

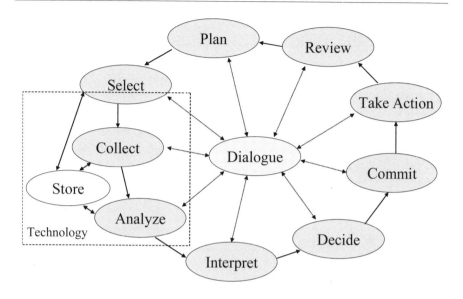

nantly social one. There is no substitute for understanding what the data is really 'saying' and turning the data into wisdom.

As a result of depending too much on technology, many organizations are not able to identify the critical few measures, differentiate them from the trivial many, and manage with them effectively. For example, having data about every kind of transaction with your customer does not in itself mean that relationships will improve. Most performance measurement challenges turn out to be more about *culture* than about *technology*. Spending vast sums on computer systems will do little to create a culture conducive to real customer relationship improvement. Too often, sales or marketing executives spend a lot of time staring at some potentially valuable analytical data trying to figure out how to respond effectively. The problem is that they can't respond based on data, or even information. As Larson and Resney tell it, "Expensive sales automation systems that promise to achieve higher sales and leaner staffs too often deliver far less: unchanged sales with a higher cost base, plus lots of information that no one knows what to do with."[5]

The promise of technology will not be realized as long as the *implementation* issues are viewed as secondary. Any breakthrough in organizational performance measurement will eventually require technology, but technology "solutions" aren't *real* solutions unless the social and organizational enablers are in place. It is surprising to me that the lesson is only now beginning to sink in.

## Failure to Address the Social Issues

Fred Smith, founder and CEO of FedEx, has observed that unsuccessful IT projects are usually run by people who have unrealistic expectations of human nature on the one side, and are funded by corporate executives who have a very poor knowledge of what the technology can do on the other side. He adds, "I think that people who follow that model in the future are going to be competitively annihilated."[6] Almost every failed technology project fails because it was rejected, sabotaged, misused, or otherwise undermined by *people*. As the following example will demonstrate, the technology *adoption* process is as important, if not more important, than the design of the technological system itself.

Consider this representative comment from a participant observer regarding a newly implemented CRM program in his organization: "During the training, it became obvious that the new CRM program was not a hit: the reps were complaining; few knew how to use it properly; the supervisors were continually running to the IT group for help; the IT people would often come by and be helpful but roll their eyes in annoyance as they left; meetings would ensue between the IT professionals and the management to discuss misunderstandings, new needs in the software function, and support needs that were arising—it was a mess. No one was happy. Everyone was annoyed with everyone else—the techies with the managers and users, the users with the managers and the techies, and the managers with the users and techies. Everyone felt they were doing their part, and doing a fine job given the problems they had to deal with. The CRM solution got lost in a tangle of blame and annoyance, resistance and resentment."

## Critical Issues in Adopting Measurement Technology

Despite the technology's rapid development, availability, and overall increasing adoption rate, many challenges to successful adoption and use abound. In the sections that follow, I will present and discuss some of the most difficult ones.

### The Challenge of Automating Emergent and Transformational Measures

Technology is very effective for automating routine measures. In fact, I believe that in the future not only will routine measurement be automated, but so will routine responses to those measures. This will free up organizational attention to focus on those things that contribute most to truly differentiating competitive advantage. However, my biggest concern is that automated performance measurement, when used inappropriately, can pose a very real threat to transformational measurement and the development of emergent measures.

The natural tendency to focus on the measures that are highlighted in an automated system can discourage the use of measures that might have to be handled manually and presented in a much more complex way. Transformational measures cannot be treated as "just another metric" on a scorecard, and they usually need to be considered in a much broader context than a traditional automated system can provide.

It is very difficult, if not impossible, to automate emergent measures. They are usually quite tentative, exploratory, and are often qualitative (rather than quantitative). Furthermore, newly identified measures, especially those with transformational potential, take a considerable period of time before they can become adequately operationally defined and standardized so that eventually they can become established "metrics."

## The Challenge of Integration

As we have seen, most aspects of an organization are linked in some way, and effective performance measurement requires a holistic, integrated view of performance. However, organizational integration is impossible without measurement integration when measures of organizational performance are seen as isolated elements. It is impossible to see the whole picture, the whole supply chain, the whole customer. Furthermore, real transformational innovation is unlikely to come from partial perspectives.

Integration of measurement must include integrated data, which I already identified as quite a problematical area. According to Accenture's McMinn and Puts, "The most significant challenge all companies face is information integration." It has been said that "what is not designed to fit together only does so by chance."[7]

We know that data is growing exponentially. Poorly managed data becomes a liability, rather than an asset. Research firm Gartner indicates that the average Fortune 1000 company has more than eight data stores, fifteen information platforms, ten critical systems, and hundreds to thousands of business applications![8]

Given this state-of-affairs how can companies "see" the whole customer, and how can we even consider really transformational CRM with such a foundational problem? For CRM and many other performance measurement related transformations, cross-functional collaboration is the next step, but without the platform for cross-functional data, this kind of collaboration will be very difficult to achieve.

In fact, business technology experts say that the greatest issue in customer information management is the variety of sources from which they must pull data. That is why there is a desperate need for serious "house-cleaning" of legacy systems and measures before the data can be trusted.

## Cultural Constraints to Data Integration

The threat of data dis-integration is a serious one. It has been estimated that data quality problems cost U.S. businesses $1.5 trillion per year—and that is just the direct economic cost. It doesn't include the opportunity costs, such as lost collaborative innovation opportunities! Poor data or poor use of good data can be disastrous. Clearly much more emphasis needs to be placed on data quality (data integrity, data accuracy, data ownership, and data accessibility)—not just on the technical issues.

Although one doesn't ordinarily think of data as a "cultural" issue, at its core, it is. Most data is stored in functional silos. Functions and departments in organizations, which represent different disciplines, cultures, and perspectives, generally have their own "measurement frameworks" and "reference models" that have evolved from a variety of disciplines. Although these frameworks and models are often very effective, they reflect a functional perspective and exhibit significant diversity in their design and use. But the biggest problem is that these inconsistent and conflicting measurement systems are also a reflection of a deep lack of *agreement* about priorities and value creation drivers. Add to this the threat of intentional "gaming," and there is a real potential for serious problems. What's more, as information scientist Arno Penzias warns, the overlay of technology has already made it more difficult to detect measurement problems. Says Penzias, "Most of today's abuses of numbers are far harder to spot because they lie deeper in the problem."[9]

Some of the systemic constraints include data ownership issues, intellectual property issues, and internal competitiveness. Overcoming this "information politics" can be daunting. Too often it is assumed that new technologies will lead to new behaviors, but experience contradicts that belief. Zuboff and Maxmin insist, in their book *The Support Economy*, that cross-functional collaboration around common models, methods, and data will require changes in the "deep structure" of the enterprise.[10]

## Scorecards and Dashboards

Scorecards and dashboards are not stand-alone "solutions." But when they are developed along with measurement frameworks, they often present positive opportunities for social interaction around measurement.

### Scorecards

The concept of a well-designed and dynamic scorecard, like a lot of good ideas, has become commercialized into a form that has compromised the intent of the original concept. To be successful, a balanced scorecard must be more than just a collection of measures distributed into four perspectives. There is no doubt that balanced scorecards have *the potential* to increase the clarity of business strategy and enhance the organization's ability to communicate (cascade) the strategic direction to others. But the success of this tool, and the related technology, depends on how it is implemented and used. Kaplan and Norton themselves caution that unless the scorecard is tied to the management system, nothing will happen from it.[11] Scorecard expert Nils Goren-Olve adds, "The discussion concerning the scorecard will determine whether it will have any effect."[12]

Without *interactivity* around a scorecard, the great value will be lost. Furthermore, score-carding implies "scoring," and it is easy to include the measures that you want to use to "win the measurement game," not the "game of business." Because three out of four of the balanced-scorecard perspectives are internally-focused, a company can "ace" almost all of the scorecard and still not deliver any value to the customer!

The potential problems with scorecards are not really the fault of the concept. The major problem I see is that, in the zeal to adopt the concept as a "quick fix" and to short-cut the pain of proper implementation, organizations have adopted labor-saving templates that preserve the style of the balanced scorecard, but miss the substance of it. Unfortunately, when scorecards are automated, the problems tend to be exacerbated and hardened. By deemphasizing the crucial interactive and interpersonal components, technology contributes to the problem. When technology presents the data so clearly, it is so easy to assume that the data is the answer!

It appears as if virtually every automated measurement system has a scorecard—balanced or otherwise—but not necessarily a good one. The truth of the matter is: No pain, no gain! Instant, off-the-shelf scorecards are the order of the day, and will leave organizations devoid of any real value, especially after the initial glow has worn off, and the consultants are gone. It should not surprise that, as has been variously estimated, 70 percent of all scorecard and dashboard projects have failed to provide any positive business results for the companies adopting them.

## Dashboards

Performance dashboards use a vehicle or control panel metaphor (with performance measurement data displayed graphically using symbols and color-coding) to assist people to make performance data more visible, and presumably more actionable. In most cases, a dashboard is the user's "front-end," and it is built on top of an enterprise "Business Intelligence" or "Business Performance Management" application. In reality, dashboards are not much more than visual "exception reports." But exception-based measurement can be of real value if it is done well. Kenneth McGee says, "I spent years investigating business surprises, such as revenue shortfalls, bankruptcies, and market share erosion. In every case, I found there was a warning—some information available early that would have told managers of coming events."[13]

Richard Brath and Michael Peters explain it this way: "Dashboards and visualization are cognitive tools that improve your 'span of control' over a lot of business data. These tools help people visually identify trends, patterns and anomalies, reason about what they see and help guide them toward effective decisions."[14] If well designed, dashboards might help detect major danger signs or even obvious causes of the problem, but few "pilots" feel comfortable flying entirely by their instrument panel. Performance dashboards can help you navigate, but they must be pointed *in the right direction*, or else you are going end up traveling faster *in the wrong direction*.

The biggest danger is that dashboards will "dumb down" performance measurement and reduce visibility of "what lies beneath." They may not provide enough data to take action on the alerts that show up on the dashboard. Dashboards typically show lagging *indicators,* not drivers. They may also gloss over data quality problems that usually arise when trying to integrate data from multiple systems. The key is that they need to be built on a robust data management infrastructure based on a sound business logic.

That is why, to be effective, these tools must embody a business architecture that aligns users and groups with strategic goals, using leading and lagging metrics to translate objectives into visual indicators tailored to each individual function. It has been recommended that organizations deploy dashboard measures at all levels, with each level using its own set of measures that presumably are aligned to the level above. In this way, in theory at least, the measures "flow down" from the top and data "rolls up" from the bottom of the organization.

I find it both amusing and frightening that dashboards often incorporate indicators we call "idiot lights"—a derogatory term for an instrument panel warning light. They're called idiot lights because they're for "idiots" who don't know how to read or understand gauges. Actually they're not all bad. But an idiot light won't give you any indication that a problem is developing until it happens. That's why it is important to include gauges as well.

Initially dashboards were implemented manually using presentation applications like Excel and PowerPoint. But, as the technology developed, some dashboards began to look more like the cockpits of 747s! The tools vary greatly: Some have a lot more glitz than substance; others are downright scary—either because of their simplicity or because of their complexity. I have a real problem with managing anything other than a simple project when I have data like "green" means good, "red" means bad, and "yellow" means caution. Dashboards, unfortunately, appeal to the measurement illiterate and those who prefer to escape any "negative accountability" by blaming their dashboard gauges!

## The Future of Scorecards and Dashboards

One commentator has described the challenge and the threat of both scorecards and dashboards this way: "It seems that all too often senior managers decide that a scorecard (a.k.a. 'dashboard') will provide the answers they need for accountability and key decisions. Once approved, the effort is delegated to a team of specialists—often led by outside consultants—to implement the initiative. In the end, despite cosmetic changes to the naming and positioning of 'perspectives,' groups often sadly end up with a generic set of measures, foisted on the organization from the top-down. There is little or no attention paid to the key elements of strategy, roles, relationships and the logic of the 'performance story' underneath the measures."

The good news is that *all* the potential problems associated with scorecards, dashboards, and other performance measurement technology can be overcome. But it will take more than the technical people to do it.

On the technical side of the ledger, there are certainly advances that can, and should, be incorporated into the designs. William Fonvielle proposes "dynamic business scorecards" to replace or complement balanced scorecards.[15] These dynamic versions would more clearly display the underlying causal logic and be less rigid about perspectives. For example, a broader perspective of "business results" is more likely to provide a more relevant, and balanced, picture of organizational health than just "financial results."

Furthermore, while there is nothing inherent in scorecards or dashboards that prevents the incorporation of more innovative and transformational measures (even if they are tentative), future designs are going to have to be more flexible. A key to the scorecard or dashboard of the future is being able to quickly change what you measure. In today's ever-changing business environment, it is vital for organizations to appreciate that what is valid today might well be obsolete tomorrow!

## Adopting and Implementing Measurement Technology

There are three keys that are essential for the successful adoption of technology to support transformational performance measurement:

1. Setting project priorities
2. Considering organizational readiness
3. Preparing the Context

### Setting Project Priorities

Shockingly, failure rates for new technology implementations range from 40 to 60 percent, and only 20 percent achieve "full satisfaction." Considering the vast capabilities of technology, it makes one wonder whether technology has gotten ahead of our abilities to properly assimilate it. Research has indicated that the key failure factors for technology projects are: unclear requirements, poor definition of scope, unrealistic expectations, poor project planning, incompetent staff, passive leadership, start-up difficulties, bureaucracy and politics, lack of user involvement and teamwork, and inadequate resources.

For IT solutions delivered by an external supplier, the client-supplier relationship is crucial, and poor communication is the major reason for relationship failure, with expertise and honesty as close second and third. Underlying most project failures is the lack of synergy between IT and the larger organization. But just turn those around and you have the success factors! Surprisingly, hardly any of these problems relate to the technology itself.

*Just as with performance measurement, technology adoption is primarily related to people and context.*

It is sometimes thought that more expensive systems are better, as in, "My technology costs more than your technology!" However, research does not bear this out. Success in adopting new measurement technology is not primarily about the purchase price. Certainly you want to technology to possess the basic features your organization wants and needs. I see so many organizations trying to please everyone, adding to a requirements document as if it were a wish list, and just generally over-engineering their systems. In fact, the Standish Group found that 45 percent of features in a typical system are seldom used, and 19 percent are never used. Furthermore, the greater complexity, the greater the possibility of failure.[16] You will be best off if you initially acquire a modest version of what the system might some day evolve into. Flexibility is the key, so that you can fairly easily add on functionality in the future. Whatever you do, don't get locked into an inflexible technology! And make as many decisions as possible reversible.

The way to avoid inappropriate commitment to a particular technology is not to let technical people take the lead. Part of the problem with "technical people" is that they are . . . well, technical. According to Matthew Treagus, a former CIO himself, information technology (IT) people "are operations people and they understand technology. They have no experience of customers and so they do not understand customers."[17]

As for costs, consider the "total cost of ownership" rather than the initial purchase price. Clearly the total costs relate more to planning, leadership, communication, training, support, and ongoing commitment than to the technology itself. Also, make sure you are prepared for the significant amount of work done that may be required to integrate databases.

## Considering Organizational Readiness

Secondly, before embarking upon a technology search, make sure you have a *solid measurement system* before you "harden" all its flaws. There will always be flaws, but I strongly recommend that you enhance your measurement system before you automate it. Also, consider the interaction between the measurement system and other related systems, such as the budgeting process. In many organizations, budgeting is so powerful that all other aspects of performance measurement are subordinated to it. So be sure to assess how ready your organization's measurement system is for automation.

The next element to assess is *leadership.* As discussed in Chapter 9, measurement leadership might well be the single most important factor in transforming performance measurement. Clearly, there are many challenges to successfully implementing technology-enabled performance measurement, the most daunting of which are the ability to clean up the data mess and the ability to measure cross-functionally.

It is truly amazing what good leaders can do, even in the face of adversity and deficient resources. Do you have the necessary executive sponsorship to launch the new technology? But even more important, does your organization have sufficient measurement leadership in place to at least begin the journey?

Next, it is crucial to assess whether *your people* are up to the challenge. Consider potential resistance. Be sensitive to the often passive resistance that exists on the part of many employees (and even managers), whose lack of support and interactivity can kill a measure. While perceptions may not be valid, one still has to tread carefully, and take the resistance to the adoption of technology very seriously—understanding that the positive interaction between people and technology is essential to effectively utilizing it.

Finally, there is *capability.* Do your people have the performance measurement capabilities to make the most out of the technology without becoming infatuated, or deceived, by it? These capabilities don't have to be very deep, but there does need to be a sufficient level of "measurement literacy" to insure effective use of the performance measurement system and related technology. Otherwise, you could find that the defects in the measurement system might never be detected, and at least part of your organization will be "flying blind."

## Preparing the Context

Although some think that technology is "anti-social," that is not the case. We all know that technology can make people passive and reduce interpersonal interaction, but it can also do just the opposite! The problem is that almost nothing is done with this enormous potential to support the social-ization of measurement vision.

If there is going to be synergy between socialization and technology, it must be *designed in*, not just *added on* later. This is because social interaction must be part of the overall architecture, or it will not be integral to it, and it will almost never happen *after the fact*. So how should it be built in?

According to Jeff Woods, Gartner supply chain analyst, it's about *empowerment*, and it's also about *organizational learning.* As he says," Each time you face one of these unanticipated situations, do you have a way to consult with colleagues? Can you look across your company and build a team of people who understand what's going on and have similar relevant experience? There's a technical hurdle here as well. A lot of the time people spend responding to a problem is devoted to gathering data. If you can put in place technical capabilities to put information at your fingertips and you have sensory networks that tell you what's going on, then you're spending less time trying to figure out what's going on."[18]

Unfortunately most organizations don't encourage their people to take the time to understand the "performance logic" of their business model, strategy, and value creation process, which underlies their measurement and management systems. If that is the case in your organization, then the real power of performance measurement is being lost.

## Steps for Successful Technology Investment

By providing appropriate access to the right kind and quality of data at the right time, technology can actually facilitate the "socialization of measure-ment." The following is a checklist summarizing the major recommenda-tions (and accompanying issues and questions) to remember as your organization moves toward investing in technology that will support and enhance performance measurement:

1. *Perform "due diligence."* Before adopting a technology tool, get "the facts," not just success stories presented as "best practices." If you look hard enough, you can find testimonials for anything. Beware of tools being presented as "solutions."

2. *Start small.* Don't try to do too much too quickly. The best adoption of measurement technology is thoughtful and well-paced, more like a mara-thon than a 100-yard dash.

3. *Don't expect too much of any tool.* Improvement initiatives shouldn't be tool driven. Success has less to do with the tools selected than with where and how they are applied. Ultimately, it's not the running shoes that make the difference, but the skills of the person running in them.

4. *Don't expect immediate ROI.* Realizing that reaping the benefits of technology is an ongoing process.

5. *Establish clear expectations.* What does your organization expect to gain from the adoption of the performance measurement technology? Many companies provide a measurement system, but don't give guidance on what to do with it.

6. *Identify the key stakeholders and what their involvement should be.* Determine the key performance measurement roles, responsibilities, and accountabilities. What provisions are being made to achieve initial and on-going stakeholder commitment, buy-in, and appropriate involvement?

7. *Determine who will be providing measurement leadership.* Who owns the measurement system and/or the various components? Who owns the measurement technology? Who should own the "socialization of measurement" process? Be aware of the potential conflicts.

8. *Determine what will be done to facilitate dialogue.* What will be done to stimulate dialogue around the "performance logic"? What will be done to explore the trade-offs among measures?

9. *Determine support levels.* How much initial and ongoing communication, education, training, informal learning, and technology and performance measurement support should be provided?

10. *Determine other resources.* What other resources may be needed to ensure the success and sustainability of the performance measurement technology implementation?

11. *Assess the larger organizational/cultural issues.* For example, what kind of functional/disciplinary constraints might exist? What barriers might exist to openness and transparency? Are there strong incentives that could undermine the impact of any performance measurement system?

12. *Define the scope of the technology-enabled measurement system.* One particularly crucial issue is how the "extended enterprise" (e.g., supply chain partners and alliance members) will be included in the measurement system.

13. *Consider who will design the measurement system.* Do they have any apparent biases? Andrew Cohill advises: "Beware of vendors who do not take the time to understand organizational needs before recommending 'solutions'."[19]

14. *Determine how measures will be selected and reviewed.* Make sure that there is a well-defined selection process for measures, especially new and emergent measures. Who is involved? Should measures be weighted in terms of importance? Is there a continuous improvement process? Make sure there is a strong single- and double-loop feedback process. Above all, avoid "hardening of the metrics."

15. *Consider measurement cycles.* At what intervals should measurements be taken and reported? Will the time lags of certain measures be a problem? Businesses are run on a continuous basis, not on a quarterly basis. But since real-time measurement is quite costly, perform an assessment of what absolutely needs to be reported in real-time.

16. *Make sure that the system is dynamic and easy to modify.* It is important to be able to experiment with new and emergent measures. Furthermore, changes in company strategy can radically change performance measurement. There can be a ripple effect of changing a single measure.

17. *Determine how performance measurement will be used along with other information.* View the technology-enabled performance measurement system in the overall decision-making process. For example, exception-based measurement can be extremely valuable, but make sure that the criteria for normal and abnormal performance patterns are clear.

And do keep remembering the image of the concealed Wizard of Oz. I strongly urge you to keep asking the question: "What's behind the curtain?"

# Performance Measurement Maturity

The concept of maturity is popular today, with new models emerging describing many aspects of individual maturity, professional maturity, team maturity, process/program/project maturity, and organizational maturity. All of these models attempt to define, and foster, development over time. Because of the pivotal importance of performance measurement in any organization, the potential benefits of increasing its maturity are enormous. Debra Hoffman explains it this way: "Performance measurement maturity determines a company's ability to continuously improve, and is a key determinant of its future performance."[1] Although some maturation occurs naturally through normal learning and experience, it is generally accepted that systematic development interventions will enable the attainment of higher levels of maturation more quickly. One of the main reasons I wrote this book is to help organizations *accelerate* the transformation of their performance measurement systems to higher levels of maturity.

Performance measurement maturity is built on the foundation of the concepts, principles, and practices already discussed. This chapter will provide you with a useful synthesis of the content previously presented. In addition, the "Transformational Measurement Maturity Assessment" located at the end of this chapter is a valuable tool both for communicating the concept of performance measurement maturity and for gauging your organization's progress along the transformational measurement journey.

## The Concept of Maturity

To some, the term "maturity" means old, tired, and stuck in a rut; to others, it connotes experience, wisdom, and effectiveness. I like the expression: "You're not getting older; you're getting better." Performance measurement systems that are maturing are getting better—*much better*.

Searching the human development literature, some concepts emerge that

177

are very clearly associated with maturity. They include: development of wisdom; eagerness to confront reality; learning from the past; being willing to act independently; knowing when to conform; being adaptable to ongoing change; being open to new ideas; willingness to question one's own belief system; not being threatened by questions from others; not taking the easy (expedient) way out in problem situations; willingness to take risks; and many more. As we progress through this chapter, you will notice that many of these qualities are very analogous to qualities of performance measurement maturity.

The table in Figure 12-1 contrasts the major categories of factors in human development maturity with those of performance measurement maturity. In the table, you will notice that "psychological well-being" on the human development side is similar to what we have been discussing in terms of a "positive context" of measurement. "Personal efficacy" relates to the capacity to make a difference in life and is analogous to "focus" in performance measurement, which relates to the power or leverage that certain measures have. "Integrity/balance" relates to the capacity of people to balance the various parts of their personality and therefore maintain their integrity, which I see as analogous to "integration" in performance measurement.

On the human development side, "socialization," or effectiveness in human relationships, relates to "interactivity" in performance measurement. You will notice that I have placed "leadership" and "learning" on both the human development and the performance measurement sides of the table. This is because the ability to lead and to accept leadership, as appropriate, is essential to both the mature personality and to mature performance measurement. Similarly, "learning" (both single-loop and double-loop) is crucial for both human development and performance measurement development.

FIGURE 12-1. CONTRASTING HUMAN DEVELOPMENT WITH
PERFORMANCE MEASUREMENT.

| Human Development | Performance Measurement |
| --- | --- |
| Psychological Well-Being | Positive Context |
| Personal Efficacy | Focus |
| Integrity/Balance | Integration |
| Socialization | Interactivity |
| Leadership | Leadership |
| Learning | Learning |

Arie de Geus describes the maturation of an organization in the following way: "Like all organisms, the living company exists primarily for its own survival and improvement: to fulfill its potential and become as great as it can be."[2] In the case of performance measurement, maturity is the progressive realization of its *full potential.*

Maturation has no destination. There is no final end of the road. Rather, it is a state of "becoming"—becoming more relevant; becoming more functional; becoming more powerful. Maturation in performance measurement provides the possibility that it will continue to develop beyond anything that is currently known. Attaining the highest level of maturity takes time; it does not happen overnight. There is no such thing as "instant transformation," or "instant maturity."

## Maturation Requires Transformation

Attaining the highest levels of development requires a specific and intensive program of action—a *transformation* process. The transformation of performance measurement and its maturity are closely related. Figure 12-2 depicts the performance measurement transformation process as a continuous improvement process loop—progressing from improving context, to improving focus, to improving integration, to improving interactivity—the four transformational keys. While this transformation doesn't necessarily occur in this particular order, it is important that all four keys be continu-

FIGURE 12-2. PERFORMANCE MEASUREMENT TRANSFORMATION CYCLE.

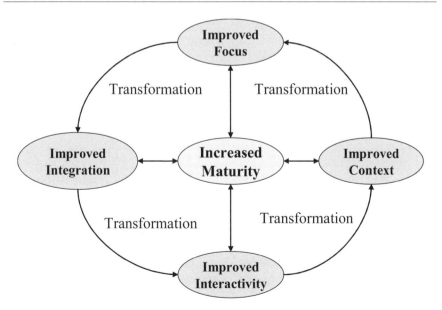

ously improved. While the transformational cycle is occurring, maturity (in the center of the diagram) is also increasing.

Whereas transformation is about "change of form," maturation is about movement to a higher level of development. Furthermore, as we consider performance measurement maturity, it is important to remember that it is not about strength in any one aspect of performance measurement, but about the health of the "total system."

Research has indicated that only twenty percent of organizational change efforts—only one in five—achieve long-term improvement. I believe that this is because there is rarely an understanding of the requirements for real transformation, or for real maturation. Piecemeal, tool-based, and other short-term changes are seductively easy, but they are ultimately ineffective. This is because they just add a part to the machine. The machine might run better for a while, but only until the next part needs to be changed. As Peter Senge has said, "Seeing a company as a machine implies that it is fixed, static." That is why technological changes alone are usually superficial and have been proven to be so ineffective in promoting permanent, transformational change.

## The Importance of the Social Factors

As far as performance measurement is concerned, a change in method or technology is unlikely to change the organization because it is primarily a social entity. The technical and technological aspects might improve things temporarily, but the key to the deep and sustainable improvement is the *social aspects*. Without them, the technical and the technological aspects might take a leap forward, but the change will not be dynamic or self-renewing. The transformation must be continuous, or it will stop when the method or technology is deemed "implemented."

## Assessing Transformational Performance Measurement Maturity

The "Transformational Measurement Maturity Assessment" located at the end of this chapter is divided into four parts, one for each of the key areas discussed in this book: Context, Focus, Integration, and Interactivity.

In the following sections I will briefly review the four keys to transforming performance measurement, including the outputs of the improvement process and the factors that are instrumental for driving that improvement. At the end of each section, indicators of transformational performance measurement maturity are presented, derived from the analysis. These indicators will comprise the items that appear on the "Transformational Measurement Maturity Assessment."

## Improving the Context of Measurement

Improving the context of measurement is one of the best investments your organization can make, since the context affects all other aspects of the measurement system across the entire organization. If the context is not transformed, then most people, if they use performance measurement at all, will just be "going through the motions"—and will very likely also continue using the measurement system for their own self-serving purposes.

Figure 12-3 depicts some of the highlights for the improvement of the context of measurement. You will notice in the figure that the major output of improving the context of measurement is "positive attitudes." As attitudes toward performance change in a positive direction and as positive experiences occur, performance measurement will become more highly valued, which reinforces the improvement. Measurement dysfunction will also decrease, because there will be less of an adversarial approach to performance measurement. When significant changes in the context of measurement start taking hold, past negative associations will be replaced by current positive experiences. Dysfunction will virtually disappear, and the culture will be much less likely to tolerate the negative behavior of those who attempt to "game" the system.

Major factors that contribute to the improvement of the context of measurement are provided on the left side of the diagram. They include:

• *Relevance*: Numbers aren't inherently relevant to most employees. Most employees view measurement as "a waste of time." That is why it is so important to clarify how measurement relates to what employees care about—their work. When measurement is part of work, its relevance becomes obvious. Furthermore, when employees can clearly see the "line-of-sight" between their measures and organizational results, they will understand how their actions will affect both, and performance measurement will become even more relevant.

FIGURE 12-3. CHANGING THE CONTEXT OF MEASUREMENT: SUMMARY.

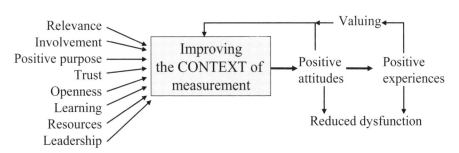

• *Involvement*: As the context transformation progresses and the maturity level increases, more and more people in the organization will become involved in performance measurement (from the lowest level to the highest level of the organization) and will begin to experience its positive side. Often, involvement starts with the "early adopters," but it increases as additional measurement opportunities are identified, and employees experience personal involvement in using their own measures to guide their own performance, and have input into the measures of their internal customers, suppliers, and teams. As the transformation process continues, employees will develop more ownership in measurement.

• *Positive Purpose*: Organizations that are transforming their performance measurement systems place great emphasis on using measurement for improvement and learning (rather than for control). Certainly, control is important, but it should be control of the quality of the process, rather than control over people. To repeat, unless you reduce the tight linkage between measurement and judgment, defensiveness will prevent honesty and learning from measurement. No matter what is said, employees are smart enough to discern the true purposes of measurement.

• *Trust*: As long as performance measurement is used to monitor, control, and manipulate, it will not be trusted as an information source. However, when employees and managers view it as enabling high-performance and improvement, then it tends to be valued, and trust is built. When employees trust measurement, and feel confident that it won't be used against them, they will much more eagerly embrace it. And then there will be growing commitment throughout the organization to continuous improvement of measures and the measurement system.

• *Openness:* As the context of measurement becomes more positive and measurement is perceived as being more pivotal to success, there is no longer any reason for secrecy about measurement. All measurement data is available to whoever wants and needs it. Discussions about measurement are open and honest. In fact, the degree of openness and honesty about measurement is a good way to gauge performance measurement maturity.

• *Learning*: Nothing contributes to transforming the context of measurement like providing opportunities for learning about and from measurement. When employees understand performance measurement, they can be proactive in using it. Transforming organizations are discovering that measurement is essential for effective learning, and learning is essential for effective measurement.

• *Resources*: Providing ongoing resources to support organization-wide performance measurement sends a powerful message that it is important and valued by the organization. Providing a variety of internal measurement resources to support performance measurement activities in the right places at the right time (including funding, appropriate technology, measurement specialists, etc.) is key. For example, use measurement specialists to work with business line people to make the best use of statistics, data mining, and modeling, and other such methods, but not to interpret the data or make business decisions for them. Done correctly, this allows executives, managers, and employees to focus on the *meaning* of the measurements, rather than on the calculations.

• *Leadership*: Measurement leadership is crucial for transforming the context of measurement and for increased performance measurement maturity. Organizations with the most mature performance measurement systems will have someone who is responsible for performance measurement organization-wide.

## Improving the Focus of Measurement

As you can see in Figure 12-4, the key output of improving the focus of measurement is "increased use of high-leverage measures." The right performance measures can provide enormous leverage to achieve competitive advantage. Increasing the use of high-leverage measures should also drive "reduced routine measurement." Increasing high-leverage measurement and reducing routine measurement enables the transforming organization to achieve progressively greater focus. On the left side of the figure, you can see the major factors which drive this transformation in the focus of measurement. They include:

• *Measure what matters most*: Organizations that are transforming their focus of measurement are continually looking for performance measures that reflect the factors that are most critical to their success. In Chapter 6 we discussed how Dell Computer measured "cash conversion cycle time" and Southwest Airlines measured aircraft "turnaround time." When these measures were developed, they represented factors that mattered most to these companies.

FIGURE 12-4. IMPROVING THE FOCUS OF MEASUREMENT: SUMMARY.

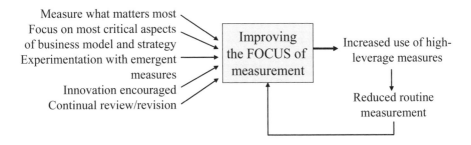

• *Focus on the business model and strategy*: Transforming organizations constantly reassess and recalibrate their measures against their business model and strategy. Then, they focus on the measures that are most crucial for managing their strategic priorities.

• *Experiment with emergent measures*: Transforming organizations are constantly developing new measures to drive innovation, and to supplement or replace obsolete measures. Many of the emergent measures will be measures of difficult-to-measure intangibles. Not deterred by the difficulty, these organizations realize that if they don't measure these intangibles, they can't effectively manage them.

• *Encourage innovation*: Transforming organizations encourage innovation in the measurement system. Knowing the importance of viewing performance through different lenses, they encourage employees to discover new measures, rather than just continuing to rely on the same old ones.

• *Continually review/revise*: In transforming organizations continually review and revise performance measures in terms of how valuable they are in providing high-leverage information on how well the organization is performing. They are not reluctant to changing or discarding poorly performing measures.

## Improving the Integration of Measurement

When organizations are improving the integration of measurement, they realize that performance measurement shouldn't be primarily about isolated measures or even functional measures. Figure 12-5 provides a quick overview of what the transformation of the integration of measurement looks like.

The major output of improving the integration of measurement is "progress toward one integrated measurement system," including replacing the functional "silo" measurement systems and data repositories. However, nothing is more difficult than overcoming the forces of functional parochialism and data politics. Moving forward with the integration of measurement is enabled by the following factors:

FIGURE 12-5. IMPROVING THE INTEGRATION OF MEASUREMENT: SUMMARY.

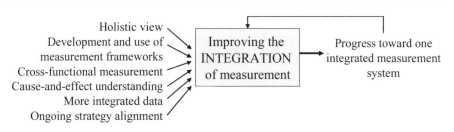

• *Holistic View*: Transforming organizations are working hard to take a holistic, "big picture" view of performance measurement, increasingly measuring performance constructs that reflect a broader understanding of all essential value creation activities and being more aware of their trade-offs. A good indicator of measurement maturity is the extent to which decisions are made based on multiple measures, rather than single measures, and how many measures are, in fact, being considered in making those key decisions.

• *Development and Use of Measurement Frameworks*: Transforming organizations realize that isolated measures—even transformational ones—must be integrated into larger "measurement frameworks." These frameworks include both vertical integration (the connection of measures up and down through the organization) and horizontal integration (the connection of measures across organizational functions). Transforming organizations are finding that they are often dealing with abstract concepts, exploring in areas where many do not feel very comfortable, and adopting new and emerging measures in areas of considerable uncertainty. Measurement frameworks enable organizations to address these issues.

• *Cross-Functional Measurement*: In transforming organizations, cross-functional measures contribute greatly toward breaking down long-established functional silos. New cross-functional measures, which are viewed as a key to collaboration across the organization, are being regularly adopted.

• *Cause-and-Effect Understanding*: It is through understanding the relationships and the trade-offs among measurable factors that organizations can gain valuable predictive insights from their measurement systems. They realize that the key to transformational performance measurement is to "understand first; measure second." One of the indicators of measurement maturity is that the causal relationships are being frequently being hypothesized *and* tested. Too many organizations hypothesize, but do not test. Insight into important cause-and-effect relationships *and* healthy skepticism about these relationships are features of performance measurement maturity.

• *More Integrated Data*: In transforming organizations, increased cross-functional collaborations are energizing the development of central data repositories with high data integrity. As a result, more data can be relied on, and a more holistic picture of the organization and its customers is emerging. This richer and more consistent data can then be converted into more useful information, knowledge, wisdom, and appropriate action. Until this maturity characteristic is realized, most of the knowledge that comes from measurement is likely to be incomplete or seriously flawed.

• *Ongoing Strategy Alignment*: In transforming organizations, there is ongoing commitment to increasing deeper understanding of the key strategic drivers of organizational success. This is not a one-shot alignment exercise, but an ongoing process. One of the major contributions of the work of Kaplan and Norton has been to gain greater awareness of the importance of increasing the "strategic alignment" of measurement systems.[4] However, as you have seen, this is just one element of measurement system maturity.

## Improving the Interactivity of Measurement

Organizations that are improving the interactivity of measurement are well on their way to transformational measurement. Most of them have already improved through some degree of transformation of the context, focus, and integration of measurement. Now, they are looking for new and better ways to "socialize" measurement. These organizations are using interaction to develop and continually review new measures, supplemented by the appropriate use of technology.

Transforming organizations have typically established a "social architecture" to promote discussion of measurement data and information. This formal or informal structure enables executives and other key stakeholders to carry on regular dialogues about performance measurement issues. Measurement is built into the social fabric of the organization, and is no longer just a program or an add-on.

Transformational measures, and the emergent measures that are precursors to them, require the synergy and support that interactivity provides. Most of the mistakes and shortfalls in attempts at transformational measurement have, in fact, been due to a lack of interactivity.

Figure 12-6 shows the process of improving the interactivity of measurement. As you can see in the figure, the major output of improving the interactivity of measurement is "increased speed and quality of conversion of data to insight to action."

Transforming organizations use extensive internal and external interactions around the data that facilitate the data-to-wisdom conversion process. Because the forums for interactivity are more formally in place, rather than simply being done *ad hoc* (if at all), there is increased speed of the conver-

FIGURE 12-6. IMPROVING THE INTERACTIVITY OF MEASUREMENT: SUMMARY.

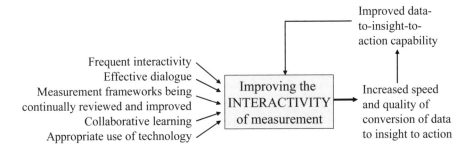

sion process. Christopher Meyer has said, "The hallmark of any powerful measurement system . . . [is that] it creates the maximum insight with the minimum of data." Practice builds capability, and using interactivity leads to continually improving "data-to-insight-to-action capability."[5] If a measurement program does fail, it is very rare that the information is the problem; it is usually the organization's inability to turn it into effective action.

The factors contributing to transforming the interactivity of measurement include the following.

• *Frequent Interactivity*: Organizational stakeholders realize that performance measurement is not primarily about the numbers, but about clearer perception, deeper understanding, and greater shared insight, knowledge, and wisdom. Interpretation is not usually something that happens through a sudden flash of insight; more often it requires study, summarizing, listening, discussing, comparing, reflecting, visualizing, questioning, and the like—involving lots of interactivity. In most organizations, each function does its own measurement and rarely interacts with people in other functions. This is incompatible with the fact that most of what adds value in organizations today is cross-functional.

• *Effective Dialogue*: As Larry Bossidy and Ram Charan have stated, "How people talk to each other absolutely determines how well the organization will function."[6] A lot of this interaction occurs through dialogues. Regular dialogue meetings within teams and between functions will help to integrate functions and lead to higher levels of collaboration and performance. One characteristic that differentiates effective dialogues from other meetings is that they are more about asking the "right" questions than providing the "right" answers.

• *Continual Review and Improvement of Measurement Frameworks*: Transforming organizations realize that what is optimal at a particular time might not be optimal in a month or a year, so the refinement of the measurement frameworks must be continuous. Measures must be continually calibrated and realigned with strategy, and then integrated across the entire organization.

• *Collaborative Learning*: Most learning from measurement is "collaborative action learning." Through using measurement, people in transforming organizations are engaging in both single-loop *and* double-loop learning, and they are not afraid to challenge the traditional assumptions about performance and existing measurement frameworks. There are regular "dialogue" meetings between functions to discuss existing measurements, develop actions plans, review measurement frameworks, and consider transformational measurement issues. Organizations are finding that dialogues about their measurement frameworks will help identify cross-functional measures that will make a transformational difference to the organization. Nothing will break down the traditional functional barriers like collaborative learning through cross-functional measurement.

• *Appropriate Use of Technology*: In transforming organizations, technology is viewed as an enabler of a robust performance measurement system, but not the system itself. The emphasis is on automating routine measurement and administrative functions, and on performing advanced analysis and reporting, but not replacing the uniquely human capabilities or detracting from the social aspects of transformational performance measurement. Care is taken that technology facilitates interactivity, and doesn't diminish it. Although technology can analyze data and produce information, when it comes to generating knowledge and wisdom, there is no substitute for human interaction.

## Levels of Performance Measurement Maturity

The "Performance Measurement Maturity Model" in Figure 12-7 is offered to help organizations better gauge their performance measurement maturity level.

You can assess the performance measurement maturity of your organization based on the score on the "Transformational Measurement Maturity Assessment," located at the end of this chapter, There are three major levels in the model: *Ad Hoc, Systematic, and Transforming.* Level 1, the lowest level of performance measurement maturity, is *Ad Hoc*. At this level, there is relatively little performance measurement above and beyond what is legally required. Any performance measurement that does exist can best be described at sporadic and unplanned.

FIGURE 12-7. PERFORMANCE MEASUREMENT MATURITY MODEL.

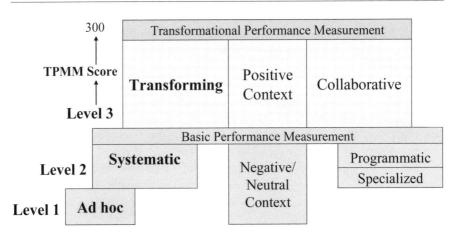

Level 2, the second level, is *Systematic*. At this level, there is a well-planned, systematic measurement effort. Level 2 provides the kind of foundational performance measurement that I referred to in Chapter 4 as "basic performance measurement." This basic level enables organizations to take advantage of at least some of the functionality that performance measurement has to offer. However, in order for an organization to tap into the real power of performance measurement, it is important to progress far beyond this basic level.

Both Levels 1 and 2 have a "negative or neutral context" of measurement (either negative, or somewhere in between positive and negative), while Level 3 is the only one that has a "positive context." Also, Level 2 includes first "specialized" and then "programmatic" measurement. *Specialized* performance measurement is indicative of measurement that is delegated to measurement specialists (including business and financial analysts). *Programmatic* performance measurement refers to the existence of programs like Balanced Scorecard and Six Sigma. While these programs are beneficial in themselves, they do not indicate that performance measurement is being transformed *systematically* throughout the entire organization, nor do they necessarily indicate maturity beyond Level 2.

Thus, it is important for organizations to move performance measurement to Level 3, termed *Transforming*. An organization's performance measurement system has attained this level of maturity when it has made significant strides in its performance measurement transformation. When your organization's performance measurement system attains Level 3 status, all four keys to transformational performance measurement are at least beginning to work together synergistically. This allows powerful performance measurement to make a real difference—a transformational difference—in the organization.

The "Transformational Measurement Maturity Assessment" score will give you a good idea of how far your organization has progressed overall and in each key area of the transformation. Although comparing your organization's total score to the maximum score of 300 will give you some idea of its performance measurement maturity, the primary purpose of this assessment is to help make improvement more visible, not to provide a static measure of the current level of measurement maturity. By administering this assessment over time, as performance measurement is being transformed, you should be able to discern improvements. More importantly, this assessment should be used as a diagnostic and to foster dialogue about crucial performance measurement issues.

Scoring instructions are provided at the end of the assessment. Of course, no one wants correspondence to take wild guesses at items about which they have no knowledge. That is why there is an adjustment in the scoring to permit "Don't Know" responses, without any penalty. However, you should realize that a high number of "Don't Know" responses would indicate that whatever transformation might be occurring may not be visible enough to organizational stakeholders—which is clearly a problem.

As with any emergent measure, its greatest value is the interactivity that it can stimulate and its ability to drive positive change. Of course, its value will depend heavily on the willingness of those performing the admittedly "subjective measurement" to be honest in their assessments. As for who should participate in the assessment, I suggest involving those managers and employees from all functional areas who have a variety of perspectives regarding the performance measurement system.

## TRANSFORMATIONAL MEASUREMENT MATURITY ASSESSMENT

*Instructions:* Please rate your organization on each of the 50 aspects of performance measurement listed in the left-hand column. Place a checkmark in the appropriate column according to the following scale:

*Exemplary*: The organization is clearly outstanding in this aspect.
*Good*: This aspect is evident to a considerable extent throughout the organization.
*Fair*: This aspect is evident to some extent throughout the organization.
*Poor*: This aspect is not in evidence to any significant extent in the organization.
*Don't Know*: Respondent is not aware of the status of this aspect in the organization.

| Please score your organization in terms of the following: | Exemplary | Good | Fair | Poor | Don't Know |
|---|---|---|---|---|---|
| **Context Maturity** | | | | | |
| Performance measurement is widely used by all levels of employees throughout the organization. | | | | | |
| The importance and value of performance measurement are widely appreciated. | | | | | |
| Employees perceive performance measurement as relevant, timely, and actionable in their jobs. | | | | | |
| Employees actively use performance measurement in their jobs. | | | | | |
| Understanding and acting upon performance measurement data are viewed as key responsibilities of all employees. | | | | | |
| Performance measurement is generally viewed as a positive force in the organization. | | | | | |
| Performance measurement is used to empower and enable self-management. | | | | | |
| Performance measurement is rarely used to blame or punish. | | | | | |
| Fear of measurement is low. | | | | | |
| Performance measurement is trusted. | | | | | |
| Manipulation of measurement for self- | | | | | |

| Please score your organization in terms of the following: | Exemplary | Good | Fair | Poor | Don't Know |
|---|---|---|---|---|---|
| serving purposes is very low or nonexistent. | | | | | |
| Performance measurement data is discussed openly and honestly. | | | | | |
| Employees are educated about measurement. | | | | | |
| Employees are given the time and other resources they need to use performance measurement well. | | | | | |
| *Context Totals* | | | | | |
| **Focus Maturity** | | | | | |
| This organization measures the things that matter most and not those that don't matter. | | | | | |
| Performance measures accurately reflect the most critical aspects of the organization's business model and strategy. | | | | | |
| Performance measures are regularly reviewed and revised or eliminated (as appropriate). | | | | | |
| This organization has the right number of measures (not too many nor too few). | | | | | |
| Routine measures are reduced when new high-leverage measures are added. | | | | | |
| Routine measurement is being increasingly automated. | | | | | |
| Progress is being made in measuring intangible assets and other difficult-to-measure aspects of performance. | | | | | |
| Experimentation with emergent measures is encouraged. | | | | | |
| Transformational measures are being widely adopted and used. | | | | | |
| *Focus Totals* | | | | | |

| Integration Maturity | | | | | |
|---|---|---|---|---|---|
| There is a holistic approach to performance measurement across the organization. | | | | | |
| Measurement data is becoming more integrated. | | | | | |
| Employees understand the cross-functional implications of their measures. | | | | | |
| Cross-functional measures are developed and used. | | | | | |
| There is increasing understanding of the relationships and trade-offs between performance measures. | | | | | |
| There is widespread commitment to understanding the causal relationships among performance measures. | | | | | |
| Integrative measurement frameworks are developed and used. | | | | | |
| Ongoing effort is being made to align measurement frameworks with strategy, and keep them aligned. | | | | | |
| Progress is being made toward creating one integrated organization-wide measurement system. | | | | | |
| Performance measurement integration efforts have organization-wide leadership. | | | | | |
| *Integration Totals* | | | | | |
| Interactivity Maturity | | | | | |
| There is widespread and frequent interaction throughout the organization about measurement. | | | | | |
| Frequent interactivity occurs regarding the selection of performance measures. | | | | | |
| Developing and revising measurement frameworks are highly interactive. | | | | | |

| Please score your organization in terms of the following: | Exemplary | Good | Fair | Poor | Don't Know |
|---|---|---|---|---|---|
| Insights from performance measurement information are discussed in many forums. | | | | | |
| The organization places a high priority on learning from measurement. | | | | | |
| Time is made available to learn from measurement. | | | | | |
| There are frequent and high-quality dialogues about performance measurement. | | | | | |
| Executives are deeply engaged in measurement-related dialogues. | | | | | |
| Measurement frameworks are continually and interactively reviewed and revised when appropriate. | | | | | |
| Interpretation of data is as highly valued in this organization as data collection and analysis. | | | | | |
| Collaborative cross-functional learning from measurement occurs throughout the organization. | | | | | |
| Revealing questions are constantly being asked about measurement. | | | | | |
| Measured experiments and pilot projects are occurring throughout the organization. | | | | | |
| The organization has effective social mechanisms for translating performance measurement data into appropriate action. | | | | | |
| The capability of the organization for converting data into actionable insight is high. | | | | | |
| The organization is effective at sharing insights from performance measurement. | | | | | |

| | | | | | |
|---|---|---|---|---|---|
| Technology is being used appropriately to support interactivity around measurement. | | | | | |
| *Interactivity Totals* | | | | | |
| **Assessment Totals** | | | | | |

*Instructions for computing the assessment score:*

Total the checkmarks in each column. Multiply the column totals as follows:

|                        | # Items Rated |            | Score      |
|------------------------|---------------|------------|------------|
| *Exemplary* responses  | _____       | × 3 =      | _____  |
| *Good* responses       | _____       | × 2 =      | _____  |
| *Fair* responses       | _____       | × 1 =      | _____  |
| *Poor* responses       | _____       | × 0 =      | _____  |
| Total:                 | _____       |            | _____  |

# of "Don't Know" responses: _____

Divide the total score by the number of items rated (50 total items minus the number of items with "Don't Know" responses). Multiply this value by 100. The maximum possible score is 300.

# Transformational Measures

N ew, emergent, and transformational measures are beginning to radically change the way people and organizations view measurement. It is
vital to appreciate how far we have come in using performance measurement as a new lens to transform the way we understand and drive some of
the factors that were once ignored (or not seen), but which we now know
are vital to organizational success. Unfortunately, organizations are still
quite reluctant to change their performance measurement systems (which
they see as almost sacrosanct), and, as far as we have come, there is still a
long way to go.

## Defining Transformational Measurement

Transformational measurement is about changing organizations so that new
ways of measuring can become part of the DNA of the organization. Even
so-called "change management" programs will ultimately fail unless the
measurement *system* changes, because the measurement system ultimately
"tells" all the other management systems what is important, and what to do.

Transformational measurement is, first and foremost, about transformation—"a change in form"—which is, by definition, *deep change*. Most
breakthroughs result from looking at things differently. The key to transformation is to change *perspective*. In many organizational areas, dramatic
shifts in vision have taken place because of relatively minor changes in perspective, such as from "product-line profit" to "customer profit," or from
"on-time delivery" to "perfect orders." Transformational measures measure
many of the same things, but from a *different* perspective.

In an influential *Harvard Business Review* article, "The Ambidextrous
Organization," Charles O'Reilly explained that successful organizations
have to balance two needs—(1) the need to *look backward* in order to maintain the existing organization and its current customers and (2) the need to

*look forward* in order to explore and achieve performance breakthroughs and to identify and attract new customers and new sources of value. This second need includes much of what we are calling "transformational measurement."[1]

## From Exploration to Transformation

According to Napier and McDaniel, the first step in developing new measures is "a clear understanding of what you wish to measure and a willingness to ask the tough questions that may lay bare the underbelly of the issue being explored."[2] While digging deeply may seem daunting, the reality is that *not* doing so will ultimately prove detrimental to the future growth and prosperity of your organization! The key to developing emergent transformational measures is *exploration* and *experimentation,* which requires the willingness to take risks and an environment that fosters risk-taking and a spirit of exploration.

Transformational measures are not difficult, but they require new thinking and someone willing to propose a new lens to view things. Transformational measures begin with concepts that are potentially transformational. We all have the capacity to begin to view things differently, and to propose suggestions for improvement, however small and tentative, or bold and sweeping.

James Brian Quinn describes just such a transformational concept that has caused a quantum change in the focus of marketing—the "shift in focus from individual product profitability to the total profit potential in a customer's relationship." This conceptual shift gave rise to an enormous measurement shift—a "reorientation from short-term transaction measures to long-term customer outcome measures."[3]

## Traditional vs. Transformational Thinking

The biggest challenges you and your organization face will come from those who say it can't be done, or that you are transgressing an "incontrovertible" rule of measurement. However, if you don't break any rules, there won't be any innovation! So, if you and your organization want to embrace transformational measures, get ready to tolerate some of those measurement concepts and practices that you have been taught are "wrong," as well as the resistance of those who will tell you that "You just can't do that!"

The fact is that while most of business has become extremely advanced, measurement has remained a bastion of traditional thinking. Performance measures in most organizations tend to reinforce the "old rules" and the mental models that gave rise to them. Worse still, our belief systems and conventional wisdom often run so deep that we find it difficult to believe what the actual facts are telling us.

The biggest problem of performance measurement is that the world has changed, but the measurement of performance has pretty much stayed the same. If you were to compare the workplace of today with the workplace of fifty years ago, the difference is dramatic. But if you were to compare how most performance is measured, it looks like a throwback to yesteryear. Just think how little progress has been made in performance appraisal! And those who "mind the gates" are not particularly encouraging of those who want to change the measures—much less the "metric system"—because, after all, these gatekeepers have benefited enormously, and continue to benefit, from the legacy systems.

Many existing measures seriously constrain performance and prevent breakthrough performance improvements (especially in services and knowledge work), but most workplace environments still discourage trying anything new. Take for example the following typical scenario: A company sends out a team with instructions to "improve" a specific project. More often than not, the team comes back with a set of *incremental* improvement recommendations that only end up further entrenching the status quo, while declaring victory because the project came in on time and under budget! Trying to innovate without the freedom (and the mandate) to explore unconventional approaches and take risks ultimately leads to more of the same old measures and, of course, the same old managing.

However, despite the obstacles, change does happen. An example I cited earlier is "customer profitability." Most organizations, as well as the traditional accounting community, couldn't "conceive" of it, because there was no way to calculate it. Activity-Based Costing changed this, and now it is possible to determine customer profitability by allocating all the "costs to serve" to specific customers. Customer profitability is finally a *measurable* concept, not just a theoretical one. It is revolutionizing marketing by helping people realize that, for years, companies were diluting their profits by selling *unprofitably* to most of their customers.

In fact, a profitability analysis on just a few well-selected customers will almost always shock company executives and motivate a change in the way the company does business. It can even be used as a conceptual discussion tool even before you start actually measuring it. When you take even a cursory look at some qualitative indicators of cost-to-serve, it often becomes clear which customers are costing the most. If you think of your customers as you would your "investment portfolio," would you really hold on to the "dogs" without doing something about the situation?

Isn't that amazing, and *transformational*—an accounting innovation revolutionizing marketing? But that's how it happens! Activity-Based Costing vividly demonstrates what can occur when someone sees the world differently, and has the courage to formulate and communicate a *new* construct. It is indeed possible to change the world!

Deep change is impossible without changing the measures that underlie management. Because measures reflect our "mental models," it is impossible to change the way people think and act unless they measure differently.

Transforming performance measurement is not optional. It is not a matter of *whether* your organization wants to change the way it measures; it is a matter of *when* those changes are going to happen and *how much* change there will be. But changing a long-established infrastructure of "legacy" measures won't be easy. Changes in performance measurement have never come easily, and they will continue to be resisted. The question is whether sufficient measurement innovators, early adopters, and most importantly, measurement leaders, will emerge quickly enough to save companies from the consequences of obsolete thinking.

## Taking the Lead in Transformational Measurement

Performance measures are often viewed as hard-wired into the organization. There are literally thousands of things that could be measured and managed better in any organization. Unfortunately most organizations tend to default to easy-to-measure things, for which data is readily available. Force of habit causes most people to continue collecting the data they already have without considering *why* they are doing it, and whether the data is providing any real *value.* That is why too often the operational minutia are measured, while the key drivers of business value are not.

Fortunately, today more and more people are realizing how much the measurement system affects what happens, and that performance measurement is potentially one of the highest leverage activities any organization can perform. While organizations do a great deal of measuring, a lot of value is *not* being effectively measured or managed, and this needs to change. It is important for organizations to realize that one of the most important functions of *emergent* performance measures is to increase stakeholders awareness through measurement of the factors that are important to organizational success.

The following are some thoughts that organizational leaders can use to stimulate creative thinking about incorporating and utilizing emergent and transformational measures:

• *Beware of metricizing.* The question of where your organization should invest your limited resources is a critical management decision. Most performance measurement that is done is, in fact, just cost analysis. As Tony DiRomualdo has explained, "Nowadays there seems to be a scorecard or measurement index for just about everything from the cost of living to the cost of dying and everything in between. The problem with many of these measures is that they take a pure economic view of whatever is being measured. But conclusions about the economy or business can often be misleading when drawn from only those indicators that are easy to quantify."[4]

That is why it is essential to avoid the institutionalization of "metrics that will remain around forever"—even when their usefulness has long passed. In order to avoid this, performance measurement must be *reconceived* as something an organization *does*, not as something it *has* (like a set of metrics.)

- *Search for new truths.* It is important that measurement not be viewed as "the truth," but as a "search for truth." Furthermore, *transformational* measurement is not only a search for truth, but it is a *continuing* search for *new* truths. Every organization's mental models, beliefs, and assumptions about what really "matters" are not always valid, or may simply be obsolete. Review your organization's business model and strategy in order to understand what really matters. Chances are your organization is measuring too many things that don't really matter, and not measuring many that do. The truth often defies conventional wisdom.

- *Usefulness is key.* There is also a strong tendency, especially by measurement specialists, to demand a high level of validity, reliability, accuracy, and precision in performance measurement. Unfortunately, this is too high a bar for most emergent and transformational measures. As Karl-Erik Sveiby has said, "It is not possible to measure social phenomena with anything close to scientific accuracy."[5] But that is okay. Initially at least, transformational measurement is not so much about reliability or precision as it is about relevance and usefulness. It is much better to have the *right* measures in their formative stages than completely accurate measures that are wrong.

- *Overcome skepticism.* One of the most difficult barriers to overcome is skepticism about the value of subjectivity in performance measurement. Admittedly, subjective perceptions have many weaknesses associated with them, but they also have many strengths—especially in the early stages of measurement. Don't expect any emergent measure to be perfect from the start. You can enlist the assistance of measurement specialists to help you to operationalize the construct, but don't let them determine what should be measured. Performance measurement innovation requires tolerance for error and ambiguity, especially during the initial stages.

- *Avoid "rigor" mortis.* Transformational measurement should not be judged by the traditional criteria, at least not for a while. Excessive rigor will undermine innovation. Unfortunately, most measurement specialists are trained to value validity and reliability over relevance and usefulness. These priorities are antithetical to measurement creativity. Don't adopt too rigorous an attitude, since too much rigor kills innovation! Start with creativity, and add validity and reliability over time.

## The Transformational Lens

Defining transformational measures (measures that help people *see* things *differently* so that their organization can increase its competitive advantage) is not as difficult as it might seem. As Stanford University organizational systems expert John Sterman has said, "Once we recognize the importance of a concept, we can always find ways to measure it." Obviously some constructs are more difficult to measure, but they *all* can be measured.

Consider the lifecycle of an "emergent measure." It first comes from a decision to change *perspective* about how a particular performance is viewed. Then, the emergent measure is tested on a small-scale trial basis, and, if it is not working as desired, it can be revised or discarded. When an emergent measure passes the test, it can then be adopted more widely within the organization as a "transformational measure."

## An Experimental Attitude Is Essential

What differentiates emergent from transformational measures is that the emergent measures are not yet "ready for prime time." You need to try them out on a small scale before spreading them widely, to determine whether they are triggering the right behavior and discouraging the wrong ones, and whether they have any unanticipated side-effects. You will find that the mere effort to measure some constructs differently will add new knowledge, even if the measure itself is changed or discarded.

Some emergent measures might seem too simple to be effective. For example, The Acelera Group has come up with a simple, but creative, indicator that they are convinced is one of the best measures of organizational health: "It's the number of times each quarter that your CEO meets with clients."[6] Try it out! See if it works for your organization.

One of the keys to transformational measurement is the trial use of emergent, or experimental, measures. However, just as through the ages people have been looking for the Holy Grail, so have many people in organizations been looking for "the magic metric," and many won't accept anything less. I hate to disappoint those who are still looking, but it doesn't exist, and never will. At its best, measurement is a continual process of trial and discovery.

## The Challenge of Measuring Intangibles

Where tangible assets have become increasingly commoditized and are no longer the source of competitive advantage, the most important drivers of value in today's organizations are mostly *intangible*. As Herb Kelleher, former CEO of Southwest Airlines, put it: "It's the intangibles that are the hardest things for competitors to imitate. You can get an airplane. You can get ticket-counter space. You can get baggage conveyors. But it is our *esprit de corp*—the culture, the spirit—that is truly our most valuable competitive asset."[7] If your organization wants to excel, then it better start measuring its sources of intangible value.

That's the problem: *Most of what is valuable is intangible, but most of what is measured is tangible!* But rather than shrink from the challenge of "unmeasurabililty," I encourage you to seize the opportunity of helping find the pathway to measurability. As David Skyrme points out, there is growing criticism that the traditional balance sheet does not take account of the intangible factors that largely determine a company's value and its growth prospects.[8] The unreported assets of all but the most traditional major companies are on average five to ten times those of the tangible assets. Although very few people can make the link, it is generally accepted that intangibles underlie most future financial results.

## Difficulties of Measuring Intangibles

Organizations must more effectively measure and manage all their major sources of intangible value. For example, there is enormous value tied up in organizational relationships: customers, suppliers, employees, partners, and other stakeholders who contribute to organizational success. Although there is currently little understanding of how to effectively measure and manage the value of those relationships, at least some progress is being made in terms of the *quantity* of intangibles measurement, if not the *quality*. For example, ten years ago almost none of the top companies reported on environmental performance; now more than 35 percent do.

On a scale of 0 percent to 100 percent, ask yourself to what extent you think your organization measures and manages its *entire* portfolio of assets. Most experts would say that if you respond higher than 30 percent, you are probably exaggerating your estimate! Rest assured that those assets of your organization that are not being measured, or are being poorly measured, are also being poorly managed. Did you ever think that one of those unmeasured and unmanaged assets might be the key to your organization's next competitive advantage?

Where attempts are made to measure intangibles, the focus is generally on trying to place a *financial* value on a few of the intangibles that are currently in fashion, and then estimating how much each is *worth* by how much it *costs*.

Calculating the theoretical return on investment (ROI) of assets and investments is big business. Certainly a credible predictive ROI can help prioritize investment alternatives. But how often are these financial estimates based on credible assumptions? Ask yourself why you are doing the measurement: Is it for political reasons (e.g., to show how well your function has spent its budget), or to understand how you can better manage the resources, to learn and improve? With only slight tongue-in-cheek, I call the former version of ROI "Return on Insecurity!"

Unfortunately, the perceived need to fall back on the tried-and-true measures of "units produced" and "dollars and cents" is widespread and has caused people to shy away from the less precise, but probably more useful, measures. Karl-Erik Sveiby, a pioneer in the measurement of intangibles, has put it this way: "So entrenched are the traditional measuring paradigms that executives and researchers have not even started to explore the most interesting reason for measuring intangibles: the learning motive. Measuring can be used to uncover costs or to explore value creation opportunities otherwise hidden in the traditional accounts."[9]

The "Value Creation Index"[10] is one early attempt at producing a composite index of the value of intangibles (such as innovation, ability to attract talented employees, alliances, process quality, environmental performance, brands, technology, and customer satisfaction), which could be used, in theory at least, to compare a company's future value creation potential with a benchmark sample. However, this effort has not gotten much traction, because few organizations have figured out how to effectively assess and use that information.

Another effort is the "Skandia Intangible Assets Navigator."[11] However, if you look beneath the surface of these and many of the other attempts to *count* and to *monetize* intangible value, you will find that the estimating methodologies do not justify the confidence that many people place in them. The numbers trivialize rather than illuminate the real power of the concepts they attempt to measure. While they may provide an interesting exercise, at this point they are not yet adept at helping to measure intangible assets in any meaningful way.

## The Need to Think Differently About Intellectual Capital

One of the most valuable forms of intangible assets is intellectual capital, which is typically divided into three categories: *organizational capital* (patents, copyrights, trademarks, brands, infrastructure, culture), *relational capital* (customer knowledge and relationships, suppliers, partners, competitors, governments, communities), and *human capital* (skills, knowledge, and attitudes of employees, depth of talent). How much potential value do you think is represented by those three categories of intellectual capital in your organization? How much of that value is being effectively used? How much is being wasted?

Michael Malone has long advocated the more *creative* measurement of intangibles like intellectual capital. As he said, "Traditional accounting gives us half or less of the information we need to make an intelligent judgment about corporate value. Intellectual capital is indeed our best hope for continued prosperity into the twenty-first century. And learning how to measure it is the only path for getting there."[12]

Despite the difficulty, intellectual capital is a prime area just crying out for transformational measures. And without the *experimental* process of discovering *new* measures, organizations will continue measuring inappropriate surrogates, such as the cost of training or the number of "pieces of knowledge" deposited in a repository, rather than value-based measures.

True *transformational* change will not happen until organizations begin to *think much more creatively* about the value of the assets, how to connect them with strategy, and how to link them to competitive advantage. The way you measure them will determine how you treat them. For example, your organization probably has already begun to manage *people* differently because it is at least beginning to view them as assets worthy of investment, rather than just as costs to be expensed. If so, this is a sure sign that transformation is beginning to happen.

## Transformational Measurement of Intangibles

The key to competitive advantage going forward is primarily an issue of better measurement and management of intangible sources of value. Few realize that one of the key success factors for supply chain management is the ability to measure trust throughout the system, and a key measure is "supply chain trust." A relatively short time ago, this kind to thinking would have been viewed as "just crazy!" Today, it might still be viewed by traditionalists as "unmeasurable," but it is no longer crazy. It is *transformational.*

Figure 13-1 lists a number of high-value intangibles, and two possible emergent measures of each. The purpose of this figure is to show you that everything—no matter how intangible—*can* be measured! None of the proposed measures are difficult to implement, nor are they esoteric or intimidating. Some of the measures are surveys or questionnaires, others are audits, self-assessments, and inventories. Any of these measures can yield extremely rich data that can be rather easily converted into knowledge and even wisdom. Several of these methods are discussed further in the Transformational Measurement Action Plans in Chapter 14.

But don't look for numbers (quantitative measures) that can be easily put into a financial statement or reported in columns of numbers in monthly reports without further explanation. Remember: transformational measurement is seeing things differently, which is neither as difficult nor obscure as you may have believed.

FIGURE 13-1. MEASURING INTANGIBLES: SELECTED EXAMPLES.

| Intangible | Measure 1 | Measure 2 |
|---|---|---|
| Partnership | Partner attitudes survey | Partnership audit |
| Trust | Behavioral audit | Questionnaire |
| Collaboration | Collaborative activity audit | Collaboration climate survey |
| Knowledge | Knowledge assets (stock) | Knowledge map (flow) |
| Intellectual Capital | IC inventory | IC usage patterns |
| Employee Equity | Expertise self-assessment | Employee talent inventory |
| Innovation | Innovation climate survey | Innovation productivity index |
| Strategic Skills | Strategic alignment ratings | Time to proficiency |
| Customer Equity | Customer survey | Customer equity inventory |
| Leadership | Succession plan audit | Climate survey |

## Qualitative Measurement

Many emergent and transformational measures are, by their very nature, *qualitative*. Too often it is wrongly assumed that measurement is about assigning numbers to things. Based on her extensive research, D. Lynn Kelley arrived at the followed definition of measurement: "Assessing the degree to which a variable is present." She adds, "Notice that there is no reference to counting or quantifying the variable in the definition."[13] Furthermore, when you are not really clear about the variable you are measuring, it is important to perform some qualitative study. The real purpose of *qualitative measurement* is exploratory—to generate hypotheses. On the other hand, quantitative measurement is primarily for the purpose of confirming our existing hypotheses.

According to Pfeffer and Sutton, "From our research, we are convinced that when companies base decisions on evidence, they enjoy a competitive advantage. And even when little or no data is available, there are things executives can do that allow them to rely more on evidence and logic and less on guesswork, fear, faith, or hope. For example, qualitative data, such as that gathered on field trips to retail sites for the purpose of testing existing assumptions, can be an extremely powerful form of useful evidence for quick analysis."[14] However, because of the exploratory nature of qualitative measurement, it is important to have realistic expectations for it.

One of the most positive things about qualitative measurement is that it is infinitely flexible. But its disadvantage is that it is cumbersome for our existing information systems to handle. Virtually everything *can* be "reduced" to numbers for ease of data handling, but that doesn't mean that everything *should* be. Many qualitative dimensions are extremely difficult to quantify. As D.Q. McInerny explains in his book *Being Logical*, "We regularly express quality in quantitative terms, a practice that can bring with it considerable practical benefits, but we should be aware of its limitations."[15]

One of the biggest limitations is when qualitative aspects of performance are quantified and then used inappropriately or given too much credibility. Says McInerny, "We indulge in a false sense of precision if we suppose we know the quality better, *as a quality*, because it has been quantified."[16] That is why I strongly advocate *experimenting* with new and emerging measures, and avoiding prematurely institutionalizing new "metrics." The key is to *use* the information received to answer important questions, not to conform to rigid methodological criteria.

Ethnographic market researchers are well known for their creative use of measurement. They are trying to collect rich data unobtrusively, rather than shoving a survey in someone's face. Roger Dow and Susan Cook recount the story of market research pioneer, Louis Cheskin, who wanted to learn more about women's preferences for fabric colors. He paid women to select scarves stacked on tables. The women were asked to rate the colors on a scorecard. When finished, the women were allowed to select a scarf to take home. When asked when they should start tabulating the scorecards, Cheskin replied, "We are not going to look at the scorecards. Each table had the same number of scarves, so we're going to count the scarves that remain on each table. Who cares how the colors were rated on the scorecard? We're interested in the color women actually chose."[17]

Organizations often are surprised to find out how much resistance there is to such "radical" ideas as using unconventional measures. Much of the resistance comes from impatient executives who "want 'the metrics' now!" In addition, many are concerned that subjective and softer measures will be used for self-serving purposes—and, in a negative context of measurement, they will—but so will financial numbers! If you are offering big rewards for hitting a target, you are inviting dysfunction—so don't be surprised if you get it—whether you are measuring quantitatively or qualitatively.

## Estimating

Arno Penzias points to estimating as a particularly difficult practice for traditionalists to accept. "A high barrier stands between us and the habit of making rough estimates—the fear of getting the 'wrong' answer. There is nothing wrong with educated guesses as long as the uncertainty is acknowledged and managed. Contrary to what most of us have learned in school . . . an inexact answer is almost always good enough."[18]

In many measurement efforts, approximations are acceptable because it is the underlying logic that is important, not massive data collection and analysis exercises. The key to estimating is not just figuring out how to arrive at acceptable estimates, but how to determine the right constructs to estimate. After all, it doesn't matter if your thermometer is a few degrees off when you're deciding what clothes to wear, but it does matter when you're taking someone's body temperature. So, the key is not accuracy, but *appropriate* accuracy. And sometimes when you are measuring something emergent and the purpose is learning, then perhaps accuracy is not very important at all.

## Subjective Measures

Nothing is more difficult for measurement traditionalists to accept than the validity of subjective measures. However, when objective measurement is not feasible, subjective measurement is a reasonable alternative. In fact, sometimes subjective ratings are all that we can rely on for measuring some of the intangible, leading-edge, predictive constructs.

Many people are justifiably fearful that subjective measurement is particularly prone to bias, either intentionally or unintentionally. But subjective measurement is not really the biggest problem; being *subjectively judgmental* in using the data is. While unintentional bias can be reduced through the design of creative measurement methods and tools, the more difficult and dangerous problem, intentional bias, can only be reduced through changing the context of measurement in order to remove the motive for this kind of dysfunction.

Using safe but inappropriate quantitative measures isn't going to solve the root-cause problem, and it will only generate more meaningless numbers that are useless for managing real value creation. According to Karl-Erik Sveiby, "All social measurement systems are very fragile and open to manipulation and there is very little we can do about it."[19] What we *can* do about it is to be aware of the limitations of whatever measurement methods we are using, and create a positive context for their use. At least in the short-term, the best remedies for the inevitable distortion that is caused by an emergent "lens" is to acknowledge, and accommodate for, that distortion, not throw out the new lens!

It is most certainly possible to satisfy all the key requirements of a good performance measure with a subjective measure. While subjective experiences are very real to the person experiencing them, there are many psychological phenomena that can cause the *reporting* to deviate from objective reality. So, due care must be taken in eliciting that reality. We already know that there are multiple causal factors that contribute to most effects. One of the biggest problems with subjective measurement is the inability of those responding to distinguish one contributory factor from another.

Take, for example, the case of customer service surveys. The customer might be responding to an item on the "speed of the transaction," which might be rated high. But in fact the customer had wanted *information,* not service at the cash register, provided speedily. So, the wrong question was asked. That is why it is so important in customer measurement to understand the context, in this case the customer's expectations. If a subjective measurement instrument doesn't capture performance against expectations, then the data might be worthless. However, if it does capture the right data, then the data can be translated into actionable knowledge much more effectively than all the objective measurement data could ever collect.

Nothing generates more wisdom and less respect from many measurement traditionalists, than self-assessments. But I would bet that most of us have learned an enormous amount of valuable personal information by tracking our time, keeping a budget, completing a personality assessment, and other such highly subjective measures. In fact, there is probably no better learning and performance improvement experience than a manager or a team receiving feedback, discussing it, and committing to behavior change. This can then be followed up with repeated measurements to provide productive, ongoing feedback on progress achieved.

## Rating Scales

Careful definition of the constructs and appropriate design of the measurement tools can overcome most of the weaknesses of subjective measurement. Rating scales and interpretive guidelines cause people designing survey and questionnaires much heartburn. My recommendation is to review the response scale options (and there are a lot of them, such as true-false, "strongly agree" to "strongly disagree," "to a great extent" to "not at all," "very confident" to "not confident at all," 5-point scale, 10-point scale) and choose one that seems to fit your items. The key is to determine what response options best fit your situation and how much variation you need in the responses.

There are many ways to avoid the risks of subjective measurement, including using rating scales with better "anchored" (more descriptive) rating points, increasing the variance of the ratings scales, adding confidence estimates ("How confident are you in your rating?"), using even-numbered rating points to avoid the "undecided" mid-point problem, and eliciting textual comments that clarify the ratings. (Note: Several rating scale recommendations are made in the Transformational Measurement Action Plans, in Chapter 14.) There are also many sources listed in the Bibliography that you can draw upon, if interested.

Remember, it is not so much the scores that are important, but what to do about them. This is why, especially with subjective measurement, the context of measurement is so important.

## Cross-Functional Measures

One of the biggest problems hindering the diffusion of emergent and transformational measures has nothing to do with the measures themselves, but rather with the lack of cross-functional collaboration. That is why almost every performance measurement today is a functional one, which continues to reinforce the "silo mentality." But many, if not most, of the best new and emerging measures will need to be cross-functional or they won't have much of an impact. If a measurement innovation remains within a silo, not much will change. The most successful organizations will increasingly be based on well-measured and managed end-to-end processes, such as the supply chain and customer experience, both of which cross functions and span the entire enterprise.

One of the greatest opportunities and challenges facing organizations today is how to get buy-in from the various stakeholders for at least experimenting with—*trying out*—the new, emergent, and cross-functional measures. Today, the best measures of supply chain effectiveness are "percent perfect orders" (an objective measure of the percent of *complete* orders that arrived at the customer on-time) and "trust among supply chain partners" (a subjective measure of attitudes), both of which require extensive cross-functional collaboration. Another good example is "new product time-to-market," which also requires the collaboration of a large number of stakeholders in different functions throughout the organization.

Probably the greatest "opportunity" for cross-functional transformational measurement is in sales and marketing. The marketing people seem to be coming up with all the new measures, and the sales folks seem to be stuck on "opportunities in the pipeline." The problem, of course, is that sales is so locked into its commission structure that dominates its measurement system, and not much will change until sales figures out a way to commission people based on "profitable long-term customer relationships"!

## Predictive Measures

Today, most measurement still focuses on the past and the present, and it does not serve effectively as a guide for the future. This is because traditional measurement can do nothing except collect data on what has *already* happened. The winners in business must be able to see beyond the obvious, and be able to *manage the future*.

According to DiPiazza and Eccles, "Although measurement is inherently based on information about events that have already happened, certain measures can be predictive in nature when they relationship among value drivers are well understood."[20] That is a major reason why measurement frameworks are so important. Intense competition today necessitates that organizations constantly improve and transform themselves and their measurement systems. Unfortunately, many organizations become complacent with their successful business model and strategy until they are "blind-sided" by something they didn't anticipate. This recently happened to Dell Computer. The company became too internally-focused, failed to modify their critical measures, missed some crucial customer insight that the company should have captured and acted upon, and is now suffering the consequences.

I see blindness to the obvious all the time when leaders are steering their organizations though the turbulent seas with their eyes fixed on the rear-view-mirror of their financial statements and antiquated assumptions. Our mental models and our existing measures keep us stuck in the past.

Most of the future is fairly predictable (I'd say about 90 percent). There is some future that is almost unpredictable, but new measures and new mental models can help us prepare better for that future.

Greater use of predictive measures will enable progressive companies to make and manage better investments, understand the crucial trade-offs, and optimize their portfolio of assets. This kind of *transformational* measurement will require a lot more focus, integration, and interactivity than currently exists. It will not be sufficient to simply extrapolate data from isolated measures into the future. It will require sophisticated predictive thinking and modeling based on sound measurement frameworks, and, most of all, courage to experiment. This is not as difficult as it might sound. For example, developing a rough model and creating "order of magnitude" estimates can be stimulating, as well as useful.

## Multiple Measures

Even though I have stressed the importance of reducing the number of routine measures, this is not necessarily true for the most strategic emergent and transformational ones. When you don't understand something, it is dangerous to measure just one aspect rather than the whole. When thinking strategically and transformationally, rather than looking for one measure of something that is somewhat abstract, it is usually better to settle for multiple measures. That is why dashboards, while a good idea in principle, can be dangerous in practice if not used with care.

We all know the perils of relying on isolated numbers, and, even though data can be very impressive, until it is converted into knowledge it can be extremely misleading. And, while intuition is a great capability to have, it is deeply flawed because it still relies on individual subjective perceptions and habits. Relying on any one person's subjectivity, even the CEO's, to make decisions is like giving a survey to one person and generalizing it to the entire organization.

Just as there is no single test that is adequate to assess the overall condition of health of the human body, no one measure of a complex organizational dimension is adequate for organizations, especially in the early stages of measuring a construct, or when the situation is unstable.

Using multiple measures together, while considering their relationships and trade-offs, can lead to a much more effective organizational "diagnosis." Multiple measures can also lead to the development of a single measure, or an index (which can also be disaggregated into its component parts, if need be). It isn't a matter of "just improving" things *anywhere,* because improvement in one area might be another case of suboptimization. The key is to improve the *right* things, and ensure that the improvement is *aligned* with what is needed for the organization as a whole.

## Introducing the Transformational Measurement Action Plans

In Chapter 14 you will find 34 Transformational Measurement Action Plans (TMAPs) that are directed at important measurement areas. The TMAPs provide discussions of the new, emergent, and transformational measures being developed and tested today or that should be considered for tomorrow. These measures can be used as springboards to stimulate *dialogue* within your organization to create your own transformational measurement action plans.

Some of the measures discussed are in fairly wide use today, but I still consider them transformational because they have significantly altered the measurement lens, or mental model, that organizations used to view phenomena in particular areas. Others are newer transformational measures that are starting to gain traction, but are not yet widely used. Still others are emergent measures that are just being experimented with. However, every measure or measurement methodology included was deemed to be at least worthy of being tested in any appropriate organizational context. Interestingly, I can't think of a single measure highlighted among the TMAPs that was even on any organization's radar screen twenty years ago!

Although changing to new performance measures might seem scary to some, remember that the experimental use of even the most emergent performance measures is low risk—especially if they are used for learning and improvement. The only risk is in using the experimental measures to evaluate people and make personnel decisions, especially before their validity has been established.

The Transformational Measurement Action Plans contain some natural clusters of measures, including quite a few customer-related ones, such as Customer Delight, Customer Loyalty, Customer Experience, Customer Engagement, Voice of the Customer, Customer Profitability, and Customer Lifetime Value. All provide a valuable piece of the total puzzle. Some focus on the attitudes and emotions of customers, and others on the value received by the company *from* the customer. Some are more qualitative and subjective than others. But what they have in common is that they have all, to some extent, changed the *lens* through which organizations view their customers. Because of that, all of them are potentially *transformational*. These measures show just how far we have come in the transformation from a traditional transactional customer satisfaction approach, but also highlight how far we still have to go! I also encourage you to experiment with measurement frameworks that show the hypothesized or actual relationships among the measures, such as shown in Figure 13-2.

You will also find emergent and transformational measures of financial constructs (Economic Value Added, Total Cost of Ownership, Activity-Based Costing); employee health and safety constructs (Employee Safety, Employee Presenteeism); human resources constructs (Emotional Intelligence, Employee Engagement, Learning Effectiveness); information technology (Information Orientation, Information Proficiency); research and development (Innovation Climate); the extended enterprise (Partner Relationships, Organizational Trust); knowledge management (Knowledge Flow); and others, including Organizational Agility, Strategic Readiness of Intangibles, Project Scheduling, Collaboration, Reputation, and Service Quality.

I could have included scores of additional emergent and transformational measures. For example, there is some exciting work being done in the areas of social performance,[21] corporate social responsibility,[22] and sustainability.[23] There are interesting measures being developed for organizational health,[24] employee vitality,[25] and becoming an employer of choice.[26] There are also new measures of executive intelligence,[27] people equity,[28] visionary leadership,[29] and many more.

There are even new financial measures, which are supposed to be quite transformational. Jim Collins tells of how some companies have transformed their marketing by moving from one financial measure to another, such as from "profit per store" to "profit per region," or from "profit per division" to "profit per customer," or from "profit per sales region" to "profit per global brand category," and (would you believe?) from "profit per postage meter" to "profit per customer"![30]

FIGURE 13-2. CUSTOMER MEASUREMENT FRAMEWORK.

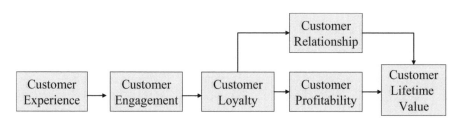

Who said performance measurement isn't creative? But, oddly enough, the least innovative measures seem to be coming from those in the innovation business—Research & Development—which still seems to be stuck on a product-centric approach. For example, how do you measure the "pipeline" of innovative ideas?

## Don't Get Discouraged

But whatever you do, don't get discouraged! For example, one of the measures included in Chapter 14 is SERVQUAL, a transformational measure of Service Quality. Since its development, SERVQUAL has had its detractors, especially among measurement purists who have criticized it for being overly complex (multiple rating scales), subjective, and statistically unreliable. However, it provides a very useful model for exploring and assessing customers' service experiences, is now being used widely by service organizations, and will continue to provide value until some better measurement tool takes its place. It might not be a perfect measure, but it is an extremely effective way to get an organization focused on customer service, to gain valuable feedback on its performance, and to motivate continuous improvement.

Now dive into the Transformational Measurement Action Plans in Chapter 14 with an open mind and an exploratory attitude. And don't forget to read the Epilogue.

# CHAPTER 14

# Transformational
# Measurement Action Plans

This chapter is composed of Transformational Measurement Action Plans (TMAPs) of emergent and transformational measures that are intended to stimulate your thinking, challenge your mental models, and, in some cases, provide examples and guidance for measurement. Review those that cover problematic areas in your organization, use them as ongoing references, and add your own emergent and transformational measures to the list.

## 1. Customer Experience

Meeting the high standards of doing business successfully today requires more than the standard customer satisfaction measurements. Customer experiences include not only the "core transaction" (the purchase) itself, but also everything that precedes *and* follows it—all of the points of *interaction* between the organization and its customers. For example, for an airline "transaction," there may be as many as twenty individual experiences involved in making reservations, check-in, travel, and arrival that cannot be reduced to a single satisfaction rating.

Organizations are beginning to realize that providing a product or service is only the "tip of the iceberg" in terms of what the customer *experiences* about the organization. A Bain and Company study reveals just how companies tend to misread their customers' perceptions: Of 362 firms surveyed, 80 percent believed they delivered a "superior experience" to their customers, but customers rated only 8 percent of the companies as delivering a truly superior experience.[1]

Transactions are easy to measure, but experiences aren't. Most customer satisfaction measures average customer experiences, when in fact the customers don't see the average, but they see every "defect" as an issue.

When used effectively, Customer Experience measurement can be a very powerful tool for transforming the way that organizations view themselves and their customers. For each incident made visible through a customer comment or complaint there might literally be hundreds of incidents that are *never* reported.

Changing from measuring and managing "customer service" (what you give the customer) to measuring and managing Customer Experience (what the customer gets) represents a major paradigm shift. This is a *transformationally* different approach from what is traditionally measured and managed, which tends to make organizations and their employees much more aware of the total cross-functional customer experience. Because it focuses on well-defined interactions, Customer Experience measurement is also more actionable than customer satisfaction measurement. A great example of this is at the Inn at Little Washington in Virginia, where restaurant staff assign a "mood rating" (from 1 to 10) to each customer party when they enter the establishment and throughout the meal. The goal is to raise the mood rating, with the standard that no one should leave the restaurant with a mood rating below a 9.[2] Although subjective, this is a innovative tool to help the staff keep focused on Customer Experience and to obtain feedback on how well they are orchestrating the experience.

One of the best ways to measure Customer Experience in a less centralized environment is through the use of "event-driven surveys"—surveys that are automatically deployed when a customer has completed a particular interaction, such as a reservation, a purchase, a service inquiry, or a refund.[3] However, one of the biggest challenges with measuring complex customer interactions is how to do so relatively nonintrusively. Retail stores and banks use trained observers, video surveillance, and mystery shoppers to monitor Customer Experience. With some creativity and a good sampling strategy (of both experiences and respondents), organizations can still collect considerable data without offending customers or creating data overload.

## 2. Customer Engagement

One of the oldest measures to have dominated the business measurement landscape is "customer satisfaction." However, increasingly, customer satisfaction has become acknowledged as a measure that tends to focus on and reinforce low expectations (the extent to which customers' minimal expectations have been met). Furthermore, it tends to be based on the myth of the entirely "rational customer" who makes rational decisions. However, research indicates that buying decisions are also *emotional*. Organizations need to tap something deeper than mere "satisfaction."

New measures are beginning to acknowledge the customer in a more holistic way. That's why the concept of Customer Engagement is a potentially transformational one. An "engaged" customer is very different from a merely "satisfied" one.

The Gallup Organization has developed and is distributing a Customer Engagement measurement instrument[4] that endeavors to measure the strength of the *emotional bond* between a customer and a company or brand. The Gallup survey shown below includes eight statements to which customers are asked to respond on a 5-point scale (from "Strongly Agree" to "Strongly Disagree"). The blanks should be filled in with the company or brand name being assessed.

---

1. [ _____ ] is a name I can always trust.
2. [ _____ ] always delivers on what it promises.
3. [ _____ ] always treats me fairly.
4. If a problem arises, I can always count on [ _____ ]
   to reach a fair and satisfactory resolution.
5. I feel proud to be a [ _____ ] customer.
6. [ _____ ] always treats me with respect.
7. [ _____ ] is the perfect company for people like me.
8. I can't imagine a world without [ _____ ].

---

One of the key words in the survey is the use of the word "always," which appears in five of the eight statements. Gallup's research has shown that trust, respect, confidence, fair treatment, and the other practices have to be present *all the time*. According to the underlying theory, every time there is an interaction with a customer, the company is either building Engagement, or eroding it. Gallup researchers have found, in numerous industries they studied, that the proportion of "fully engaged" customers has ranged from around 6 percent to as high as 40 percent. In contrast, they found that 80 percent of customers reported "satisfaction" in these same industries.

## 3. Customer Delight

What is a "satisfied customer"? How does customer satisfaction relate to other customer measures (such as customer retention, loyalty, and profitability)? The research says, "Not much!" Furthermore, what do different satisfaction scores mean? For example, what is the difference between a 3.7 and a 4.1 on a five-point scale? Let's say that your organization finds that 80 percent of its customers are satisfied. What does that really mean? The reality is that 20 percent of your customers are *dis*-satisfied, and you probably don't know which or why. Even more serious is that every one of those 80 percent satisfied might be a candidate for attrition.

Recent thinking has led many advocates of traditional customer satisfaction measurement to realize that its value is quite limited and that it might even distract organizations from focusing on what is most important: "delighting" (not just minimally satisfying) their most important customers. There is now a very strong body of research indicating that, if you implement a customer satisfaction survey with a five-point response format (very dissatisfied to very satisfied), customers who report being "very satisfied" are *much different* from merely "satisfied" customers. They aren't just more satisfied, they are actually *delighted*. So, identifying the customer who are "very satisfied" or "delighted," and discovering why (through interviews or focus groups with a sample of the segment) can provide transformational insight. Interviewing "very dissatisfied" customers can also be extremely valuable, if your organization has the stomach for it!

A *Customer Delight Index* has been developed by Dr. Darrel Edwards using a 5-point Customer Delight scale (Failure, Unsatisfactory, Satisfactory, Excellent, and Delightful).[5] Only the final rating point is considered to represent true "delight." According to Edwards, "When you Delight your customer, you create a strong emotional response that commits the customer to the product, brand or manufacturer. Commitment leads to loyalty." Clearly this scale has raised the bar from the traditional satisfaction survey, with three positive choices, rather than just two. But what is more significant is that only one of them really counts.

The Net Promoter Score[6] is a rating of Customer Delight with another name. Customer loyalty guru Frederick Reichheld has introduced a similar concept, but calls these delighted customers "Promoters"—customers who are willing to recommend your product or service to friends (defined as those rating your organization a "9" or "10" on an 11-point scale). But that's not all, there are very likely to also be "detractors"—those customers who are unlikely to recommend your organization (defined as those rating your organization "0" through "6" on the scale). "Passive" customers are those who rate your organization "7" or "8." A Net Promoter Score (NPS) is calculated by subtracting the percent of detractors from the percent of promoters. What is particularly intriguing about the Net Promoter measure (and there is a substantial body of recent research to back it up) is that it can be measured using *one* simple question: "How likely is it that you would recommend this organization to a friend or colleague?"

## 4. Customer Loyalty

The importance of customer retention started being acknowledged when it became clear that even a small increase in retention rates can raise profits considerably. Many years ago, organizations developed the idea of "loyalty programs" as a way to increase customer retention. Airlines, hotels, supermarkets, and credit card companies invested aggressively in such plans. As we now know, these programs did not create truly loyal customers. Customers who buy according to incentives tend to follow the incentives and are attracted to the next good deal, no matter who is offering it. In addition, many customers who appear loyal on the surface are only staying because of the unavailability of acceptable substitutes. Clearly a new approach for understanding "loyal customer behavior" is needed.

A new transformational concept of Customer Loyalty has evolved over recent years, and is progressively being better understood and articulated. Much of this understanding has come from efforts at measuring it. When one starts measuring a construct, its meaning and significance become much clearer—and so it is with Customer Loyalty.

What caused particular interest in the loyalty construct is how consistently more profitable *truly loyal* customers tend to be because acquisition costs have already been amortized, there is less emphasis on discounting, and loyal customers typically provide recommendations, referrals, and other sources of indirect profit. Marketing expert George Day has said that "real profitability comes from keeping valuable customers by building deep loyalty that is rooted in mutual trust, bilateral commitments, and intense communication."[7]

Loyalty is really about the *depth*, not just the *length* of the relationship. Measuring the drivers of these relationships is the key to being able to create them. There is no universal agreement about what the drivers of Customer Loyalty are. However, a number of other transformational measures included in this chapter can be used to predict loyalty, such as Customer Delight, Customer Experience, Voice of the Customer, and Customer Relationship. And, of course, Customer Profitability and Customer Lifetime Value can determine the potential value of a particular customer's loyalty.

## 5. Customer Relationship

Most customers have been traditionally viewed as short-term "transactions" rather than as long-term "relationships." Transactions are rather easy to measure and manage, and the traditional assumption has been that positive transactions could be simply aggregated into positive relationships. However, the whole concept of a customer relationship is changing with the increase in long-term services relationships, and with more organizations wanting to capture larger shares of customers' spending and their "lifetime value."

As Dow and Cook say, "The most fertile ground to grow your business lies in existing customers."[8] Furthermore, as the cost of acquiring profitable customers goes up, the value of retaining and expanding existing customer relationships increases. Customer relationship is very much in vogue today as Customer Relationship Management (CRM) gains traction. The change from "transactional thinking" to "relationship thinking" is clearly potentially transformational. But realizing the transformation will require much more progress in measuring and managing relationships.[9]

Here is a sampling of the indicators that can be used to measure and manage the health and value of a customer relationship:

• *Revenue*: The ongoing flow of revenue through increased sales, cross-sales, and up-sales is an indicator of a healthy relationship.

• *Profits*: A healthy relationship is a profitable relationship, because the customer appreciates the value being received, and doesn't nickel and dime the other partner.

• *Retention*: The length of the relationship is an indicator of the quality of the relationship.

• *Loyalty*: The loyalty of the customer can be measured through longevity, frequency of purchases, and expressed loyalty.

• *Communication*: The frequency and positive nature of two-way communication between relationship partners is key to customer relationships. How positive is the communication?

• *Commitment*: A good indicator of relationship is demonstrated by unfailing commitment to the relationship despite negative experiences.

• *Trust*: Nothing better indicates the depth and quality of a relationship than trust, which can be self-reported or demonstrated by trusting behavior, such as sharing confidential information.

• *Input*: Willingness to make proactive suggestions and contribute to new product development, refinement, and trial can be of great value.

• *Referrals*: The referring of others to the relationship partner is a very strong relationship indicator.

• *Community*: Many companies—like eBay and to a lesser extent Starbucks—are building more than relationships; they are building "communities" of customers.

Clearly, there are multiple indicators that can serve as barometers of relationship quality. These indicators can be used in the form of a checklist (checking off the frequency with which each indicator occurs), an inventory (listing examples of behavioral indicators), and/or a scale that quantitatively rates the strength of each indicator.

## 6. Voice of the Customer

The real purpose of customer measurement should be to learn as much as possible about customers, and translate that knowledge into better and deeper relationships with the most valuable, and potentially valuable, customers. This stands in stark contrast to superficial quantitative customer satisfaction ratings that have been described as "Tell Us How Much You Love Us" exercises. They might make organizations feel good but tell them almost nothing valuable about what customers are really thinking.

Voice of the Customer measurement is a way to gain a more holistic (360 degree) customer understanding of what customers are *really* saying, to supplement (not necessarily replace) the quantitative data that most employees have difficulty interpreting (such as understanding the difference between a customer rating of 2.6 and 2.8). It is transformational because it attempts to move organizations from superficial "satisfaction scores" to "profound knowledge" of the customer.

The Voice of the Customer can be captured through some combination of interviews, surveys, telephone calls, focus groups and panels, observation, customer visits, warranty data, field reports, complaint logs, exit interviews with departing customers, ongoing employee interactions with customers, feedback options on websites, and so on.

Smart companies proactively gather customer feedback continuously and from multiple sources (sometimes referred to as "listening posts"). Here are some other practices that are being used successfully to tune into the Voice of the Customer:

1. *In-depth interviews*, or "personal dialogues," are being used to explore customer experiences, attitudes, beliefs, and feelings; to create a rich "picture" of the whole customer; and to fill in the gaps in the quantitative data.

2. *Customer advisory councils* are being established, representing all major customer sectors.

3. *Ethnography* (the branch of anthropology that seeks to scientifically describe human cultures, societies, and organizations) is being used to observe customers using products in their natural setting, at work, at home, or while shopping.

4. *Psycho-physiological response measurement* is being used to capture the emotions and unconscious thoughts of customers, using biofeedback devices to assess thoughts that customers might not be consciously aware of.

The real shift in perspective is away from atomism (reducing complex phenomena to simplistic elements) to holism (viewing things organically, as unified wholes that are greater than the simple sum of their parts). Those who embrace this kind of "Voice of the Customer" measurement welcome input from multiple sources, realizing that all data can be valuable, that there are multiple viewpoints, and that diversity is good.

When companies measure what's important for the customer, rather than just for them, a transformation occurs. Chris Carey, the CEO of Datatec Industries, explained that they used to ask customers things that were important to Datatec. "But once we began talking to customers to understand what *they* cared about, everyone in our organization learned exactly what to concentrate on. Our measures took on a whole new look."[10]

## 7. Customer Profitability

If you asked an average person on the street how much profit a typical company makes, most would say around 25 to 50 percent. However, it has been found that "the real aggregate profit margins of companies in most developed industrialized companies lie dangerously close to zero."[11]

When Customer Profitability finally started to be measured, it surprised almost everyone that between 30 and 80 percent of all customers were unprofitable. Most businesses don't realize that some of the customers they thought were "good" customers were actually "bad" (unprofitable), and many were profoundly unprofitable. Simply doing business with these customers was actually costing a lot of money! Retaining *more* customers doesn't increase profitability, unless they are the *right* customers.

Profits come *from customers*, not from products, and yet profits have rarely been linked to customers. While companies have long known how much revenue individual customers provide, it has been impossible to link specific costs to customers. Traditional cost accounting doesn't capture costs that can be assigned to particular customers, because most costs are simply amortized across the entire customer base. That is, until companies learned their ABCs! Customer Profitability measurement was originally enabled by the creation of Activity-Based Costing (ABC), through which it is possible to identify the costs of particular activities and assign them to specific customers. (See Activity-Based Costing in Section 23 of this chapter.)

When some pioneering companies started measuring Customer Profitability, executives were truly startled by all the activities that contribute cost to sales in addition to the actual product or service itself (such as promotions, discounting, rebates, salaries, commissions, bonuses, order processing, financing, credit checks, delivery fulfillment, installation, invoicing, collections, nonpayment, late payment, warranties, post-sales service, returns, and rework). One company found that just being too casual about expediting orders had made many potentially-profitable customers unprofitable. Hudson's Bay Company in Canada found that at one of its stores 30 percent of customers accounted for 325 percent of profits!

What is so transformational about the Customer Profitability measure is the extent to which it can improve decision making. A profitability analysis with just a few well-selected customers will almost always shock company executives and motivate a change to how the company does business. This also allows companies to do customer profiling by targeting the "best" customers and prospects, and to migrate customers from unprofitable to profitable and from low profit to high profit.

## 8. Customer Lifetime Value

Customer Lifetime Value (CLV), a relatively new measure with great transformational potential, helps companies to view customers as potential streams of current and future value. Like most emergent and transformational measures, it is not a measure that you're going to find on a balance sheet, an income statement, or anywhere else in the "official" corporate accounts. But it might actually have more value than most officially reported measures.

Customer Lifetime Value is essentially a forecast of the "potential value of the customer relationship," based on past history and assumptions about the future. For example, according to Gupta and Lehmann, the lifetime value of a customer is equal to 1 to 4.5 times the annual margin of the customer.[12] Some companies are starting to use CLV, both for customer selection and to target marketing investments.

More specifically, CLV is the "present value" of the *future* income stream generated by customers or customer segments. Customer Lifetime Value can actually be defined in terms of both total revenue and profit expected from customers over their lifetime. For example, an appliance store chain develops CLV profiles for each of their regular customers based on past purchases, cross-selling opportunities, the likely replacement intervals, and repairs over a ten-year period.

One common way to calculate CLV is by estimating the customer's anticipated purchases (including post-sales service and replacement parts) multiplied by profit margin on all sales and service, multiplied by purchase likelihood (expressed as a percentage), multiplied by the anticipated longevity of the customer relationship, adjusted for present value of money. Sometimes, less tangible sources of customer value (such as trends in the relationship, advocacy, or referrals) can be factored in.

Although CLV isn't a precise quantity, it can be of great value for planning purposes. As such, the major purpose of CLV is not so much to determine an accurate estimate of future profits, but to *prioritize* customers and customer segments, and decide how best to maximize opportunities. Of course, the danger of a measure like CLV is that it can become a wild guess based on questionable assumptions, such as the length of the relationship.[13]

## 9. Service Quality

As the service component of world economies grows in size (it now comprises about 80 percent of American jobs) and importance, the challenge of measuring and managing Service Quality is becoming increasingly important. But, this has proven to be no small challenge, since Service Quality is quite different from product quality.

Product quality has been the focus of most quality research and measurement. For a long time, there was little interest in developing standard measurement tools for services. Most service organizations (like hotels, restaurants, and airlines) have tended to use their own customized customer service assessments, making it virtually impossible to benchmark with other organizations.

Researchers Zeithaml, Parasuraman, and Berry developed an innovative and transformational approach to service quality measurement.[14] First, they developed a model they called SERVQUAL.[15] Then they developed a measurement instrument based on that model, with multiple items for each dimension. Their definition of service quality was not about "defects" (as it is in the manufacturing world), because in services "defects" are quite subjective. The quality of services depends on the perceptions of those being served, rather than absolute quality. Thus, the focus of SERVQUAL is on "perceived" rather than "objective" quality. It essentially measures the gaps between the level of customer "expectations" and the level of customer "perceptions."

The ten service quality dimensions originally measured by SERVQUAL (reliability, responsiveness, competence, access, courtesy, communication, credibility, security, understanding the customer, and tangibles) were eventually reduced to five, with the handy acronym RATER:

1. *Reliability* (the consistency of service quality, lack of service defects)
2. *Assurance* (the provisions for maintaining service quality and addressing service quality problems)
3. *Tangibles* (the physical environment)
4. *Empathy* (sensitivity to the customer)
5. *Responsiveness* (speed and effectiveness of the response to customer requests)

Although SERVQUAL has its detractors, it is widely used by progressive service organizations. Recent research in many different services settings indicates that the SERVQUAL instrument indeed represents accurate views of customer perception.[16]

Certainly, there will be other instruments developed for measuring service quality, and maybe even better ones. But for now, SERVQUAL is the standard, and it has already made a major contribution to service quality improvement.

## 10. Brand Equity

Brands have long been viewed as a major off-balance-sheet asset. The value of brands is powerfully exemplified by the large price premium and much greater demand that the Toyota Corolla commanded compared with the Chevrolet Prizm (which was essentially the same car) and by the success of the "Intel Inside" program (even though there wasn't much difference between the Intel and competitor's processors). When many companies are acquired, a substantial amount of the price is "goodwill" (much of that being the estimated value of any brands). For example, when Philip Morris acquired Kraft for $12.9 billion, $11.6 of it was for goodwill. According to Almquist and Winter, "The corporate brand is one of the last great under-leveraged business assets."[17]

The traditional view of a brand was about an "image" created primarily through advertising. Hundreds of billions of dollars have been spent creating and promoting brand images. The traditional advertising-based approach to brand management was more about logos, taglines, and advertising copy than anything approaching real brand management. In fact, some have referred to it as "marketing narcissism" ("Let me tell you how good we are."). But a new paradigm of branding is emerging that involves a lot more than customer messaging.

This new paradigm requires a high degree of alignment across the organization around its brand(s). To manage brands in this new paradigm, Brand Equity has become the transformational measure of choice and might soon be the only differentiator of most products and services. Brand Equity is actually what separates a product or service as a commodity from a premium product or service. Even nonprofits and government agencies can have brand equity.

The logic of the Brand Equity construct is essentially that *perceptions* (or beliefs) lead to *attitudes,* which reflect an "emotional connection" with the brand and behavioral intentions toward purchasing it.

However one analyzes it, Brand Equity is essentially a function of the brand's *image,* the brand's *performance,* and the brand's *added value.* The following are some of factors that are typically measured:

1. *Distinctiveness* (the brand's differentiation from competitors)
2. *Quality* (the reputation of the brand and how well it actually performs)
3. *Value* (the strength of preference for the brand)
4. *Image* (the extent to which the brand conveys the intended image)
5. *Loyalty* (the degree of commitment to the brand)

Another factor ("love") has even been suggested, and so-called love-marks[18] have been proposed to differentiate brands for which customers evidence passionate affection (as for Southwest Airlines and Starbucks).

Most of these factors (even love) can be fairly easily quantified. Of course, one of the keys is to determine the strength of the attitudes. One way to do this is through a technique called "conjoint analysis," whereby choice situations (involving various trade-offs) are presented, requiring respondents to make fairly realistic choices, rather than just respond to standard questions.

## 11. Intellectual Capital

Intellectual Capital (IC) can be defined as all of the intangible resources that contribute to the creation of value to an organization that are not included on the balance sheet. It includes such sources of value as knowledge (both tacit and codified in the form of documents), intellectual property (patents), competence and skills of people, and working methods, processes, and systems. It can also include the culture that supports the people, the image in the market place, and relationships with customers, alliance partners, and suppliers.

The traditional approach is to ignore these sources of value, or to value only those that are easy to place a value on, like patents. Some companies have tried to communicate their intangible value by calculating the difference between their market value (based on share prices) and book value, and attributing the difference to Intellectual Capital. Almost everything that counts as an IC "asset" is traditionally paid for, and written off, as an overhead expense and charged against current profits.

It is critical to find credible ways to measure the Intellectual Capital that underlies so much of the value of today's organizations. One method is to perform an inventory of the intellectual capital assets that exist in your organization, something that many organizations have never even done! Once the intellectual capital is inventoried, subjective ratings should be given to each major category of IC by knowledgeable internal or external "experts" (of course, you will first have to determine what constitutes an expert and develop guidelines for consistent ratings). It is then also possible, although admittedly difficult, to place a financial value on each major component of the intellectual capital inventory. The individual components can be assessed on either a value or a cost basis, or the overall intangible value of the corporation can be distributed among the IC assets. Clearly these measurement activities are primitive and time-consuming.

Another approach is a methodology for performing this inventory and rating process more systematically. The IC Rating methodology uses a standardized Intellectual Capital language and framework to help increase the consistency of the ratings. IC Rating was developed by experts in the field and has been validated through field work with over 270 ratings at more than 200 companies. The ratings are based on interviews with key stakeholders (both internal and external). Ratings are performed for current efficiency, renewal efforts underway, and the risk of each Intellectual Capital component.[19]

## 12. Strategic Readiness of Intangibles

One of the greatest challenges facing organizations today is the effective management of the multitude of intangible assets. Unfortunately, most of those assets are currently either managed tactically, or not managed at all. Intangibles must be carefully managed so that their realized value exceeds the cost of capital, or else they destroy value. Treating intangibles—such as employees, partnerships, and innovation—as assets necessitates a completely different approach from treating them as activities or costs. Another challenge with intangibles is that each one is *different,* and consequently they all need to be managed—and measured—differently.

Kaplan and Norton, of Balanced Scorecard fame, have recently started taking leadership in an areas they call the "strategic readiness of intangible assets," and how this readiness can be measured.[20] Intangible assets are said to be "strategically ready" when they can be used to support a strategic objective (like "increased new products"), which in turn is linked with measures of strategic success (like revenue, profit, or market share).

It is not enough just to have intangible assets. The competitive advantage of organizations in the new economy is increasingly dependent on how "ready" their intangible assets are for deployment in supporting strategy. Intangibles assets that are not ready are like unused inventory. If they cannot be effectively used to support strategic objectives, their value is reduced, sometimes to zero. For example, employees who have the right strategic capabilities or skills (those whose skillsets are clearly aligned with one or more of the organization's strategic objectives) are said to be "in a state of readiness" to contribute to strategic value creation. On the other hand, employees might be highly motivated and hard-working, but without the right strategy-related skills their "strategic readiness" is near zero.

Kaplan and Norton point out that organizations often have some categories of job ("job families") that are more strategic than others.[21] They recommend that much more attention be placed on those than on the myriad of more tactical jobs. In order to measure "human capital readiness," Kaplan and Norton believe that the organization must first identify the most critical internal processes (those that support key strategic objectives), and then identify the set of competencies required to perform each critical internal process. "Strategic job families" are the categories of jobs in which these competencies can have the biggest impact on enhancing the organization's critical internal processes, which are aligned with the strategic objectives.

Here is how it can be done: Link your most important intangible assets with major strategic priorities. Based on this linkage, rate each intangible asset (from 0 percent to 100 percent) in terms of "how well-aligned" it is with one or more of the components of your organization's strategy. For example, if one of your organization's intangible assets is "customer knowledge," determine its alignment with relevant strategic objectives, such as "increased customer acceptance of new product development." If "culture" is one of the key intangible assets, rate how "customer-centric" your culture is *right now* to support your "customer service" objective. Then, continue to assess each key intangible. The "alignment with strategy score" for each intangible asset constitutes the "strategic readiness" of the asset.

## 13. Innovation Climate

Organizations today have been struggling to find really good *measures* of innovation. As Davila, Epstein, and Shelton assert that in a recent survey of executives, "more than half rated their performance measurement system for innovation as poor or less than adequate."[22] Typically, organizations have defaulted to measures they can count, such as number of innovation projects, cost measures, and number of patents—a measure which Art Kleiner has called a "clueless measure"[23].

Nothing is more important *for* innovation than a climate *of* innovation! Innovation Climate is an important emergent area, because it largely determines what will happen with innovation in any organization. It is a key leading indicator of innovation results. The Innovation Climate Questionnaire (ICQ)[24] is a questionnaire for assessing the organizational climate for innovation. Adapted by the Innovation Centre Europe from the pioneering work of Goran Ekvall in Sweden, the ICQ has been completed by over 1500 respondents from organizations in the U.K. and other European countries. The instrument includes thirteen scales, listed here with brief descriptions:

1. *Commitment*: Commitment to organizational goals and operations; work perceived as stimulating and engaging.
2. *Freedom*: Opportunities to make own decisions, seek information, and show initiative; freedom from tight supervision.
3. *Idea-Support*: People encouraged for putting forward ideas and suggesting improvements.
4. *Positive Relationships*: People trust each other and get on well; absence of personal conflicts.
5. *Dynamism*: Dynamic and exciting atmosphere.
6. *Playfulness*: People laugh and joke with one another.
7. *Idea-Proliferation*: People are perceived as having creative ideas and varied perspectives toward their work.
8. *Stress*: People generally feel overburdened and under pressure at work.
9. *Risk-Taking*: People are prepared to take risks and implement new ideas.

10. *Idea-Time*: People have the time to generate and consider new ideas.
11. *Shared Views*: There is open and adequate communication among more and less senior employees.
12. *Pay Recognition*: People are satisfied with their remuneration.
13. *Work Recognition*: People receive praise for their achievements.

With the exception of Stress, higher scores on each scale relate to more favorable organizational outcomes (including lower turnover intention, increased job satisfaction, and greater organizational commitment). Risk-taking, Dynamism, and Freedom appear to account for the difference in a climate that supports *radical innovation* versus incremental improvements. Risk-taking appears to account for the biggest difference between the most and least innovative organizations.

As Dauphinais, Means, and Price insist, "Our experience suggests that the most predictive measure of whether an organization will be innovative is the level of trust between people in the organization."[25] I agree that this might be a factor that is given too little attention in the ICQ, and you might want to consider the recommendations in Section 15, Organizational Trust, to enhance trust measurement.

## 14. Reputation

Reputation has traditionally been dumped into a "general perception" category, remained the province of Public Relations or Advertising, and not given much corporate attention unless there is a Tylenol-like crisis. However, organizations are starting to become increasingly aware of the importance of a good reputation, and the perils of a bad one. According to Pate and Platt, "An enterprise's reputation is a resource that must be preserved at all cost."[26] Much of the lackadaisical attitude about reputation has been due to the difficulty of measuring it. Even if it doesn't affect the bottom-line immediately, there is a large body of evidence that shows it will eventually. It is useful to view reputation as "reputational capital," because this reinforces the financial implications of a good or poor reputation.

Reputation has been defined as how *all stakeholders* view the organization. Thus, measurement begins by measuring the perceptions of investors, employees, customers, vendors, business partners, government regulators, the community at large, and any other group for which the organization's reputation might be important.

The most transformational measure of Reputation that I have found is the Reputation Quotient (RQ).[27] It was developed by Harris Interactive in association with the Reputation Institute as an assessment tool that captures perceptions of corporate reputations across industries, among multiple audiences, and it is adaptable to countries outside the United States. A list of the top-50 corporations listed by RQ rating is also published.[28] However, like many other measures, reputation is best reflected by changes over time, rather than as a snapshot at a particular moment in time.

The RQ measures stakeholder perceptions across twenty attributes that are grouped into six dimensions, which are:

1. *Vision and Leadership*: clarity of vision, quality of leadership
2. *Financial Performance*: record of profitability, growth prospects, risk, competitive performance
3. *Workplace Environment*: quality of workplace, quality of employees, fairness
4. *Products and Services*: quality, innovation, value, fulfillment of promises
5. *Emotional Appeal*: feelings, admiration and respect, trust
6. *Social Responsibility*: philanthropy, environmental and community responsibility

The attributes are rated on a 7-point scale, ranging from 7 ("describes the company very well") to 1 ("does not describe the company well"). Harris Interactive solicits nominations of high-reputation companies and then performs interviews of the stakeholders of the nominated firms.

The same factors can be used by any company to perform their own reputation assessment. Such a "self-service" approach can provide your organization with deep insights into the perceptions of key stakeholder groups, which, in turn, can enable it to protect and enhance its reputation.

## 15. Organizational Trust

I have created the following definition of Trust by synthesizing it from a number of other definitions: "An expectancy held by an individual or group that promises will be kept and vulnerability will not be exploited." Thus, Trust is an "expectation" of dependability and benign intentions.

Trust is typically viewed as a characteristic of personal relationships. But there is also trust in institutions, in roles, in information, etc. Increased dangers in the world, and increased media portrayals of breaches in trust, have contributed to making people increasingly reluctant to trust others, and much more skeptical about organizational relationships. In addition, reduced personal interaction due to increased globalization, less colocation, more home-based employees, and fewer face-to-face meetings are further reducing trust-building opportunities. Trust is becoming a scarcer commodity by the day.

In organizations, trust is typically seen as outside the domain of most managers and even Human Resource departments. Although public opinion surveys often ask questions about political and institutional trust, there are few, if any, measurements of "organizational trust" or "organizational trustworthiness" (other than its inclusion in some organizational climate and culture surveys, and on the occasional employee attitude survey). Until very recently, there has been little effort to measure trust as an organizational construct.

Fortunately, with an increased realization that trust is a crucial aspect of relationships with customers, employees, vendor, partners, and other members of the extended enterprise, the trust measurement gap is beginning to close. One of the most crucial applications of trust relates to supply chain performance. As Tom Brunell has said, "Trust is one of the most important tools within the supply chain today and it cannot be simply turned on or applied like other technological tools. . . . The technology tools are in place, it's the trust that has to catch up."[29] Furthermore, trust is highly situational, and, because trust is so fragile, it can be destroyed almost instantaneously by a single act that is perceived to be a "betrayal of trust."[30]

I have developed the questionnaire below for measuring Organizational Trust based on extensive research. The terminology can be adjusted to fit the terms used in your organization. And, as with all emergent measures, it is recommended that the items be tested and fine-tuned through pilot use, before broader implementation.

I suggest that you use the standard 5-point scale: 5 = Strongly Agree; 4 = Agree; 3 = Neither agree nor disagree; 2 = Disagree; 1 = Strongly Disagree. Interpretation guidance follows the questions.

---

### Organizational Trust Questionnaire

1. I trust the expectations that have been communicated in this organization/group/team.
2. I feel that people in this organization/group/team are honest.
3. There is mutual respect among members in this organization/group/team.
4. People in this organization/group/team are good at listening without making judgments.
5. I feel good about being a member of this organization/group/team.
6. I feel that the people in this organization/group/team are competent.

7. I feel confident that this organization/group/team has the ability to accomplish what it says it will do.

8. People help each other learn in this organization/group/team.

9. Learning is highly valued in this organization/group/team.

10. I feel that I can be completely honest in this organization/group/team.

11. Honesty is rewarded in this organization/group/team.

12. There are clear expectations and boundaries established in this organization/group/team.

13. Delegation is encouraged in this organization/group/team.

14. People keep agreements in this organization/group/team.

15. There is a strong sense of responsibility and accountability in this organization/group/team.

16. There is consistency between words and behavior in this organization/group/team.

17. There is open communication in this organization/group/team.

18. People tell the truth in this organization/group/team.

19. People are willing to admit mistakes in this organization/group/team.

20. People give and receive constructive feedback non-defensively in this organization/group/team.

21. People maintain confidentiality in this organization/group/team.

22. I can depend on people to do what they say in this organization/group/team.

23. People are treated fairly and justly in this organization/group/team.

24. People's opinions and feelings are taken seriously in this organization/group/team.

25. I feel confident that my trust will be reciprocated in this organization/group/team.

*Interpretation Key*: Highest score is 125. High score range is 100–125. Moderate score range is 70–110. Low score is below 70. Danger zone is below 50.

## 16.  Partner Relationships

Clearly partnerships, alliances, and other relationships are crucial to success in business today, and being able to effectively manage them is becoming a strategic necessity. It is not longer acceptable to leave priorities like this to chance and to the good intentions of the partners. The key to competitiveness today is not so much about the advantage of a single firm, but the competitive advantage of *networks* of firms—partnerships and alliances of all kinds. Leonard Greenhalgh says that today, "relationships are the most crucial element of organizational architecture."[31] This is yet another area in which traditional performance measures fall far short of the mark, which is particularly problematic for organizations wanting to achieve outstanding results through a high-performing "extended enterprise."

Successful partnerships and alliances require careful management, which requires thoughtful and collaborative measurement. In *Getting Partnering Right*, Rackham, Friedman and Ruff say, "Almost all of the successful partnerships we studied had spent considerable time and effort setting up measurement systems to track their progress.[32]

The most flexible measurement methodology for partnerships and alliances is the one used by Vantage Partners. In *Measuring the Value of Partnering*, Larraine Segil presents the Vantage Partner approach, which includes a comprehensive set of "metrics" to use as benchmarks throughout the alliance life-cycle to make sure that the alliance gets off to a good start and that it stays on track.[33]

There are two major types of metrics: those used during start-up ("development metrics") and those used during implementation ("implementation metrics"). Some of the metrics are quantitative, but most are more qualitative, such as determining how *well aligned* the partners are. Just as in contemplating a marriage, if there are large divergences in values and expectations that are not reconciled, the alliance will be off to a rocky start and is likely to end in "divorce." Lack of alignment on key alliance "metrics" is a major reason for alliance failures.

For example, before consummating the partnership, consider how consistent the partners' missions and visions for the alliance are, how mutually beneficial the partnership is perceived to be, their expectations for things like "time to market," their typical "time to decision" (decision-making cycle time), their "competitive positioning," and their "project personalities" (management styles). Many of the most crucial considerations are usually masked by the emotions of the moment. Just like in pre-marriage counseling, forcing the partners to consider the "metrics" will very likely avoid a lot of heartache "after the honeymoon." Many problems can be avoided or resolved through greater awareness. The mere act of measurement that brings the importance of these factors to awareness is often the most important part.

## 17. Collaboration

Collaboration is a powerful force that is transforming working relationships within teams, across functions, in all kinds of organizations, and in the extended enterprise. The international research company, The Aberdeen Group, has emphasized "the very strong correlations between collaboration and success—particularly when formalized."[34]

Because collaboration is so important to the success of organizations, both private and public sector, I looked for the measurement tool that will at least be a good starting point: the OMNI Institute's *"Working Together: A Profile of Collaboration" Assessment Tool.*[35] The tool is based on extensive research and has been successfully used in a variety of settings over many years. It contains forty questions and measures five dimensions of collaboration: the context, the structure, the members, the process, and the results.

Another related construct is Climate for Collaboration. A conducive climate is the primary condition required for effective collaboration. You can measure Climate for Collaboration by adapting items from the *Wilder Collaboration Factors Inventory,*[36] which follows:

1. There is a history of successful collaboration
2. There is a shared vision and interest in achieving common goals
3. There are sufficient resources
4. There is skilled leadership
5. Diversity is appreciated
6. Clear expectations for collaboration exist
7. Roles, responsibilities, and policies are clear
8. Methods exists for addressing conflict
9. There is a favorable political and social climate
10. There is mutual respect, understanding, and trust
11. Collaboration is seen as in everyone's best interest
12. Members have a personal stake in both process and outcome
13. Members believe that the benefits of collaboration outweigh the risks
14. There is a safe environment
15. There is willingness to be flexible and adaptable
16. There is open and frequent communication
17. Sharing of ideas and information is encouraged
18. There is incentive to collaborate
19. There are no disincentives (penalties) for collaboration
20. There is adequate time and a process for team building

You can ask respondents, "How confident are you that each of the following collaboration enablers are in place?" and use a rating scale such as "very confident," "somewhat confident," and "not confident." This will certainly give you a good idea of what enablers need to be strengthened to foster a more collaborative environment.

## 18. Productivity

Productivity is the ultimate measure that both nations and organizations tend to use to measure progress. In fact, entire countries often base their economic and social policies on increasing productivity over time. However, as a short-term measure of performance, it is virtually worthless.

The traditional approach to productivity measurement is to look at either the production of employees or organizational units or to look at the total production of the entire organization. The individual or functional approach tends to create "busy-ness" ("See how long and hard I am working?"), suboptimization (how much output can Function A produce for Function B to process?), while the organizational approach can lead to production of a lot of output (even if it goes into inventory), and cost reductions (which might look good in the short-term, but can hobble the organization longer-term).

Most organizations measure their total output divided by their total in-puts (costs). Output can be anything from patients treated, tons of steel produced, airline miles flown, to revenue generated. The most familiar or-ganizational productivity measure is "labor productivity," which is simply dividing the total output by the number of workers, the number of hours worked, or the payroll of the workforce. In many cases, the typical actions aimed at increasing the productivity of labor don't really increase their pro-ductivity, just their *activity*. Productivity also tends to focus on what is easy to count, and customers, quality, service, innovation, or other important factors are almost never considered. But the biggest problem with tradi-tional productivity measurement is that it doesn't do anything to identify what is constraining productivity, and what can be done about it.[37]

Eliyahu Goldratt has proposed a much better, and potentially transfor-mational measure of productivity: Throughput.[38] Throughput is basically revenue *received* from sales, or alternatively, the rate at which the system generates money through sales (for the public sector and nonprofits, it could relate to the other value received by clients or beneficiaries). At least in the private sector view, no Throughput can be claimed until the cash has been collected (which avoids the accounting dysfunctions, such as claiming credit for producing unsold inventory).

Throughput measurement facilitates more timely visibility of how value flows *through* the organization to the customer. But, most importantly, it helps people in the organization realize that increasing Throughput cannot occur just by people working harder or increasing overall capital investment in the system without regard for work flow. As Eli Schragenheim said, "The importance of the concept of Throughput lies in its ability to support decisions by predicting how much those decisions add to the bottom line."[39] No traditional measure of productivity can do that.

Throughput is limited by "constraints." These constraints form "bottlenecks" at various points in the system, which make it impossible for additional Throughput to flow to the customer, no matter how hard employees work or how much technology is applied at other points in the system. It is all-too-common for organizations try to improve everything, but miss the key constraint. Ironically, the way most organizations try to improve productivity actually reduces *true* productivity!

Using Throughput as the measure of productivity leads to more holistic thinking about the organization as one productive system, rather than a collection of units "doing their own thing" to increase *their own* production. This approach also makes prioritization of improvement options much easier, because, once the most immediate constraint to Throughput is identified, the decision about what to improve is obvious. With Throughput as the working measure of productivity, managers and employees can now finally *do something* about it, rather than wait for disappointing productivity numbers to be announced at the end of the year.

## 19. Organizational Agility

Agility is becoming increasingly important in today's turbulent times. Many experts are proclaiming that the most successful organizations of the future will be the most agile ones, but few have offered a vision of an "agile organization."[40] While some emergent measurement attempts have been make, the measurement of Organization Agility is still in its infancy.

I have attempted to synthesize some of the major research findings[41] on Organizational Agility in the following questionnaire. I suggest that you use the standard 5-point rating scale: 5 = Strongly Agree; 4 = Agree; 3 = Neither agree nor disagree; 2 = Disagree; 1 = Strongly Disagree. Interpretation guidance is listed at the end of the questionnaire.

---

**Organizational Agility Questionnaire**

____ 1. This organization can implement changes in its business processes quickly.

____ 2. This organization can implement changes in its technology infrastructure quickly.

____ 3. This organization can implement small changes quickly.

_____ 4. This organization can implement large-scale changes quickly.

_____ 5. This organization has the capability to re-deploy and re-train employees quickly.

_____ 6. Major changes in this organization can be made relatively easily.

_____ 7. Minor changes in this organization can be made relatively easily.

_____ 8. This organization has a high capacity to adapt to change.

_____ 9. There is a high degree of collaboration across boundaries in this organization.

_____ 10. There is a great deal of modularity in this organization.

_____ 11. This organization is quite flexible compared to its competitors.

_____ 12. This organization does a good job of capturing knowledge.

_____ 13. This organization encourages learning from experience.

_____ 14. There is considerable error tolerance in this organization.

_____ 15. This organization is breaking down barriers to cross-organizational collaboration.

_____ 16. This organization is *not* bureaucratic.

_____ 17. In this organization, scenarios and guidelines are used more often than rules.

_____ 18. In this organization, work is designed to permit experimentation.

_____ 19. Problems are solved quickly and effectively in this organization.

_____ 20. Decisions are made and implemented quickly in this organization.

_____ 22. There is considerable cross-training being done in this organization.

_____ 23. This organization is designed to enable change.

_____ 24. The anticipation of change is a competency in this organization.

_____ 25. There is fast feedback in this organization.

_____ 26. Unpredictability, flexibility, and risk management is more highly valued than predictability, stability, and high assurance in this organization.

_____ 27. This organization is designed to be simple, lean, and flexible.

_____ 28. This organization is designed around processes, rather than functions.

_____ 29. This organization is transitioning from stable jobs to more flexible roles.

_____ 30. This organization is not reluctant to outsource non-core capabilities.

_____ 31. This organization is quick to respond to market opportunities and threats.

_____ 32. People in this organization are trained to deal with varied situations.

_____ 33. This organization has a high ability to acquire or absorb innovation.

*Interpretation Key*: Highest score is 160. Very high score range is 100–160. High score range is 80–100. Moderate score range is 60–80. Low score is below 60.

The most valuable use of this survey or some variation of it is for stimulating discussion. When repeated on a regular basis, it can help drive and track changes in Organizational Agility over time.

## 20. Waste

In today's hyper-competitive world, organizations are realizing that waste is a major impediment to effective competition. The time when enormous waste could be tolerated, because profit margins were so high, is long gone. Measuring waste, in order to *remove* it, has become a competitive necessity.

Measurement for the purpose of waste reduction can be truly transformational, but it is not necessarily new. It has been around since the beginning of the Industrial Revolution. Unfortunately, while traditional measurement systems are great at measuring costs, they cannot really determine which costs are value-adding and which are not. Consequently, when "fat" is cut so is some of the "muscle." Furthermore, historically, almost all waste measurement has been internally focused, concerned with reducing inefficiency, not necessarily with increasing effectiveness. That is why new, more holistic measurement tools were needed.

Although most waste reduction methods, like quality improvement methods, originated in the United States, it is the Japanese who have long been recognized as the leaders in measuring and reducing waste (or what they call "muda").[42] Shigeo Shingo, a Japanese industrial engineer, and Taiichi Ohno developed the Toyota Production System (TPS), from which the

"Lean" movement derived. Shingo defined "7 Wastes" of manufacturing: overproduction, inventory, motion, waiting, transportation, over-process-ing, and not doing it right the first time (which causes scrap, rework, and defects). He later added an eighth waste: the waste of human creativity.

In order to systematically reduce waste, rather than just cut costs, an organization needs to be able to "see" the waste. But waste is not always easy to see with existing quantitative or observational measures. People may look straight at waste without recognizing it, and they may see "waste" that is not really *wasteful* (such as excess capacity that increases flexibility).

That's why Value Stream Mapping can be such a transformational mea-surement tool. It visualizes the "value streams" (all activities required to bring a product from vendors' raw material into the hands of the customer) in your organization. It also enables the calculation of "lead times" for each activity. A transformation often occurs when people can "see" all the time that is wasted in the process—time that consumes resources but adds no value. It works backward from customer value, rather than just making more efficient what is already being done. It is not uncommon that value-adding activities comprise only 10 percent of the elapsed time, while as much as 90 percent of the elapsed time adds no value, increases inventory, and hides quality problems—not to mention, increases customer waiting time, which leads to dissatisfaction. Redesigning this value chain provides the customer with the same or better product or service more quickly, and at a much lower cost for the producer.

Lean production experts Womack and Jones observed to their chagrin that "despite a growing variety of better products with fewer defects at lower cost . . . the experiences of consumers seem to be deteriorating."[43] This led them to a unique application of Lean principles and Value Stream Mapping to services. Because the customer is so integrally involved in the provision of services, Womack and Jones realized that the manufacturing "value stream" provided only a partial view. The customer is no longer just at the end of the process, but involved throughout.

As a result of this epiphany, they advocated the depiction of the "value stream" as two parallel maps: a Provision Map (from the perspective of the service provider) and a Consumption Map (from the perspective of the consumer). This enables service providers to compare the "lead times" from both their own and the consumer's perspectives, providing a clear view of why so many customers become extremely frustrated. This new perspective provides a completely new lens, and that is exactly what transformational measurement is all about!

## 21. Inventory

Inventory traditionally has been viewed as either a major source of waste or a necessary buffer against unanticipated demand. In a business classic, *The*

*Goal*, the leading character, Jonah, a consultant, tells his client what a mess he's made of his company: "Take a look at the monster you've made. It did not create itself. You have created this mountain of inventory with your own decisions."[44] Inventory is not, in itself, bad. In today's turbulent business climate, organizations need some protective buffer, but too much of inventory ("the mountain of inventory") is clearly undesirable. Excessive inventory can place a heavy burden on the cash resources of a business, can use up space, can hide quality problems, and can become waste. But, insufficient inventory can result in lost sales, delays for customers, and lack of protection against supply disruptions and demand surges.

New thinking about production systems is that large inventories prevent production and supply chain innovation because it buffers an organization from the challenges that would otherwise stimulate innovation. It is easier to hold excess inventory than to improve planning, forecasting, production systems, and supply chain management. For example, while American auto companies were working at full capacity to produce supplies for inventory (and then selling it off through aggressive price reductions and rebates), Toyota was moving to a "just in time" manufacturing model that was producing to demand (which "pulled" the production process), rather than "pushing" it into inventory ("just in case" it's ever needed) like its American competitors.

The key to maximizing efficiency is to have the *right amount* of inventory available in the right spots in the organization, which requires the most appropriate measurement. Unfortunately, traditional inventory measurement isn't very helpful, because it is accounting-driven and one-dimensional. Depending on what the accountants say, sometimes it is good to value inventory high and sometimes it is good to value it low. But this decision is always made *after* the fact, which doesn't help to manage inventory during the process. To make matters worse, inventory is treated in accounting as an "asset," so there is typically little motivation to reduce it.

One thing appears quite clear: If a company wants to reduce inventory, it is best to make inventory as expensive as possible. Otherwise, even high levels of inventory will be viewed as "acceptable," and there will probably not be much motivation to reduce it.

Eliyahu Goldratt has developed a multi-dimensional measure of inventory: Inventory Dollar Days (IDD).[45] Inventory Dollar Days, the cost of the inventory for each day that it sits, is calculated by multiplying the monetary value of each inventory unit on hand by the number of days since that inventory entered the responsibility of a particular link in the supply chain.

Contrast this with the traditional measure of inventory, which is based on volume or monetary value alone. Inventory could sit for weeks or months, and it is still counted the same. Goldratt's approach makes it clear that excess inventory that sits around is negative, and the longer it sits in inventory, the worse it is. It can be quite transformational for a company to discover that there is more than $100,000 in Inventory Dollar Days in many locations, rather than simply knowing that the company is carrying $20,000 in inventory "assets." Furthermore, Inventory Dollar Days is a *cross-functional* measure, because it measures all kinds of inventory, wherever it is in the supply chain.

## 22. Total Cost of Ownership

Purchased materials and services can account for 65 percent to 85 percent of operating costs in manufacturing companies, and 30 percent to 65 percent in service companies.[46] It is an area of very high leverage, but it also one that is rarely scrutinized very carefully. It is an area ripe for transformational measurement.

For a long time, purchasing decisions have routinely been made on the basis of initial acquisition costs alone. The cheapest price tends to get the sale. Clearly getting the lowest price is important, but there are many other factors that should be considered. Lower cost suppliers might not provide best (or even acceptable) quality and on-time delivery.

Total Cost of Ownership (TCO) has become an important *transformational* measure. TCO is the total cost of a purchase through the entire period of ownership. It takes into account the enormous number of hidden costs in purchasing decisions. The initial purchase price is truly "just the tip of the iceberg." The total cost of purchasing an item or service can include a vast number of items, such as other purchase costs (communication, contracting, invoicing), transportation and delivery costs, set-up costs, training costs, anticipated maintenance costs, repair costs (repair likelihood, cost to repair).

Most post-purchase costs are not anticipated, and therefore they are not *managed*. This often results in huge unanticipated costs—often three to ten times the initial purchase price! For example, a computer can cost $1,000, but the Total Cost of Ownership through its lifetime (including software, upgrades, maintenance, service, and replacement) can be as high as $10,000. Obviously, the key trade-off in purchasing decisions is between "total price" and "total performance." TCO is a single measure that can reflect both sides of the trade-off. Much of the value of measurement of constructs such as TCO lies in the discipline they promote, and the visibility they provide. In Purchasing, there definitely needs to be more "full spend visibility."

## 23. Activity-Based Costing

It has been said that financial reporting systems provide tremendous detail about what has happened, but not much insight for what to do about it.

This couldn't be more true of cost accounting. For example, there is a traditional belief that increased sales will almost automatically increase profits. However, the unprofitability of parts of the organization can come as a big shock to companies that assume an *overall* profit meant that *everything* was profitable. In fact, it has been shown that, in many companies, certain products, product lines, and customers may be draining a significant amount of profits because of extraordinarily high costs that are not detected using traditional cost accounting methods. Traditional accounting provides only one response: Cut costs "across the board."

Given the traditional cost accounting approach, there is really no other viable option, since costs are *allocated* "equitably," but not "economically." When costs are being cut across the organization, we often find value-creating parts of the business robbed of capital they need, while business activities that are actually destroying value are generously funded.

Activity-Based Costing (ABC) is an accounting method that allows an organization to determine the *actual* cost associated with each product and service produced by the organization. Instead of using broad arbitrary percentages to allocate costs, ABC seeks to identify the cause-and-effect relationships between costs and activities in order to assign costs more objectively.[47]

The logic of ABC is as follows: *Outputs* (products, services, and customers) consume *activities*; activities consume *resources*; the consumption of resources is what drives *costs*. So, activities drive costs. Once the cost of each activity has been identified, it is attributed to each product, service, or customer to the extent that the product uses the activity. This allocation has been performed in various ways, but most ABC practitioners think that time studies of activities tend to produce the most accurate cost estimates.

ABC can identify the true drivers of cost. Understanding the cost drivers is powerful for *maximizing* value creation. ABC can also identify areas of excessively high overhead costs per unit for particular products, services, or customers. Identifying costs that do not add value focuses attention on these activities so that efforts can be directed at reducing specific cost drivers rather than cutting costs across-the-board. Even more impressive is that ABC can also be used to determine the costs associated with particular customers or customer segments, so that unprofitable customers can be stopped from draining resources (this topic is discussed in Section 7, Customer Profitability). Because activities are cross-functional, ABC is inherently a cross-functional measurement process, which facilitates cross-functional collaboration and decision making.[48]

However, Activity-Based Costing is not without challenges, such as the difficulty of assigning some shared costs and the need to satisfy traditional cost accounting conventions for external reporting. However, like many other emergent measures, even when it is not practical to use it fully, ABC can still be used *conceptually*. For instance, simply making your sales force more aware of customers' costs-to-serve can improve customer profitability. Even with incomplete knowledge of activity and cost relationships, some organizations are using ABC thinking to make much better decisions about products and customers than they could have done under the old model.

## 24. Economic Value Added

Even though its revenue fell 12 percent, one company reported an increased net income of 74 percent, because the company benefited from an $11.4 billion asset write-off that cut its expenses, even as it posted steep declines in sales. Another company reported an unexpected profit for the fourth quarter occurred because of an inventory adjustment that triggered the payment of executive bonuses for the year. Reports like these explain why accounting systems are increasingly being viewed with skepticism and contempt.

Although profit might seem quite straight-forward, it is actually one of the most inconsistent financial measures. Accounting profit incorporates so many assumptions and adjustments that it's no wonder people are confused, and that many accounting statements have more footnotes than a scholarly dissertation!

There are basically two types of profit: "accounting profit" (which includes only the explicit costs and revenues in its calculation) and "economic profit," which measures the revenue minus both explicit and implicit costs (also referred to as "opportunity costs"). The most distinctive characteristic of economic profit is that it includes an expense deduction for the "cost of capital," which is really the "opportunity cost" of the capital tied up in the organization.

The problem is that people have tended to use capital as if it had no cost consequences. Many companies still report earning a profit, even when their "profit" does not exceed the cost of capital. While they might be able to report an "accounting profit," they have not earned an "economic profit." Peter Drucker said it this way: "Companies do not earn a profit until their revenue exceeds all costs. . . . By that measurement . . . few U.S. businesses have been profitable since World War II."[49]

Economic Value Added (EVA) is a specific form of economic profit that attempts to capture the *true* profit of an enterprise by removing some distortions from accounting profit. The abbreviation EVA® is a trademark of Stern Stewart and Co., which has popularized the measure.[50] Put most simply, Economic Value Added is net operating profit minus an appropriate charge for the opportunity cost of all capital invested in the enterprise. The actual formula for EVA is:

$$\text{EVA} = \text{Net Operating Profit After Taxes (NOPAT)} - (\text{Capital Employed} \times \text{Cost of Capital}).$$

EVA is considered to be a good proxy for value creation. When EVA is positive, the firm is viewed as creating value for shareholders; when it is negative, the firm is said to be destroying shareholder value.

Most companies use a confusing array of measures to express financial objectives. EVA can eliminate this confusion by using a single financial measure that creates a common focus for all decision making: "How can we improve EVA?" Using EVA, all parts of an organization can become aligned around the value creation goal. Every business unit and every project can be assessed in terms of whether it is creating or destroying value.

## 25. Organizational Intangible Value

Intangibles are extraordinarily important today, including partnerships, suppliers, collaborations, skills, knowledge, innovation, patents and other intellectual property, leadership, reputation, and culture. Obviously there is a lot of value that is not listed on a company's balance sheet. But how much value? The value of companies has been shifting markedly from tangible to intangible assets. These invisible assets are the key drivers of shareholder value in the new economy, but accounting rules do not permit the proper acknowledgement of this shift in terms of the valuation of companies. Statements prepared under generally accepted accounting principles (GAAP) do not record these assets. As a result, stakeholders are blind to the real value of a company.

Some are simply attributing the difference between market value (current market value of the company's stock) and book value (the current value of the tangible assets of the company) to intangibles. Not only is this not a very accurate estimate, but it also provides little insight as to how the valuation was achieved.

New approaches to valuing intangibles are beginning to surface. More and more economists and business thinkers are beginning to (or, at least attempt) the difficult task of measuring the real and full value of a company.[51] Ben McClure has come up with a way of doing this. He calls it Corporate Intangible Value, and he illustrates the approach using microprocessor giant Intel as his example.[52] The approach goes something like this:

1. Calculate average pretax earnings for the past three years. For Intel, that's $9.5 billion.

2. Go to the balance sheet and get the average year-end tangible assets for the same three years, which, in this case, is $37.6 billion.

3. Calculate Intel's return on assets (ROA), by dividing earnings by assets: 25 percent.

4. For the same three years, find the industry's average ROA. The average for the semiconductor industry is around 11 percent.

5. Calculate the excess ROA by multiplying the industry average ROA (11 percent) by the company's tangible assets ($37.6 billion). Subtract that from the pretax earnings in step one ($9.5 billion). For Intel, the excess is $5.36 billion. This tells you how much more than the average chip maker Intel earns from its assets.

6. Calculate the three-year average *income* tax *rate* and multiply this by the excess return. Subtract the result from the excess return to come up with an after-tax number, the premium attributable to intangible assets. For Intel (average tax rate 34 percent), that figure is $3.53 billion.

7. Calculate the net present value of the premium. Do this by dividing the premium by an appropriate discount rate, such as the company's cost of capital. Using an arbitrary discount rate of 10 percent yields $35.3 billion.

Based on this calculation, the intangible value of Intel is $35.3 billion! As McClure rightfully says, "Assets that big deserve to see the light of day."

But the larger question is: So what? Once you have calculated it, what do you do with that information? The reason why I believe that this information is valuable, and potentially transformational, is that it provides all corporate stakeholders with a better understanding of the value they are managing, investing in, working with, or partnering with. We all know that you have to measure something in order to manage it effectively. When we can measure it, the scope of the management responsibility becomes clearer. However, the challenge is not to store up intangible value that is never used; it's a matter of using that value, increasing it, and turning it into shareholder value and value for the other stakeholders of the corporation. Section 12, Strategic Readiness of Intangibles, deals with the more qualitative aspect of this important subject.

## 26. Project Scheduling

Much of the work done in organizations today is project work. Most organizations are full of project teams. Although project managers often are able to claim "on-time completion," there is considerable evidence that projects, especially multiple projects, are late more often than they are on-time, because that "lateness" often doesn't show up due all the "slack" built into project schedules. (One international study found that 91.7 percent of respondents admitted that their projects were finished late![53]) Obviously, if you leave sufficient time, you will never be late, but doing so is very inefficient. That is why the way projects are currently estimated is so problematic.

The typical practice today is to ask every resource independently how long their tasks will take. Because of human nature and the punitive experiences people have had when their tasks have been late, each resource tends to estimate conservatively, based on a "worst case" scenario. This means that when all the estimates are rolled into the project plan there are implicit "buffers" built into everyone's estimates. Furthermore, when the project is implemented, almost none of those resources will "give-back" their slack time if they don't need it by waiting until the deadline date to report task completion—doing otherwise would be an admission that the original estimate was faulty. This method of project planning has resulted in a lot of "on-time" project completions of project that should have taken half that time!

Eliyahu Goldratt, who has developed as number of transformational measures as part of his Theory of Constraints, has created a brilliant solution to the problem of bogus project estimating. It is called the "Critical Chain" method.[54] The key to this approach is to schedule each task in a project based on "average" time, rather than "worst-case" time. In order to mitigate the risk of certain estimates being wrong, a single buffer for the entire project allows for some activities to be late. This means that each resource doesn't build its own "safety buffer" into its estimate, and that it is considered okay for some resources to miss their estimates because the project buffer will absorb that extra time.

The other related measurement innovation is the major tracking measure for the project: the Buffer Index, which provides timely information on the work completed as a proportion of the amount of buffer consumed. This way, the entire project team knows exactly where the project stands relative to on-time completion based on the proportion of time left in the buffer. This simple but powerful measure gives everyone a single number on which to gauge the status of a project. In addition, with this method projects have extraordinary on-time performance compared to what used to be the case.

## 27. Employee Engagement

While most organizations say that "employees are our most important assets," their measurements seldom reflect it. Few organizations perform much more than a perfunctory employee satisfaction survey to measure how "their most valuable assets" are doing. And just as with the results from many customer satisfaction surveys, the results from employee satisfaction surveys end up in a data warehouse *somewhere* because no one really knows what to *do* with the data.

So, what should be done with the trusty old employee satisfaction survey? Should it just be thrown out? Many progressive organizations are beginning to come to the realization that just as "customer satisfaction" is an obsolete construct in today's hyper-competitive marketplace, the same is true for "employee satisfaction." The major problem is that, as with customer satisfaction, employee satisfaction tends to be a transactional (moment-to-moment) rating and doesn't necessarily reflect any strong underlying emotion attachment.

Employee Engagement has been shown to be a construct that is linked to emotions, while satisfaction is simply a cognition (an opinion). It is also much more predictive of retention.

There are quite a number of Employee Engagement measurement instruments that can be used. Probably the best known is the one developed by the Gallup Organization, called the **Q$^{12}$** (12 question) survey.[55] The survey questions are as follows:

1. Do I know what is expected of me at work?
2. Do I have the right materials and equipment I need to do my work right?
3. At work, do I have the opportunity to do what I do best every day?
4. In the last seven days, have I received recognition or praise for doing good work?
5. Does my supervisor, or someone at work, seem to care about me as a person?
6. Is there someone at work who encourages my development?
7. At work, do my opinions seem to count?
8. Does the mission/purpose of my company make me feel my job is important?
9. Are my coworkers committed to doing quality work?
10. Do I have a best friend at work?
11. In the last six months, has someone at work talked to me about my progress?
12. This past year, have I had opportunities at work to learn and grow?

It's easy to perceive the difference between these questions and the typical "Tell us how much you like all the things we do for you" satisfaction surveys. This one is based on what Gallup found are most *personally* important to employees, regardless of organization. The respondents are asked about their "feelings," not just their "thoughts." This is another great example of how a relatively minor "mental model" shift can make a *transformational* difference.

Interestingly, Gallup's research has found that in a typical organization, 19 percent of employees are "actively disengaged," 55 percent are "not engaged," and only 26 percent are "engaged." On a traditional employee satisfaction survey, the "not engaged" employees might very well have indicated being "satisfied."

Other Employee Engagement surveys are offered by Satmetrix Systems, called the "Employee Acid Test"[56] (which is modeled after the "Customer Acid Test"—see Section 4, Customer Loyalty) and Mercer Human Resource Consulting's "Employee Commitment Assessment,"[57] which measures the following dimensions of the work experience: fit and belonging, status and identity, trust and reciprocity, economic independence, and emotional reward. As you can tell from these dimensions, this is also a far cry from the traditional employee satisfaction survey.

Obviously, measuring a construct like Employee Engagement won't automatically make your employees more engaged. However, when you have begun to measure contributory factors, and when you know where you stand (the baseline), then you can begin to do something to bring the score up closer to the goal level you and your organization wish to attain.

## 28. Emotional Intelligence

For a long time, it was assumed that traditional (intellectual) intelligence (I.Q.) was all it took to succeed. I.Q. (Intelligence Quotient) tests have been the standard measurement tools for selecting people for educational placement and jobs. But recent research has indicated that there are "other intelligences" (such as verbal intelligence and spatial intelligence) that might be as important, or even more important, for personal and organizational success than traditional intellectual intelligence.

Originally popularized by Daniel Goleman, Emotional Intelligence (variously referred to as either EI, or EQ (for Emotional intelligence Quotient), has created considerable excitement in the fields of human resources and leadership.[58] Emotional Intelligence has been shown to be a major differentiating factor in success.

EQ has been shown to be two times as important as IQ and technical expertise combined.[59] Emotional Intelligence skills are distinct from, but synergistic with, intellectual abilities. These performance competencies together explain from 65 percent to 90 percent of "star performer" success in a professional field.[60] According to John Grumbar, the most significant determinant of managerial failure was low EQ. Grumbar said, "Most people are hired on IQ, but fired because of EQ."[61]

Emotional Intelligence typically has four components (understanding yourself, managing yourself, understanding others, and managing relationships with others), and more than twenty competencies, including:

1. Emotional Self-Awareness (recognizing our emotions and their effects)
2. Accurate Self-Assessment (knowing our strengths and limits)
3. Self-Confidence (a strong sense of our self-worth and capabilities)
4. Self-Control (keeping our disruptive emotions and impulses under control)

5. Trustworthiness (maintaining standards of honesty and integrity)

6. Conscientiousness (demonstrating responsibility in managing oneself)

7. Adaptability (flexibility in adapting to changing situations or obstacles)

8. Achievement Orientation (the drive to meet an internal standard of excellence)

9. Initiative and Optimism (readiness to act)

10. Empathy (understanding others and taking an active interest in their concerns)

11. Leveraging Diversity (cultivating opportunities through many kinds of people)

12. Organizational Awareness ("savvy," understanding and empathizing issues, dynamics, and politics at the organizational level)

13. Stewardship Orientation (recognizing and meeting customer needs)

14. Developing Others (sensing others' development needs and responding to them)

15. Leadership (inspiring and guiding groups and people)

16. Influence (wielding interpersonal influence tactics)

17. Communication (sending clear and convincing messages)

18. Change Catalyst (initiating or managing change)

19. Conflict Management (resolving disagreements)

20. Networking and Building Bonds (cultivating and nurturing a web of relationships, seeking partnerships)

21. Teamwork and Collaboration (working with others toward shared goals)

Three popular EQ tests are the MSCEIT (Mayer-Salovey-Caruso Emotional Intelligence Test), the ECI (Emotional Competence Inventory), and the EQ-i (Emotional Quotient Inventory).[62] They are showing that not only is Emotional Intelligence measurable, but it appears to be "trainable" to a greater extent than IQ.

Emotional Intelligence might be the most relevant transformational measure for this book, since it is a crucial factor in how well measurement is "socialized." Those with high Emotional Intelligence are clearly more oriented toward socialization, and better able to make it happen throughout the organization.

## 29. Employee Safety

Workplace safety may sound like an unlikely area for transformational measurement, but you may be surprised about the significant individual and organizational impact the transformational measure can have.

As Daniel Patrick O'Brien explains, most safety measurements "measure past efforts, loss events, problem areas, and past trends. They are totally dedicated to how things *were* . . ."[63] Safety measurement tends to focus on injury statistics (such as lost-time accidents) and safety rule compliance issues (safety violations). Almost all accident data are failure-based measurements, such as: the number of injuries/deaths, number of lost work days, number of spills, cost of accidents, number of safety violations, and so on. To make matters worse, accident statistics tend to be incomplete, because some accidents aren't reported because of peer pressures ("We don't want our safety streak ended . . .") or because they don't result in lost-time injuries.

Trying to manage safety by counting accidents is like trying to fight a battle by measuring the number of casualties. Measurement used to show how well, or poorly, you *did* is going to be of little help for improving things. Furthermore, accident rates are due to chance as much as any other factor. This is because there are a lot of unsafe conditions in workplaces and people engage in many unsafe behaviors that do not result in accidents. Research has indicated that, on average, a worker would have to engage in an unsafe behavior 330 times before it resulted in an accident! When an accident does occur, it is often due to bad luck. Companies with low injury rates may actually have big safety problems; they are often just lucky.

The inherent problems with the traditional approach to safety measurement have given rise to a transformational approach to measuring safety. The measure is Safe Behavior,[64] a primarily qualitative/subjective measure that can also be converted into quantitative statistics. The concept behind it is that it is much more useful to measure something positive that you want to happen than something negative, especially since measuring accidents is more a measure of "bad luck" than of employee behavior.

According to this new paradigm, measurement occurs during random "peer observations." Rather than waiting for accidents and injuries to be reported, the observers proactively look for critical "safe behaviors"—those that would prevent the most common accidents—listed on a behavioral observation form. Although the observers are not specifically looking for "unsafe behavior," if they do happen to see it, they will give helpful feedback (but not criticism), and they will *not* record the unsafe behavior on the observation form. Only the safe behaviors listed on the observation form are recorded. Although the measurements are based on subjective judgments, observers are trained to recognize the Safe Behaviors, and their observations tend to be quite accurate.

Further, because the measurement is *positive,* there is little or no defensiveness by those being observed. Safe Behavior scores are computed for each team (not individually). These scores are recorded on a scorecard and trends are graphed and displayed, so that teams can see their progress. Employees are encouraged to discuss the measurements and exert "positive peer pressure" to encourage one another to work more safely. When predetermined "goal levels" are reached, some recognition is often provided. The idea is to use "the power of positive measurement" to increase Safe Behavior, not just to monitor it. And, unlike in traditional "accident measurement," Safe Behavior is completely under the control of the employees.

## 30. Employee Presenteeism

Current measures in attendance and health ignore probably the most serious problem faced in the workplace: Presenteeism.[65] While the presenteeism problem has existed in some form or another for centuries, the term itself is relatively new. Presenteeism occurs when people show up for work with illnesses and other issues that reduce their productivity and spread disease. Like any other construct, Presenteeism cannot be effectively managed until it is measured.

Presenteeism is widely thought to be caused by a fear of loss of income or employment on the part of the employee. Many companies do not offer sick leave benefits for illnesses lasting three days or less. On top of that, the recent dramatic increases in health insurance rates and skyrocketing health care costs have caused many employees to be more reluctant to seek medical attention.

Presenteeism can have catastrophic effects on a company's output, as well as present hidden long-term costs and wider social problems. Employees who arrive at work ill may operate at only a fraction of their normal capacity despite receiving the same wages and benefits as employees operating at 100 percent. They may also be more prone to mistakes and injuries, and they are more likely to transmit contagious diseases to fellow employees, causing even more work efficiency problems.

Now that Presenteeism has been identified and defined, it *can* be measured and managed. When the Employers Health Coalition of Tampa, Florida first studied the problem and analyzed seventeen diseases, it found that lost productivity from Presenteeism was 7.5 times greater than productivity loss from absenteeism. For specific problems, like allergies, arthritis, heart disease, hypertension, migraines, and neck or back pain, the ratio was more than 15 to 1.[66]

Researchers at the Institute for Health and Productivity Studies at Cornell University found that up to 60 percent of the total cost of employee illnesses came from Presenteeism.[67] Studies such as the above are in the forefront of emergent efforts that are beginning to deal with this problem, which has been ignored for so long because it was never measured.

## 31. Learning Effectiveness

Despite the more than $300 billion American companies spend annually on training, there is little data to show any positive impact of learning on business results. In fact, most companies and government agencies don't even try to measure the impact, either because they don't know how or feel that it is too difficult. That is why training and other learning programs are still measured by such indicators as the number of programs run, the number of participants, the number of course days, training investment per capita, and end-of-course satisfaction surveys.[68] These are not really measures of learning *effectiveness*; they are measures of learning *activity*.

While almost everyone believes that there must be a causal relationship between training and business results, few have seriously looked, and even fewer have been able to find one. There has been recent attention to isolating the ROI of training programs, but most of that activity has focused on "easy pickings," like showing that basic job skills training of employees improves performance. Actually, that is pretty obvious without an ROI calculation!

Furthermore, in this era of knowledge management, coaching, and mentoring, traditional training programs are becoming more difficult to isolate from everything else that is being done to improve employee performance. That is why I developed Learning Effectiveness Measurement (LEM) at IBM to address the weaknesses in the traditional approach to training measurement.[69]

One of the biggest challenges in learning has been how to bridge the gap between learning and real organizational impact. To bridge this gap, a systematic process was needed in order to trace the *chain of causality* between typical learning measures (acquisition of knowledge and skills) and more results-oriented organizational measures. The centerpiece of LEM is the concept of "causal chains," diagrams that are used to trace the impact of learning through a "chain" of causes and effects: from "acquisition of knowledge and skills," to "behavior change," to "individual or team performance improvement," to "organizational performance improvement," and culminating with "organizational results measures."

What is most important is not the diagram, of course, but rather the understanding that is obtained through the process of developing, examining, and interacting. The causal chain provides a roadmap for designing more effective learning programs and a measurement plan for tracking the impact of the learning programs to the desired results. This causal understanding has long been the missing link in training that attempts to achieve a *business* impact. Not only does this causal logic help identify measures that can be used for tracking all the key links in the "learning to business impact chain," but, more importantly, it provides visibility to the critical linkages needed for driving that impact.

LEM is more than just a conventional learning measurement methodology. It is an approach for *planning* and *managing* the learning and performance improvement process to achieve the desired organizational impact.

## 32. Information Orientation

While organizations can measure almost every aspect of the operation of their IT infrastructure in excruciating detail, the nontechnical aspects of information *use* are rarely measured at all. Existing measures tell us little or nothing about how well a company profiles the information needs of employees, filters information to prevent overload, identifies key knowledge sources, trains employees to use information, shares information, or reuses information. What people *do* with information is as important as, or more so than, the technology they use to manage it. Without the ability to measure "information use," most of what twenty-first-century organizations actually do can't be *managed.*

Information Orientation (IO) is an emergent measure of how well an organization uses the information it has. It is based on the extensive research by Donald Marchand, William Kettinger, and John Rollins, who have studied IO in hundreds of companies in many industries worldwide.[70] Until the development of new measures such as this, the indicators of effective information use had been largely invisible.

The IO of an organization comprises three "capabilities," only one of which relates to IT application and infrastructure management. The other two IO capabilities are concerned with 1) "managing information" over its lifecycle and 2) the ability of the organization to instill and promote "behaviors and values" conducive to the effective use of information.

IO is composed of the following practices, behaviors, and values:

• *IT Practices (ITP)*: IT for operational support (controlling operations); IT for business process support (deployment of hardware, software, and expertise to facilitate business processes); IT for innovation support (hardware and software support for employee creativity); IT support to facilitate management decision making

• *Information Management Practices* (*IMP*): sensing information (how information is detected and identified); collecting information (gathering relevant information); organizing information (indexing, classifying, and linking information); processing information (accessing and analyzing information prior to decision making); maintaining information (re-using, updating, and refreshing information)

• *Information Behaviors and Values (IBV)*: information integrity (improving security and reducing manipulation of information); information formality (increasing the trustworthiness of formal information); information control (disclosure of business information to appropriate stakeholders); information sharing (facilitating the free exchange of information within functions and across the enterprise); information transparency (increasing trust and honesty relative to information); information proactiveness (increasing the propensity of people in the organization to seek out and enhance information)

Information Orientation isn't just about doing the things listed above, but about doing them well. While organizations with low IO do many of these things, they do not do them well or thoroughly. It's not enough to just collect and organize a lot of data; you must be able to turn the data into the *right* knowledge and action.

## 33. Information Proficiency

Charles Leadbeater, author of *The Weightless Society*, said, "Our capacity to generate information far outstrips our ability to use it effectively."[71] Information work will not really become true knowledge work until individuals and organization develop better capabilities for transforming data into information, information into knowledge, and knowledge into wisdom.

I know of no measures of employee "information use" other than what Thomas Buckholtz calls Information Proficiency. For the most part, organizations hire smart people, and then throw them into a system that is drowning in data. Most of the employees barely stay afloat, much less do anything proactive or creative with this data. I know of no curriculum on Information Proficiency, though it might exist somewhere.

Ironically, a company might have the greatest IT infrastructure in the world, but if Information Proficiency is low, it is likely a cause of enormous waste. Most organizations are measuring "information availability" rather than "information use."

According to Buckholtz, "Information Proficiency is the effective use of information to define and achieve goals. Operationally, information proficiency denotes quality in making and implementing decisions."[72] There are two aspects of Information Proficiency:

1. Measuring proficiency with information to *make* decisions
2. Measuring proficiency through information to *implement* decisions

The measurement method suggested by Buckholtz is an interesting one, involving the reflection on a representative decision in which the respondent was involved. The complete questions and scoring system are contained in his book. To give you a sense of the measures, the following questions are used by Buckholtz to measure "proficiency with information to make decisions":

1. Objectives were clear relative to the decision.
2. The right participants were involved in the decision-making process.
3. An effective decision-making process was used.
4. There was appropriate management of the decision-making process.
5. Progress of the decision-making process was appropriate for the priority of the decision.
6. The key issue in the decision was determined early.
7. The participants were well coordinated during the decision-making process.
8. Communication around the decision-making process was appropriate.
9. The decision was made at the right time for optimal impact.
10. The decision (or nondecision) was well communicated.
11. Learning occurred from the decision-making process.
12. There was learning from past decisions.
13. The decision was reviewed at an appropriate time.
14. The decision included a plan for implementing it.
15. Sufficient information was used for making the decision.
16. The quality of information used in making the decision was appropriately verified.
17. "Meta-information" (information about information) was appropriately used.
18. The quality of the information used for decision-making was appropriately considered.
19. Optimal results on organizational goals were achieved from the decision.

Although Buckholtz's response options are fairly complex and tailored to each item, I see no reason why a standard 5-point (5 = Strongly Agree to 1 = Strongly Disagree) rating scale, or another appropriate rating scale, could not be used.

Information Proficiency measurement can have a truly *transformational* impact on an organization. I can't imagine an individual, team, function, or entire organization not improving the quality of its decision making if it were to diligently use this construct and spend time developing plans for improving it.

## 34. Knowledge Flow

No one doubts that better management of knowledge within an organization will lead to improved collaboration, innovation, and competitive advantage. It has been pointed out that, while an organization's "data" resides in its computer systems, its "intelligence" is found in its *social* systems. In this knowledge-intensive economy, organizations need better understanding of how knowledge is being shared so that they can manage it more effectively. In the future, "who knows what" and "who shares with whom" will be more important than the traditional symbol of status, "who knows whom."

Social Network Analysis (SNA), originally called Organizational Network Analysis (ONA), is the mapping and measuring of relationships and information flows between people in a social group or organizational network.[73] The insights resulting from such analysis are often quite compelling and counter-intuitive.

This is how SNA works: Those selected for an analysis complete a survey asking them questions about with whom they share knowledge, and what kind of knowledge they share. As a result of the survey data, knowledge networks are mapped that uncover interactions within and across the boundaries of the organization.[74] This analysis results in a map of *how* knowledge and expertise is shared. Each person in the analysis is represented by a "node" on the network map. The primary nodes are the people who are most central to this network. They are typically the acknowledged experts, who are sought out for critical information and knowledge, or people who are just prolific networkers.

In addition to the network maps, there are a number of measures that are computed by the software. Several of the measures relate to the "centrality" of nodes. These measures help determine the importance, or prominence, of a node in the network. It is always interesting to see that network location often differs significantly from location in the formal hierarchy or on the organization chart. "Degree centrality" is the measure of network activity for each node using the concept of "degrees" (the number of direct connections).

Contrary to what people may think, in personal networks, having more connections is not always better. What really matters is *where* those connections lead. "Betweenness centrality" is the measure of how many connections a particular node is *between*. For example, someone who is between many other connections is seen to play a "'broker" role in the network. A node with high "betweenness" has great influence over what flows in the network.

"Closeness centrality" has to do with how close a node's connections are. Those with the shortest paths to others are in a particularly good position to monitor the information flow in the network; they have the best visibility into what is happening in the network. "Network centralization" provides insight into a node's location in the network. A centralized network—one that is dominated by one or a few central nodes—presents a dangerous situation, since the removal of any of these nodes could cause the network to fragment. "Hubs" are nodes with high degree and betweenness centrality. A highly centralized network is at risk, and can abruptly fail, if any hub is disabled or removed. "Average path length" is the average length of the paths in a network. Research indicates that shorter paths in the network are the most important ones.

This brief description of some of the key SNA concepts and measures should give you an idea of how much data can derive from such an analysis. SNA can be used for many purposes, including: mapping personal influence, identifying innovators in particular areas, mapping the interactions of people involved in a change effort, improving the functioning of project teams, discovering emergent communities of interest, identifying cross-border knowledge flows, exposing possible terrorist networks, and locating technical experts in a field. Most importantly, this measurement enables more effective management of social networks.

# How to Begin Transforming Performance Measurement in Your Organization

As you have realized, this is not a traditional book on performance measurement! There are literally hundreds of other books that emphasize the technical aspects of how to measure. The focus in this book has been on the social and organizational aspects of performance measurement that are so crucial to *transforming* performance measurement. Not only is it a waste of time for most people to be mired in the minutia of calculating "metrics" and performing data analysis, but it also prevents leaders and other interested stakeholders from doing what they should be doing—using measurement to make better decisions and envisioning better measures that will improve important dimensions of organizational performance.

It is almost certain that your organization's potential is being held back by an antiquated measurement system. This is why James Brian Quinn has concluded that the best companies in the world are the ones that are using measurement *most strategically*—and *creatively*. He goes on to say that very soon "what are now considered appropriate measurement systems will be deemed inadequate and insufficient."[1] That time is has come!

As exciting as many of the existing transformational measures are, they all have been strongly resisted, and they and others like them will continue to be resisted by organizations that lack critical enablers. The kind of transformation I have been advocating in this book will only come through multiple *changes* in the Context, Focus, Integration, and Interactivity of measurement. Without these enablers, transformational measurement in your organization doesn't stand much of a chance. As you have seen throughout this book, it is the social and organizational aspects of performance measurement that impede real change, and it is in *transforming* these aspects that the promise of transformational performance measurement can be realized.

The sections that follow suggest some practical steps you can take right now to begin transforming performance measurement in your organization, or in the areas that you can influence. These recommendations are categorized according to the "four keys" to transforming performance measurement. Don't be concerned if you can't do all of these things, or even very many of them. The most successful transformations (especially those that touch virtually every aspect of performance like performance measurement does) are more likely to be *evolutionary* than *revolutionary*.

### *Recommendations for Improving the* Context *of Measurement*

• *Gain executive sponsorship for transforming performance measurement.* As in any change effort, leadership is fundamental to success. Executive sponsorship is the first step toward the kind of measurement leadership discussed in Chapter 9. If you are not at the appropriate executive level, then give a copy of this book to someone who is and explain to them how crucial it is to at least begin the transformation.

• *Be willing to start small.* Sure, it is great to be able to transform an entire organization, but when that is not possible, get a foothold. Start transforming performance measurement wherever you can.

• *Ensure empowerment.* Let people experiment with new measures. Transformational measurement requires empowerment to challenge the status quo. That is why a positive context and strong measurement leadership is so essential. Without that, you will only be getting more ways to measure the routine things.

• *Obtain the necessary resources.* A certain minimal threshold of resources is essential for transformational measurement, most importantly the time and patience needed to do it right.

• *Provide appropriate education.* Those involved in transformational measurement should be knowledgeable about the basics. Reading this book is a good place to start.

• *Involve key stakeholders.* Involvement is a key to ownership, and transformational measurement is not possible without very active stakeholder involvement. Reach out to those in other areas and functions who might want to participate.

• *Emphasize the improvement and learning purposes.* Make sure that those involved see that transformational measurement must be focused on improvement and learning purposes (which are the highest and most motivating purposes of performance measurement), otherwise ulterior motives will take over.

• *De-couple measurement from judgment and rewards.* Make it clear that the transformational measurement effort will not be used to judge, or as the direct basis of rewards. Both are incompatible with the experimental attitude that is essential for transformational measurement and receptivity to learning from the data

- *Emphasize the importance of honesty—even if the truth hurts.* Emergent subjective measures are worthless unless respondents feel safe to be honest. After all, if you don't tell your doctor where it hurts, you are not fulfilling your responsibilities as a patient.

- *Don't let it devolve into a "report the metrics" exercise.* Be vigilant. Old habits are difficult to break. There is always the possibility that transformational measurement will revert back to another reporting exercise. Don't let that happen!

### *Recommendations for Improving the* Focus *of Measurement*

- *Challenge old and outmoded assumptions.* Be willing to challenge the existing mental models. This requires that the implicit (and often hidden) assumptions behind existing measures be made explicit. Practice double-loop learning.

- *Take time to understand the breakthrough desired.* There is no substitute for taking the time to understand the situation that has given rise to the need for new measures and what is expected of the new measures.

- *Make sure any new measure is linked to the organization's business model and strategy.* All new measures should be clearly related to how the organization does business and what it wants to accomplish. Determine how the new measure will help release more of the organization's unutilized strategic potential.

- *Make sure that the measures are doing what they are supposed to do.* Test your proposed emergent measures! Make sure they are yielding valuable knowledge, driving the right improvements, and not having negative side-effects. If a problem is perceived, correct it promptly.

### *Recommendations for Improving the* Integration *of Measurement*

- *Place all measures within appropriate frameworks.* Never view any measure in isolation. Always view measures in the context of a measurement framework, which lets you see the relationships and trade-offs between measures.

- *Never stop increasing your understanding of the relationships between measures.* Most measures relate to other measures, and managing and better understanding these relationships is what measurement is really all about.

- *Continuously test and revise the measurement frameworks.* Never stop revisiting and re-testing the measurement frameworks to make sure that they are still valid and that the right combination of performance drivers are driving the right performance.

### *Recommendations for Improving the* Interactivity *of Measurement*

• *Involve all appropriate stakeholders in dialogues.* Remember that performance measurement at its best is more social than technical, but unfortunately the socialization around performance measurement tends to be very poor. If possible, get all key stakeholders, across functions, involved in dialogues about the new measures.

• *Foster cross-functional collaboration.* Since much transformational measurement is cross-functional, it is vital to foster cross-functional involvement. The measurement frameworks should be a good place to start in identifying who needs to be part of the collaboration.

• *Encourage interactivity.* Collecting and analyzing data is just the starting point. Increase the interactive dialogues about the data and its meaning. Realize that many stakeholders will have to be educated about transformational measurement before they will take time away from operations for interactions that might not pay off in immediate results.

• *Stimulate the data-to-wisdom performance measurement cycle.* Focus adequate attention on all phases of the performance measurement cycle. Particularly important are the all-too-often ignored phases of selection, interpretation, decision-making, taking action, and learning from experience, which most people still don't see as part of performance measurement.

• *Capture and share learning.* As explained often in this book, the major purposes of transformational measurement are improvement and learning. Too often the time and effort necessary for learning is not taken, and much of the potential value of performance measurement for improvement is lost. Don't let this happen in your organization.

\* \* \* \* \*

A recurring theme throughout this book has been the need for "measurement leadership"—not just at the top, but throughout the organization. Leaders must become more involved with measurement, not by making calculations, but by leading the transformation in their respective organizational areas. This book is a call for people to *lead* in the transformation of their organizations and their industries. Giniat and Libert have stated that "what companies and their leaders measure and manage reveals who they are, what they value, and what assets and relationships they invest in."[2] What do you, and your organization, value? Is it apparent from what you are measuring?

Creating and sustaining an environment conducive to innovative measurement is a key leadership responsibility. Some of the most important qualities for organizational success in the new economy are already the most important components for transformational measurement—intangible assets like talent, trust, knowledge, and collaboration. And that is why transforming performance measurement is more of a *social* than a technical issue.

Are you ready to look at things differently? Are you ready to begin to "see" the existing measurement system in your organization with a new perspective? The time has come for a major transformation in performance measurement and its management. It will take the kind of transformational leadership and transformational thinking that I am advocating in this book to take measures to the point that organizations like yours can use them to create the greatest value for all stakeholders.

I hope that you are catching the vision. So I urge you to start transforming performance measurement in your organization, or, if you have already started, to take it to the next level. Start small, or think large. But whatever you decide to do, *do* something!

And please let me know how you are doing at implementing these ideas, concepts, and methods, or if I can be of any assistance. You can contact me at spitzer@us.ibm.com.

# Notes

## Chapter 1

1. David Landes, *Revolution in Time*, Belknap Press, 2000.
2. Herbert Arthur Klein, *The Science of Measurement*, Dover Press, 1989.
3. Ibid.
4. Edward J. Geniat and Edward D. Libert, *Value Rx for Healthcare*, Diane Press, 2004.
5. Daryl Connor, *Leading at the Edge of Chaos: How to Create the Nimble Organization*, Wiley, 1998.
6. Michael LeBoeuf, *GMP: The Greatest Management Principle in the World*, Berkley Books, 1986, p. 22.
7. Frederick Reichheld, *The Loyalty Effect*, Harvard Business School Press, 2001, p. 246.
8. Eliyahu M. Goldratt, *The Haystack Syndrome: Sifting Information Out of the Data Ocean*, North River Press, 1991, p. 26.
9. Bob Frost, *Measuring Performance: Using the New Metrics to Deploy Strategy and Improve Performance*, Measurement International, 2001.
10. Larry Bossidy and Ram Charan, *Execution: The Discipline of Getting Things Done*, Crown Business, 2002.
11. H. James Harrington, *Total Improvement Management: The Next Generation in Performance Improvement*, McGraw-Hill, 1994.
12. Paul Rogers and Marcia Blenko, "Who Has the D? How Clear Decision Roles Enhance Organizational Performance," *Harvard Business Review*, January 2006.
13. Paul C. Nutt, *Why Decisions Fail*, Berrett-Koehler, 2002.
14. Will Kaydos, *Measuring, Managing, and Maximizing Performance*, Productivity Press, 1991.
15. Peter M. Senge, *The Fifth Discipline*, Doubleday/Currency, 1990.
16. Harrington, *Total Improvement Management*.
17. W. Edwards Deming, *Out of the Crisis*, MIT Press, 1994.

## Chapter 2

1. Michael Hammer, *The Agenda*, Crown Business, 2001, p. 105.
2. Frederick R. Reichheld, *Loyalty Rules! How Today's Leaders Build Lasting Relationships*, Harvard Business School Press, 2001, p. 121.
3. Philip Slater, cited in John Seddon, *Vanguard News*, March 2004.
4. W. Edwards Deming, *Out of the Crisis*, Massachusetts Institute of Technology, 1982.
5. Arthur Levitt, *Take on the Street*, Vintage Books, 2002.

6. Simon Caulkin, *The New Manufacturing: Minimal IT for Maximum Profit*, Economist Press, 1989.
7. C. Benko and F.W. McFarland, *Connecting the Dots*, Harvard Business School Press, 2003.
8. Steven Levitt and Stephen Dubner, *Freakonomics*, William Morrow, 2005.
9. Stern Stewart, sternstewart.com
10. Elliott Jaques and Stephen Clement, *Executive Leadership*, Blackwell, 1994, p. 190.
11. Hammer, *The Agenda*.
12. T. Davila, M.J. Epstein, and R. Shelton, *Making Innovation Work*, 2005, p. 144.
13. R. Dow and S. Cook, *Turned On: Eight Vital Insights to Energize Your People, Customers, and Profits*, Harper Business, 1997, p. 173.
14. Art Kleiner, *Who Really Matters*, Currency, 2003, p. 84.

# Chapter 3

1. Leonard Greenhalgh, *Managing Strategic Relationships*, The Free Press, 2001, p. 21.
2. John Seddon, Vanguard Consulting, www.vanguardconsulting.com.
3. Peter Hunter, "How to measure change," Peter Hunter, Hunter Business Consultancies, hunter-consultants.co.uk.
4. See Mercer HR Consulting, mercerhr.com.
5. Dean R. Spitzer, *SuperMotivation: A Blueprint for Energizing Your Organization from Top to Bottom*, AMACOM, 1995.
6. Eliyahu M. Goldratt, *The Haystack Syndrome*, North River Press, 1990, p. 144.
7. James Champy, *Reengineering Management*, Collins, 1996, p. 81.
8. Vijay Govindarajan, IBM Innovation Symposium, 2006, ibm.com.
9. Alfie Kohn, *Punished by Rewards*, Houghton-Mifflin, 1995.
10. David Meador in Peter Senge, *et al.*, *Fifth Discipline Fieldbook*, Doubleday/Currency, 1994.

# Chapter 5

1. David W. Krueger, M.D., *Emotional Business*, Avant Books, 1992, p. 11.
2. Gary Hamel and C. K. Prahalad, *Competing for the Future*, Harvard Business School Press, 1996, p. 152.
3. Michael Hammer, *Beyond Reengineering*, Collins, 1997, p. 81.
4. John Case, *The Open-Book Experience*, Perseus, 1998, p. xvii.
5. Paul A. Strassman, *The Business Value of Computers*, The Information Economics Press, 1990, p. 73.

# Chapter 6

1. Geoffrey A. Moore, *Living on the Fault Line*, HarperBusiness, 2000, p. 22.
2. Rod Napier and Rich McDaniel, *Measuring What Matters*, Davies-Black, 2006, p. 9.
3. Bob Phelps, *Smart Business Metrics,* Prentice Hall, 2005.
4. Robert G. Eccles and Nitin Nohria, *Beyond the Hype: Rediscovering the Essence of Management*, Harvard Business School Press, 1992, p. 160.
5. Peter Drucker, *The Effective Executive*, HarperBusiness, 1993.
6. Napier and McDaniel, *Measuring What Matters*.
7. Paul Hawken, *Growing a Business*, Simon & Schuster, 1988, p. 21.
8. Ram Charan, *Profitable Growth is Everyone's Business*, Crown Business, 2004.
9. Adrian Slywotsky, *The Profit Zone*, Wiley, 2000.
10. Eliyahu Goldratt, *The Haystack Syndrome,* North River Press, 1990, p. 53.
11. Michael Dell, *Direct From Dell*, Collins, 2006.

12. Jonathan Byrnes, "Dell Manages Profitability, Not Inventory," *Harvard Business School Working Knowledge*, June 2, 2003.
13. Debra Amidon, *Innovation Strategy for the Knowledge Economy*, Butterworth-Heinemann, 1997, p. 11.
14. R.E.S. Boulton, B.D. Libert, and S.M. Samek, *Cracking the Value Code*, Harper Business, 2000, p. 17.
15. David Meador in Peter Senge *et al.*, *Fifth Discipline Fieldbook*, Currency, 1994.
16. Frederick Reichheld, *The Loyalty Effect*, Harvard Business School Press, 2001.
17. Thomas Kuhn, *The Structure of Scientific Revolutions*, University of Chicago Press, 1996.
18. Marilyn M. Parker, *Strategic Transformation and Information Technology*, Prentice Hall, 1996, p. 345.
19. Vince Kellen, *Business Performance Management*, February 2003.
20. Hap Klopp, *The Adventure of Leadership*, Longmeadow Press, 1992, p. 45.

# Chapter 7

1. Bob Phelps, *Smart Business Metrics*, Prentice Hall, 2004.
2. Dan Burke, *Business@The Speed of Stupid*, Perseus, 2002, p. 178.
3. C. Benko and F.W. McFarland, *Connecting the Dots*, Harvard Business School Press, 2003, p. xi.
4. Leonard R. Sayles, *The Working Leader*, The Free Press, 1993.
5. Benson P. Shapiro, V.K. Rangan, and John J. Sviokla, "Staple Yourself to an Order, " *Harvard Business Review*, July-August 2004.
6. Hackett Research, thehackettgroup.com
7. G. Rummler and A. Brache, *Improving Performance*, Jossey-Bass, 1995.
8. Gartner Group, gartner.com.
9. Samuel A. DiPiazza, Jr. and Robert G. Eccles, *Building the Public Trust: The Future of Corporate Reporting*, Wiley, 2002, p. 84.
10. R. Kaplan and D. Norton, "The Balanced Scorecard: Measures That Drive Performance," *Harvard Business Review*, January-February, 1992.
11. Nils-Goran Olve, Jan Roy, and Magnus Wetter, *Performance Drivers: A Practice Guide to Using the Balanced Scorecard*, Wiley, 1999.
12. R. Kaplan and D. Norton, *Strategy Maps: Converting Intangible Assets into Tangible Outcomes*, Harvard Business School Press, 2004.
13. Michael Hammer, "Why Leaders Should Reconsider Their Measurement Systems, *Leader to Leader*, Spring 2002.
14. Peter Senge, *The Fifth Discipline*.
15. Michel Lebas and Ken Euske, in Andy Neely (ed.), "A Conceptual and Operational Delineation of Performance," *Business Performance Measurement*, Cambridge University Press, 2002, p. 68.
16. DiPiazza and Eccles, *Building the Public Trust*, p. 84.
17. Christopher D. Ittner and David F. Larcker, "Coming Up Short on Nonfinancial Performance Measurement," *Harvard Business Review*, November 2003.
18. Herbert Simon, quoted by Kevin Kelly, kk.org/outofcontrol/ch11-d.html
19. Gartner Group, www.gartner.com
20. Walter Shewhart, *Statistical Method from the Viewpoint of Quality Control*, Dover, 1986.
21. W. Edwards Deming, *Out of the Crisis*, MIT Press, 1982.

# Chapter 8

1. R. Kaplan and D. Norton, *The Strategy Focused Organization*, Harvard Business School Press, 2002, p. 13.

2. Larry Bossidy and Ram Charan, *Execution: The Discipline of Getting Things Done*, Crown Business, 2002.
3. William A. Schiemann and John H. Lingle, *Bullseye: Hitting Your Strategic Targets Through High Impact Measurement*, The Free Press, 2004.
4. Clifford Stoll, *Silicon Snake Oil*, Anchor, 1996, p. 194.
5. Jim Collins, jimcollins.com.
6. Samuel A. DiPiazza, Jr. and Robert G. Eccles, *Building the Public Trust: The Future of Corporate Reporting*, Wiley, 2002, p. 121.
7. Andy Grove, *Only the Paranoid Survive*, Currency, 1999
8. Bossidy and Charan, *Execution*.
9. Ibid.
10. Doug Finton, personal communication.

# Chapter 9

1. Barbara Dochar-Drysdale, *The Provision of Primary Experience*, Jason-Aronson, 1991.
2. Robert Mittlestaedt, *Will Your Next Mistake Be Fatal?* Wharton School Publishing, 2004, p. 5.
3. Larry Bossidy and Ram Charan, *Execution: The Discipline of Getting Things Done*, Crown Business, 2002.
4. Gerald Kraines, *Accountability Leadership*, Career Press, 2001.
5. Cyril Northcote Parkinson cited in Peter Brimelow, "How Do You Cure Injelitance?" *Forbes*, August 7, 1989, p. 42.
6. John O. Whitney, *The Trust Factor*, McGraw-Hill, 1994.
7. R. Dow and S. Cook, *Turned On: Eight Vital Insights to Energize Your People, Customers, and Profits*. Harper Business, 1997.
8. Steven Hronec, *Vital Signs*, AMACOM, 1993.
9. Christopher Hart, *Extraordinary Guarantees*, AMACOM, 1993.
10. Peter Senge, *The Fifth Discipline*, Doubleday Currency, 1990, p. 60.
11. Jeffrey Pfeffer, interviewed in Alan M. Webber, "Why Can't We Get Anything Done?" *Fast Company*, June 2000.
12. Frederick Reichheld, *The Loyalty Effect*, Harvard Business School Press, 1996.
13. Machiavelli, *The Prince*.
14. David Meador in Peter Senge et al., *Fifth Discipline Fieldbook*, Currency, 1994.
15. Bossidy and Charan, *Execution: The Discipline of Getting Things Done*.
16. Noel Tichy, *The Leadership Engine*, HarperCollins, 1997, p. 28.
17. David Bain, *The Productivity Prescription*, McGraw-Hill, 1982, p. 58.
18. Andrew S. Grove, *Only the Paranoid Survive*, Doubleday, 1996, p. 116.
19. R. Kaplan and D. Norton, *The Balanced Scorecard*, Harvard Business School Press, 1996, p. 15.
20. Michael J. Critelli, "Back Where We Belong," *Harvard Business Review*, May 2005, p. 50.
21. Bob Galvin, "Why has my company adopted Six Sigma?" http://media.wiley.com/product_data/excerpt/65/04712815/0471281565.pdf.
22. Jack Welch, *Winning*, Collins, 2005.
23. Josh Weston, in D. Carey and M.C. Weichs, *How to Run a Company: Lessons from Top Leaders of the CEO Academy*, Crown Business, 2003, p. 201.
24. Linda Tischler, "Nissan Motor Co.: Carlos Ghosn Shifts the Once-Troubled Automaker into Profit Overdrive," *Fast Company*, July 2002, p. 80.
25. Suzanne Taylor and Kathy Schroeder, *Inside Intuit*, Harvard Business School Press, 2003.
26. Jason Jennings and Laurence Haughton, *It's the Fast That Eat the Slow*, HarperCollins, 2000, p. 191.
27. Rudolph Giuliani, *Leadership*, Hyperion, 2002, p. 78.
28. Don Tapscott, "Fear No Truth," *Intelligent Enterprise*, March 20, 2004.

29. CIM Insights Team, "Singular Focus at Lloyds TSB," Chartered Institute of Marketing, January 10, 2003, shapetheagenda.com.
30. Michael Lewis, *Moneyball*, Norton, 2004.

# Chapter 10

1. Jack Mezirow, *Learning as Transformation*, Jossey-Bass, 2000.
2. Chris Argyris, "Double Loop Learning," tip.psychology.org/argyris.html.
3. Peter M. Senge, *The Fifth Discipline*, Currency, 1990.
4. Chris Argyris, "Teaching Smart People How to Learn," *Harvard Business Review*, 1991.
5. Peter M. Senge, "The Practice of Innovation," *Leader to Leader*, Summer 1998.
6. Peter Schwartz, *The Art of the Long View*, Doubleday, 1991, p. 53.
7. Adrian J. Slywotsky and David J. Morrison, *The Profit Zone*, Random House, 1997, p. 286.
8. William James, bartleby.com/73/1266.html.
9. The following are examples of the many resources available on this topic: John Allen Paulos, *Innumeracy: Mathematical Illiteracy and Its Consequences*, Hill & Wang, 1988; Karen Berman and Joe Knight, *Financial Intelligence*, Harvard Business School Press, 2006; Joel Best, *Damned Lies and Statistics*, University of California Press, 2001; Gary Belsky and Thomas Gilovich, *Why Smart People Make Big Money Mistakes and How to Correct Them*, Simon & Schuster, 1999; Massimo Piatelli-Palmarini, *Inevitable Illusions: How Mistakes of Reason Rule Our Minds*, Wiley, 1994; Derrick Niederman and David Boyum, *What the Numbers Say*, Broadway Books, 2003.
10. Senge, "The Practice of Innovation."
11. W. Edwards Deming, *Out of the Crisis*, MIT Press, 1982.
12. deming.org/theman/articles/articles_threecareers01.html.
13. James Allen, Frederick F. Reichheld, and Barney Hamilton, "The Three Ds of Customer Experience," *HBS Working Knowledge*, November 7, 2005, p. 1.
14. Eliyahu Goldratt, *The Haystack Syndrome*, North River Press, 1990, p. 18.

# Chapter 11

1. Robert Rodin, *Free, Perfect, and Now*, Simon & Schuster, 1999, p. 182.
2. R. Dow and S. Cook, *Turned On: Eight Vital Insights to Energize Your People, Customers, and Profits*. Harper Business, 1997, p. 134.
3. T. Davila, M.J. Epstein, and R. Shelton, *Making Innovation Work*, Wharton, 2005, p. 165.
4. Bernard Marr, *Business Performance Management: Current State of the Art*, Cranfield University School of Management, 2004, p. 16.
5. Mary Larson and Romney Resney, "Why 'Sales Force Effectiveness' Isn't," *Handbook of Business Strategy*, MCB UP Limited, 2004, pp. 233-237.
6. computerworld.com/managementtopics/management/story/0,10801,109087,00.html?source = NLT_MGT&nid = 109087.
7. Steve McMinn and Pierre Puts, "High Value Information Systems," in *Competitive Financial Operations, CFO Project, Volume 2*, Montgomery Research, 2003, p. 63.
8. David Davidson, Gregg Taylor, and Pierre Puts, "Information Integration," in *Competitive Financial Operations*, Montgomery Research, 2003.
9. Arno Penzias, *Ideas and Information*, Norton, 1989, p. 50.
10. S. Zuboff and J. Maxmin, *The Support Economy: Why Corporations Are Failing Individuals and the Next Episode of Capitalism*. Penguin Books, 2004.
11. R. Kaplan and D. Norton, *The Balanced Scorecard*, Harvard Business School Press, 1996.
12. Nils-Gören Olve, Jan Roy, and Magnus Wetter, *Performance Drivers*, Wiley, 1999.
13. Kenneth G. McGee, "Real-Timing the Enterprise," *Optimize*, August 2004.
14. Richard Brath and Michael Peters, "Dashboard Design: Why Design Is Important, *DM Direct Newsletter*, October 15, 2004.

15. William Fonvielle, "The Dynamic Scorecard vs. the Balanced Scorecard," Performance Measurement Associates, 2001.
16. standishgroup.com.
17. Matthew Treagus in Thomas Power and George Jerjian, *Ecosystem: Living the 12 Principles of Networked Business*, Financial Times Books, 2001, p. 77.
18. Jeff Woods, "Mitigating Supply Chain Chaos," *Optimize*, March 2006.
19. lafayetteprofiber.com/QNA/CohillInterview.html.

# Chapter 12

1. Debra Hoffman, "Performance Measurement Maturity: It's All About Improvement," *AMR Research Newsletter*, February 14, 2005.
2. Arie de Geus, *The Living Company*, Harvard Business School Press, 2002, p. 11.
3. For a detailed discussion of the Service-Profit Chain experience at Sears Roebuck, see: cc.nctu.edu.tw/~etang/Marketing_Research/Service-Profit-Chain.pdf.
4. R.S. Kaplan and D.P. Norton, *Alignment: Using the Balanced Scorecard to Create Corporate Synergies*, Harvard Business School Press, 2006.
5. Christopher Meyer, *Fast Cycle Time: How to Align Purpose, Strategy, and Structure for Speed*, The Free Press, p. 234.
6. Larry Bossidy and Ram Charan, *Execution: The Discipline of Getting Things Done*, Crown Business, 2002, p. 25.

# Chapter 13

1. Charles A. O'Reilly III, "The Ambidextrous Organization," *Harvard Business Review*, April 2004.
2. Rod Napier and Rich McDaniel, *Measuring What Matters*, Davies-Black, 2006..
3. James Brian Quinn, *Intelligent Enterprise*, The Free Press, 1992, p. 342.
4. Tony DiRomualdo, "The Future of Work II: Standard of Working Up, Quality of Work Life Down," Wisconsin Technology Network, wistechnology.com/article.php?id=1855.
5. Karl-Erik Sveiby, "Learn to Measure to Learn!" Presented at the IC Congress, Helsinki, Finland, September 2, 2004.
6. The Acelera Group, "What's in a Number?" August 26th, 2003, aceleragroup.com
7. babsoninsight.com/contentmgr/showdetails.php/id/829.
8. David Skyrme, "Measuring Knowledge: A Plethora of Methods," skyrme.com/insights.
9. Sveiby, "Learn to Measure to Learn!"
10. Michael S. Malone, "Digital Age Values," *Forbes ASAP*, April 3, 2000, forbes.com/asap/2000/0403/140.html.
11. valuebasedmanagement.net/methods_skandianavigator.html.
12. hooverdigest.org/991/malone.html.
13. D. Lynn Kelley, *Measurement Made Accessible*, Sage Publications, 1999, p. 2.
14. Jeffrey Pfeffer and Robert I. Sutton, "Why Managing by Facts Works," *Strategy & Business*, July 29, 2006.
15. D.Q. McInerny, *Being Logical*, Random House, 2005, p. 117.
16. Ibid, p. 108.
17. R. Dow and S. Cook, *Turned On: Eight Vital Insights to Energize Your People, Customers, and Profits*. Harper Business, 1997, p. 162.
18. Arno Penzias, *Ideas and Information*, Norton, 1989.
19. Sveiby, "Learn to Measure to Learn!"
20. Samuel A. DiPiazza and Robert G. Eccles, Building Public Trust: The Future of Corporate Reporting, Wiley, 2002, p. 84.
21. volresource.org.uk/briefing/planning.htm.

22. mallenbaker.net/csr/CSRfiles/definition.html.
23. sustainability.com.
24. measuringcompanyhealth.com/home.php.
25. Gregory Florez, "Vitality Self-Assessment," in *Rainmaker*, December 2004.
26. drjohnsullivan.com/articles/1998/121898.htm.
27. executiveintelligence.com.
28. metrus.com/issues/people-equity-measurement.html.
29. acumen.com/pdf/vli_sr.pdf.
30. Jim Collins, *Good to Great*, Collins, 2001.

# Chapter 14

1. bain.com.
2. Tahl Raz, "A Recipe for Perfection," *Inc.* magazine, July 2003.
3. beyondphilosophy.com.
4. Benson Smith and Tony Rutigliano, "Salespeople Who Engage Customers," *Gallup Management Journal*, March 13, 2003: gmj.gallup.com/content/content.asp?ci=1018.
5. Darrel Edwards, "Delight: Introduction to a New Metric and New Way of Thinking," strategicvision.com.
6. Frederick Reichheld, *The Ultimate Question: Driving Profits and True Growth*, Harvard Business School Publishing, 2006.
7. George S. Day, The *Market Driven Organization*, The Free Press, 1999, p. 5.
8. R. Dow and S. Cook, *Turned On: Eight Vital Insights to Energize Your People, Customers, and Profits*. Harper Business, 1997, p. 51.
9. Ian Gordon, "Measuring Customer Relationships: What gets measured really does get managed," *Ivey Business Journal*, July/August 2003, p. 5.
10. Michael Meltzer, "Customer Dialogue Builds Loyalty and Profit," amt.eu.com.
11. Hermann Simon, Frank Bilstein and Frank Luby, *Manage for Profit, Not for Market Share*, Harvard Business School Press, 2006, p. 4.
12. Sunil Gupta and Donald R. Lehmann, *Managing Customers as Investments*, Wharton School Publishing, 2005.
13. Farris, *Marketing Metrics*.
14. Valarie Zeithaml, A. Parasuraman, and Leonard Berry, *Delivering Quality Service: Balancing Customer Perceptions and Expectations*, Free Press, 1990.
15. http://en.wikipedia.org/wiki/SERVQUAL.
16. James J. Jiang, Gary Klein, and Suzanne M. Crampton, "A Note on SERVQUAL Reliability and Validity in Information System Service Quality Measurement," *Decision Sciences* 31, 3 (2000): 725.
17. Eric L. Almquist and Nicholas R. Winter, "Building Power Brands for Profitable Growth in Financial Services," Mercer Management Consulting, 1998.
18. Kevin Roberts, *Lovemarks: The Future Beyond Brands*, powerHouse Books, 2004.
19. IC Rating™ was developed by Intellectual Capital AB (ICAB): intellectualcapital.se.
20. Robert S. Kaplan and David R. Norton, "Measuring the Strategic Readiness of Intangible Assets," *Harvard Business Review*, February 2004.
21. ———. *Alignment: Using the Balanced Scorecard to Create Corporate Synergies*, Harvard Business School Press, 2006.
22. T. Davila, M.J. Epstein, and R. Shelton, *Making Innovation Work*, Wharton, 2005, p. 143.
23. Art Kleiner, *Who Really Matters?* Currency, 2003, p. 87.
24. For more information, see: innovationclimatequestionnaire.com.
25. G.W. Dauphinais, G. Means, and C. Price, *The Wisdom of the CEO*, Wiley, 2000, p. 273.
26. Carter Pate and Harlan Platt, *The Phoenix Effect*, Wiley, 2002, p. 39.
27. The authoritative book on the subject is: Charles J. Fombrun and Cees Van Riel, *Fame and Fortune: How Successful Companies Build Winning Reputations*, Prentice Hall, 2003.

28. For more on how Harris Interactive measures Reputation Quotient, see: harrisinter active.com/services/reputation.asp.

29. Tom Brunell, "Trust: Release 10.0," ITtoolbox Supply Chain, June 13, 2003. supplychain .ittoolbox.com/documents/peer-publishing/trust-release-100-2003

30. Dennis Reina and Michelle Reina, *Trust and Betrayal in the Workplace*, Berrett-Koehler, 2006.

31. Leonard Greenhalgh, *Managing Strategic Relationships*, The Free Press, 2001.

32. N. Rackham, L. Friedman, and R. Ruff, *Getting Partnering Right: How Market Leaders Are Creating Long-Term Competitive Advantage*, McGraw-Hill, 1996, p. 121.

33. Larraine Segil, *Measuring the Value of Partnering: How to Use Metrics to Plan, Development, and Implement Successful Alliances*, AMACOM, 2004.

34. aberdeen.com/summary/kpi/Q305_KPI_CSO_Fig10_2145.asp.

35. See OMNI Institute's "Working Together: A Profile of Collaboration" Assessment Tool at omni.org/instruments.php. The research underlying the tool is based on David D. Chrislip and Carl E. Larson, *Collaborative Leadership*, Jossey-Bass, 1994.

36. Wilder Collaboration Factors Inventory (Amherst H. Wilder Foundation), surveys.wilder.org/ public_cfi/index.php.

37. For more on the traditional productivity measurement, see David Bain, *The Productivity Prescription*, McGraw-Hill, 1982.

38. Eliyahu Goldratt, *Theory of Constraints*, North River Press, 1999.

39. Eli Schragenheim, *Management Dilemmas*, St. Lucie Press, 1999, p. 13.

40. Stephan H. Haeckel, *Adaptive Enterprise: Creating and Leading Sense-and-Respond Organizations*, Harvard Business School Press, 1999.

41. H T. Goranson, *The Agile Virtual Enterprise: Cases, Metrics, Tools*, Quorum Books, 1999; Alvin O. Gunneson, *Transitioning to Agility: Creating the 21st Century Enterprise*, Prentice Hall, 1996; Lee Dyer, *Dynamic organizations: Achieving Marketplace and Organizational Agility with People*, Center for Advanced Human Resource Studies, Cornell University, 2003; Alex Bennet and David Bennet, *Organizational Survival in the New World: The Intelligent Complex Adaptive System*, Butterworth-Heinemann, 2003; Steven L. Goldman, Roger N. Nagel and Kenneth Preiss, *Agile Competitors and Virtual Organizations*, Wiley, 1994; John Anderson, *Running the Corporate Rapids: Creating Agile Organizations*, Xlibris Corporation, 2004; Mike Woodcock, *Developing Agile Organizations*, Gower Publishing, 1999; Faisal Hoque et al., *When Business and Technology Run Together*, Prentice Hall, 2005.

42. Jim Huntzinger, "The Roots of Lean," May 2006, superfactory.com/articles/Huntzinger_ roots_lean.pdf.

43. James P. Womack and Daniel T. Jones, *Lean Solutions*, The Free Press, 2005, p. 3.

44. Eliyahu Goldratt, *The Goal*, North River Press, 1992, p. 208; see also: goldrattconsulting.com.

45. Eliyahu Goldratt, *The Haystack Syndrome*, North River Press, 1990.

46. Andy Neely, Chris Adams, and Mike Kennerley, *The Performance Prism*, Financial Times Prentice Hall, 2002, p. 125.

47. Gary Cokins, *Activity-Based Cost Management*, Wiley, 2001.

48. Robert S. Kaplan and Robin Cooper, *Cost and Effect: Using Integrated Cost Systems to Drive Profitability and Performance*, Harvard Business School Press, 1998.

49. Peter Drucker, *Management Challenges for the 21st Century*, Collins, 1999, p. 117.

50. Bennett Stewart, "EVA: The Real Key to Creating Wealth," Stern Stewart and Company, stern stewart.com/evaabout/whatis.php.

51. For more on the intangible value of organizations, see Jonathan Low and Pam Cohen Kalafut, *Invisible Advantage: How Intangibles are Driving Business Performance*, Perseus Books, 2002; and Karl-Erik Sveiby, *The New Organizational Wealth*, Berrett-Koehler, 1997.

52. Ben McClure, "The Hidden Value of Intangibles," *Investopedia.com*, January 6, 2003.

53. "Critical Chain Project Management: A White Paper," The TOC Center, Gurnee, Illinois, tocc.com.

54. S. Nokes, A. Greenwood, and M. Goodman, *The Definitive Guide to Project Management: the Fast-Track to Getting the Job Done on Time and on Budget*, Prentice Hall, 2003.

55. For more information on the $Q^{12}$, see the Gallup website: gallup.com.

56. For more information on the "Employee Acid Test," see the Satmetrix website: satmetrix.com.

57. For more information on the "Employee Commitment Assessment," see the Mercer Human Resource Consulting website: mercerhr.com.

58. Daniel Goleman, Richard Boyatzis, and Annie McKee, *Primal Leadership: Realizing the Power of Emotional Intelligence*, Harvard Business School Press, 2002.

59. Robert K. Cooper and Ayman Sawaf, *Executive EQ: Emotional Intelligence in Leadership and Organizations*, Berkley Publishing, 1997; Daniel Goleman, "Leadership That Gets Results," *Harvard Business Review*, March-April 2000, pp. 78–90; Daniel Goleman, *Working with Emotional Intelligence*, Bantam Books, 1998.

60. Robert K. Cooper, *The Other 90 Percent: How to Unlock Your Vast Untapped Potential for Leadership and Life*, Three Rivers Press, 2001.

61. "Executives Trade Stories on the Challenges of Doing Business in a Global Economy," *Knowledge@Wharton*, November 3, 2004.

62. Charles J. Wolfe Associates, "Measuring Emotional Intelligence," cjwolfe.com/measure.htm; J.D. Mayer, P. Salovey, and D.R. Caruso, "Models of Emotional Intelligence" in R. J. Sternberg (Ed.). *Handbook of Intelligence*, Cambridge University Press, 2000; en.wikipedia.org/wiki/emotional_intelligence_tests; Stephane Cote, "Working with Emotional Intelligence," *Rotman*, Winter 2005, pp. 58–61.

63. Daniel Patrick O'Brien, *Business Measurement for Safety Performance*. CRC Press, 1999, p. 19.

64. Terry L. Mathis and Dean R. Spitzer, *Developing a Safety Culture: Successfully Involving the Entire Organization*, Neenah, Wis.: J.J. Keller and Associates, 1996.

65. en.wikipedia.org/wiki/Presenteeism.

66. "Multiplier Effect: The Financial Consequences of Worker Absences," *Health Economics*, Wharton School, December 14, 2005, knowledge.wharton.upenn.edu.

67. refresher.com/!gslpresenteeism.html.

68. Dean Spitzer and Malcolm Conway, *Link Training to Your Bottom Line*, American Society for Training and Development, 2002.

69. For more information on learning effectiveness measurement, see: Dean Spitzer, "Learning Effectiveness Measurement," *Advances in Human Resource Development*, February 2005; Dean Spitzer, "Using Learning Effectiveness Measurement to Enhance Business Value," *Chief Learning Officer*, December 2005: clomedia.com/content/templates/clo_article.asp?articleid =1174andzoneid=67.

70. Donald Marchand, et al., *Making the Invisible Visible*, Wiley, 2001, p. 21. See also enterprise-IQ.com for information on software related to Information Orientation.

71. Charles Leadbeater, *The Weightless Society: Living Inside the New Economic Bubble*, Texere, 2000.

72. Thomas J. Buckholtz, *Information Proficiency: Your Key to the Information Age*, Van Nostrand Reinhold, 1995, p. 7.

73. Valdis Krebs, "Knowledge Networks: Mapping and Measuring Knowledge Creation, Re-Use, and Flow," orgnet.com/IHRIM.html.

74. For more detail on Social Network Analysis, see: orgnet.com/sna.html.

# Epilogue

1. James Brian Quinn, *Intelligent Enterprise*, The Free Press, 1992.

2. Edward Giniat and Barry Libert, *Value Rx for Healthcare*, HarperBusiness, 2001, p. 24.

# Bibliography

Albrecht, Karl. *The Only Thing That Matters: Bringing the Power of the Customer into the Center of Your Business*. Harper Business, 1992.

Ambler, Tim. *Marketing and the Bottom Line: The New Metrics of Corporate Wealth*. Prentice Hall, 2000.

Austin, Robert D. *Measuring and Managing Performance in Organizations*. Dorset House, 1996.

Bain, David. *The Productivity Prescription*. McGraw-Hill, 1982.

Band, William. *Creating Value for Customers*. Wiley, 1991.

Basch, M.D. *Customer Culture: How FedEx and Other Great Companies Put the Customer First Every Day*. Prentice Hall, 2002.

Becker, B.E., et al. *The HR Scorecard*. Harvard Business School Press, 2001.

Belsky, G. and T. Gilovich. *Why Smart People Make Big Money Mistakes and How to Correct Them*. Simon and Schuster, 1999.

Benko, C. and F. W. McFarlan. *Connecting the Dots*. Harvard Business School Press, 2003.

Best, Joel. *Damned Lies and Statistics*. University of California Press, 2001.

Black, A., P. Wright, and J. Davies. *In Search of Shareholder Value: Managing the Drivers of Performance*. Prentice Hall, 2001.

Boquist, J.A., T.T. Milbourn, and A.V. Thakor. *The Value Sphere: Secrets of Creating and Retaining Shareholder Wealth*. Value Integration Associates, 2000.

Bossidy, L. and R. Charan. *Execution: The Discipline of Getting Things Done*. Crown Business, 2002.

Boulton, R.E.S., et al. *Cracking the Value Code: How Successful Businesses Are Creating Wealth in the New Economy*. Harper Business, 2000.

Boyett, J.H. and H.P. Conn. *Maximum Performance Management: How to Manage and Compensate People to Meet World Competition*. Glenbridge Publishing, 1988.

Brown, Mark G. *Keeping Score: Using the Right Metrics to Drive World-Class Performance*. Quality Resources, 1996.

Bruns, William J. *Performance Measurement, Evaluation, and Incentives*. Harvard Business School Press, 1992.

Buckholtz, Thomas J. *Information Proficiency: Your Key to the Information Age*. Van Nostrand Reinhold, 1995.

Buckingham, M. and C. Coffman. *First, Break All the Rules*. Simon & Schuster, 1999.

Burkan, Wayne. *Wide-Angle Vision*. Wiley, 1996.

Carey, D. and M.C. Weichs. *How to Run a Company: Lessons from Top Leaders of the CEO Academy*. Crown Business, 2003.

Case, John. *Open-Book Management*. Harper Business, 1995.

———. *The Open-Book Experience*. Perseus Books, 1998.

Champy, James. *Reengineering Management*. Harper Business, 1995.

Charan, Ram. *Profitable Growth Is Everyone's Business*. Crown Business, 2004.

———. *What the CEO Wants You to Know*. Crown Business, 2001.

Cheyfitz, Kirk. *Thinking Inside the Box*. Free Press, 2003.

Christopher, W.F. and C.G. Thor. *Handbook for Productivity Measurement and Improvement*. Productivity Press, 1993.

Clancy, K.J. and P.C. Krieg. *Counter-Intuitive Marketing: Achieve Great Results Using Uncommon Sense*. The Free Press, 2000.

Clancy, K.J. and R.S. Shulman. *The Marketing Revolution*. Harper Business, 1991.

———. *Marketing Myths That Are Killing Business*. McGraw-Hill, 1994.

Coers, M., et al. *Benchmarking: A Guide for Your Journey to Best-Practice Processes*. American Productivity and Quality Center, 2001.

Collins, J.C. and J.I. Porras. *Built to Last: Successful Habits of Visionary Companies*. Harper Business, 1994.

Coonradt, Charles A. *Scorekeeping for Success*. The Game of Work, Inc. 1998.

———. *The Game of Work*. Liberty Press, 1984.

Crawford, F. and R. Mathews. *Why Great Companies Never Try to Be the Best at Everything*. Crown Business, 2001.

Crossen, Cynthia. *Tainted Truth*. Simon and Schuster, 1994.

Czarnecki, Mark T. *Managing by Measuring*. AMACOM, 1999.

Davila, T., M.J. Epstein, and R. Shelton. *Making Innovation Work: How to Manage It, Measure It, and Profit from It*. Wharton School Publishing, 2006.

Day, G.S. *The Market-Driven Organization: Understanding, Attracting, and Keeping Valuable Customers*. The Free Press, 1999.

Dell, Michael. *Direct from Dell*. Harper Business, 1999.

DeMarco, Tom and T. Lister. *Peopleware: Productive Projects and Teams*. Dorset House, 1996.

DeMarco, Tom. *Slack: Getting Past Burnout, Busy Work, and the Myth of Total Efficiency*. Broadway Books, 2002.

Deming, W.E. *Out of the Crisis*. Massachusetts Institute of Technology, 1982.

Dess, G.G. and J.C. Picken. *Beyond Productivity*. AMACOM, 1999.

Dixon, J.R., A.J. Nanni, and T.E. Vollmann. *The New Performance Challenge: Measuring Operations for World-Class Competition*. Dow Jones–Irwin, 1990.

Dow, R. and S. Cook. *Turned On*. Harper Business, 1997.

Drucker, Peter F. *Management: Tasks, Responsibilities*, Practices. Harper and Row, 1973.

———. *Managing for Results*. Harper and Row, 1964.

Earl, Peter. *The Corporate Imagination: How Big Companies Make Mistakes*. M.E. Sharpe, 1984.

Eccles, R.G., et al. *The Value Reporting Revolution: Moving Beyond the Earnings Game*. Wiley, 2001.

Edvinsson, L. and M.S. Malone. *Intellectual Capital: Realizing Your Company's True Value by Finding Its Hidden Brainpower*. Harper Business, 1997.

Epstein, M.J. and B. Birchard. *Counting What Counts: Turning Corporate Accountability to Competitive Advantage*. Perseus Books, 2000.

Epstein, M.J. *Measuring Corporate Environmental Performance*. Irwin, 1996.

Ettenberg, Elliott. *The Next Economy: Will You Know Where Your Customers Are?* McGraw-Hill, 2002.

Fine, Charles H. *Clock Speed*. Basic Books, 1998.

Fitz-Enz, Jac. *The E-Aligned Enterprise*. AMACOM, 2001.

———. *The ROI of Human Capital*. AMACOM, 2000.

Fleming, M.J. and J.B. Wilson. *Effective HR Measurement Techniques*. Society for Human Resource Management, 2001.

Friedlob, G.T. and F.J. Plewa. *Understanding Return on Investment*. Wiley, 1996.

Friedlob, G.T., et al. *Essentials of Corporate Performance Measurement*. Wiley, 2002.

Frost, Bob. *Measuring Performance: Using the New Metrics to Deploy Strategy and Improve Performance*. Fairway Press, 1998.

Gale, B.T. *Managing Customer Value*. The Free Press, 1994.

Gallagher, T.J. and Andrew, J.D. *Financial Management*. Prentice Hall, 2000.

Gallant, Roy A. *Man the Measurer: Our Units of Measures and How They Grew*. Doubleday, 1972.

Gerstner, Louis, V. *Who Says Elephants Can't Dance?* HarperBusiness, 2002.

Gigerenzer, G. and P.M. Todd. *Simple Heuristics That Make Us Smart*. Oxford University Press, 1999.

Gilbert, Thomas F. *Human Competence*. McGraw-Hill, 1978.

Giniat, E.J. and B.D. Libert. *Value Rx for Healthcare*. Harper Business, 2001.

Goldratt, Eliyahu M. *The Haystack Syndrome: Sifting Information Out of the Data Ocean*. North River Press, 1990.

———. *The Goal*, North River Press, 1990.

Gupta, Praveen. *Six Sigma Business Scorecard*. McGraw-Hill, 2004.

Gupta, S. and D. Lehmann. *Managing Customers as Investments*. Wharton School Publishing, 2005.

Haeckel, S.H. *Adaptive Enterprise*. Harvard Business School Press, 1999.

Hall, Doug. *Jump Start Your Business Brain*. Brain Brew Books, 2001.

Hall, R.W., H.T. Johnson, and P. Turney. *Measuring Up*. Business One Irwin, 1991.

Hammer, Michael. *Beyond Reengineering: How the Process-Centered Organization Is Changing Our Work and Our Lives*. Harper Business, 1996.

———. *The Agenda*. Crown Business, 2001.

Hammer, Michael and J. Champy. *Reengineering the Corporation*. HarperBusiness, 1993.

Hammer, Michael and S.A. Stanton. *The Reengineering Revolution*. Harper Business, 1995.

Harbison, John and Peter Pekar. *Smart Alliances*. Jossey-Bass, 1998.

Harbour, Jerry L. *The Basics of Performance Measurement*. Productivity Press, 1997.

Harrington, H. James. *Total Improvement Management*. McGraw-Hill, 1995.

Hart, Christopher W. *Extraordinary Guarantees*. AMACOM, 1993.

Hartley, R.E. *Management Mistakes and Successes*. Wiley, 1983.

Harvard Business Review. *Measuring Corporate Performance*. 1991.

Heskett, J.L., et al. *The Service Profit Chain*. The Free Press, 1997.

Hilmer, F.G. and L. Donaldson. *Management Redeemed: Debunking the Fads That Undermine Our Corporations*. The Free Press, 1996.

Holloway, J., J. Lewis and G. Mallory. *Performance Measurement and Evaluation*. SAGE Publications, 1995.

Hope, J. and T. Hope. *Competing in the Third Wave: The Ten Key Management Issues of the Information Age*. Harvard Business School Press, 1997.

Hope, T. and J. Hope. *Transforming the Bottom Line*. Harvard Business School Press, 1996.

Hronec, Steven M. *Vital Signs: Using Quality, Time, and Cost Performance Measurements to Chart Your Company's Future*. AMACOM, 1993.

Huff, Darrell. *How to Lie with Statistics*. Norton, 1954.

Huselid, M.A., B.E. Becker, and R.W. Beatty. *The Workforce Scorecard*. Harvard Business School Press, 2005.

Iansiti, Marco and Roy Levien. *The Keystone Advantage: What the New Dynamics of Business Ecosystems Mean for Strategy, Innovation, and Sustainability*. Harvard Business School Press, 2004.

Imai, Masaaki. *Kaizen: The Key to Japan's Competitive Success*. McGraw-Hill, 1986.

Jensen, Bill. *Simplicity: The New Competitive Advantage in a World of More, Better, Faster*. Perseus Books, 2000.

Johnson, C. Ray. *CEO Logic*. Career Press, 1998.

Johnson, H.T. and A. Broms. *Profit Beyond Measure*. The Free Press, 2000.

Johnson, M.D. and A. Gustafsson. *Improving Customer Satisfaction, Loyalty, and Profit*. Jossey-Bass, 2000.

Johnson, P.L. *Keeping Score*. Harper and Row, 1989.

Joiner, Brian L. *Fourth Generation Management*. McGraw-Hill, 1994.

Joyce, W., N. Nohria, and B. Roberson. *What Really Works*. HarperBusiness, 2003.

Kanter, R.M., et al. *The Challenge of Organizational Change*. The Free Press, 1992.

Kaplan, Robert S. *Measures for Manufacturing Excellence*. Harvard Business School Series in Accounting and Control, 1990.

Kaplan, Robert S. and R. Cooper. *Cost and Effect: Using Integrated Cost Systems to Drive Profitability and Performance*. Harvard Business School Press, 1998.

Kaplan, Robert S. and David P. Norton. *Strategy Maps*. Harvard Business School Press, 2004.

———. *The Strategy-Focus Organization*. Harvard Business School Press, 2001.

Kaydos, Will. *Measuring, Managing, and Maximizing Performance*. Productivity Press, 1991.

———. *Operational Performance Measurement: Increasing Total Productivity*. St. Lucie Press, 1999.

Kearns, Paul. *HR Strategy*. Butterworth Heinemann, 2003.

Keen, Peter G.W. *The Process Edge: How Firms Thrive by Getting the Right Process Right*. Harvard Business School Press, 1997.

Kelly, Kevin. *New Rules for the New Economy*. Viking, 1998.

Kendall, Gerald I. *Viable Vision: Transforming Total Sales into Net Profits*. J. Ross Publishing, 2005.

Klein, Gary. *Intuition at Work*. Currency/Doubleday, 2003.

———. *Sources of Power: How People Make Decisions*. MIT Press, 1999.

Klein, Herbert A. *The Science of Measurement*. Dover, 1974.

Knight, James A. *Value Based Management*. McGraw-Hill, 1998.

Koomey, Jonathan. *Turning Numbers into Knowledge*. Analytics Press, 2001.

Kuczmarski, T., A. Middlebrooks, and J. Swaddling. *Innovating the Corporation: Creating Value for Customers and Shareholders*. NTC Business Books, 2001.

Kuhn, T.S. *The Structure of Scientific Revolutions*. University of Chicago Press, 1962.

Leadbeater, Charles. *The Weightless Society*. Texere, 2000.

LeBoeuf, Michael. *GMP: The Greatest Management Principle in the World*. Berkeley Books, 1985.

Lewis, William W. *The Power of Productivity*. University of Chicago Press, 2004.

Liautaud, Bernard. *E-Business Intelligence: Turning Information into Knowledge into Profit*. McGraw-Hill, 2001.

Locke, Christopher. *Gonzo Marketing: Winning Through Worst Practices*. Perseus, 2001.

Low, Jonathan and Pam Kalafut. *Invisible Advantage: How Intangibles Are Driving Business Performance*. Perseus, 2002.

Lynch, R., et al. *The Capable Company*. Blackwell Publishing, 2003.

Lynch, R.L. and K.F. Cross. *Measure Up! How to Measure Corporate Performance*. Blackwell Business, 1991.

Magretta, Joan. *What Management Is*. The Free Press, 2002.

Malone, Thomas W. *The Future of Work*. Harvard Business School Press, 2004.

Manganelli, R.L. and M.M. Klein. *The Reengineering Handbook*. AMACOM, 1994.

Marchand, D., W. Kettinger, and J. Rollins, J. *Making the Invisible Visible*. Wiley, 2001.

Marcum, D., S. Smith, and M. Khalsa. *BusinessThink*. Wiley, 2002.

Martin, J.D. and J.W. Petty. *Value Based Management*. Harvard Business School Press, 2000.

Maskell, Brian H. *New Performance Measures*. Productivity Press, 1994.

Mayo, Andrew. *The Human Value of the Enterprise*. Nicholas Brealey Publishing, 2001.

McGee, J. and L. Prusak. *Managing Information Strategically*. Wiley, 1993.

McNair, C.J., W. Mosconi, and T.F. Norris. *Beyond the Bottom Line: Measuring World Class Performance*. Dow Jones–Irwin, 1991.

McTaggart, J.M., et al. *The Value Imperative: Managing for Superior Shareholder Returns*. The Free Press, 1994.

Meek, C., et al. *Managing by the Numbers*. Addison-Wesley, 1988.

Meyer, Christopher. *Fast Cycle Time*. The Free Press, 1993.

Miller, J. G. *Personal Accountability*. Denver Press, 1998.

Mitchell, D., C. Coles, and R. Metz. *The 2,000 Percent Solution*. AMACOM, 1999.

Neely, Andy. *Business Performance Measurement*. Cambridge University Press, 2002.

Neely, Andy, C. Adams, and M. Kennerley. *The Performance Prism: The Scoreboard for Measuring and Managing Business Success*. Prentice Hall Financial Times, 2002.

Neuendorf, Steve. *Project Measurement*. Management Concepts, 2002.

Newell, Frederick. *Loyalty.com*. McGraw-Hill, 2000.

Niederman, D. and D. Boyum. *What Numbers Say*. Broadway Books, 2003.

Niven, Paul R. *Balanced Scorecard: A Step-by-Step Guide*. Wiley, 2002.

Nokes, S., et al. *The Definitive Guide to Project Management*. Prentice Hall, 2003.

O'Brien, Daniel P. *Business Measurement for Safety Performance*. CRC Press, 1999.

O'Reilly, Charles A. *Hidden Value*. Harvard Business School Press, 2000.

Pande, P.S., et al. *The Six Sigma Way Field Book*. McGraw-Hill, 2002.

Pandya, M., et al. *Knowledge @ Wharton: On Building Corporate Value*. Wiley, 2003.

Paquette, Larry. *The Sourcing Solution*. AMACOM, 2004.

Paulos, John A. *Innumeracy: Mathematical Illiteracy and Its Consequences*. Hill and Wang, 1998.

Penzias, Arno. *Ideas and Information*. W.W. Norton, 1989.

Pepper, D. and M. Rogers. *Enterprise One to One*. Doubleday, 1997.

Pfeffer, Jeffrey and Robert Sutton. *The Knowing-Doing Gap: How Smart Companies Turn Knowledge into Action*. Harvard Business School Press, 2000.

Phelps, Bob. *Smart Business Metrics*. Prentice Hall Financial Times, 2004.

Phillips, J.J. and P.P. Phillips. Measuring Return on Investment: Volume 3. ASTD, 2001.

Piattelli-Palmarini, Massimo. *Inevitable Illusions: How Mistakes of Reason Rule Our Minds*. Wiley, 1994.

Pohlman, R. and G. Gardiner. *Value Driven Management: How to Create and Maximize Value over Time for Organizational Success*. AMACOM, 2000.

Quinn, James Brian. *Intelligent Enterprise*. The Free Press, 1992.

Rackham, N., L. Friedman, and R. Ruff. *Getting Partnering Right*. McGraw-Hill, 1996.

Rae, Leslie. *How to Measure Training Effectiveness*. Nicholas Publishing, 1986.

Rappaport, Alfred. *Creating Shareholder Value*. The Free Press, 1986.

Reichheld, Frederick F. *Loyalty Rules!* Harvard Business School Press, 2001.

————. *The Loyalty Effect*. Harvard Business School Press, 1996.

Rodin, Robert. *Free, Perfect, and Now*. Simon and Schuster, 1999.

Rummler, G.A. and A.P. Brache. *Improving Performance*. Jossey-Bass, 1995.

Russo, Edward J. and Paul J.H. Schoemaker. *Decision Traps*. Doubleday, 1989.

Rust, R.T., et al. *Driving Customer Equity*. The Free Press, 2000.

Schiemann, W.A. and J.H. Lingle. *Bullseye! Hitting Your Strategic Targets Through High Impact Measurement*. The Free Press, 1999.

Schragenheim, Eli. *Management Dilemmas*. St. Lucie Press, 1999.

Schwartz, Peter. *The Art of the Long View*. Doubleday/Currency, 1991.

Scott, M.C. *Value Drivers*. Wiley, 1998.

Segil, Larraine. *Measuring the Value of Partnering*. AMACOM, 2004.

Selden, L. and G. Colvin. *Angel Customers and Demon Customers*. Portfolio, 2003.

Senge, P.M. *The Fifth Discipline*. Doubleday/Currency, 1990.

————. *The Fifth Discipline Fieldbook*. Doubleday/Currency, 1994.

Shank, J. and V. Govindarajan. *Strategic Cost Management*. The Free Press, 1993.

Shapiro, E.C. *Fad Surfing in the Boardroom*. Addison-Wesley, 1995.

Shenk, David. *Data Smog: Surviving the Information Glut*. HarperSanFrancisco, 1997.

Shillito, L. and D. DeMarle. *Value: Its Measurement, Design, and Management*. Wiley, 1992.

Siciliano, Gene. *Finance for the Non-Financial Manager*. McGraw-Hill, 2003.

Siebel, Thomas and Michael Malone. *Virtual Selling*. The Free Press, 1996.

Sink, D.S., et al. *By What Method?* Industrial Engineering and Management Press, 1995.

Sloma, Richard S. *How to Measure Managerial Performance*. Macmillan, 1980.

Slywotzky, Adrian J. *Value Migration*. Harvard Business School Press, 1996.

Slywotzky, Adrian J. and D.J. Morrison. *The Profit Zone*. Random House, 1997.

Smith, Debra. *The Measurement Nightmare*. St. Lucie Press, 2000.

Smith, Douglas K. *Make Success Measurable*. Wiley, 1999.

Smith, P.G. and D.G. Reinertsen. *Developing Products in Half the Time*. Van Nostrand Reinhold, 1995.

Spitzer, Dean R. *SuperMotivation: A Blueprint for Energizing Your Organization from Top to Bottom*. AMACOM, 1995.

Stack, Jack. *The Great Game of Business*. Doubleday/Currency, 1992.

Stalk, George and Thomas Hout. *Competing Against Time*. The Free Press, 1990.

Stallkamp, Thomas T. *Score!* Wharton School Publishing, 2005.

Stewart, G. Bennett. *The Quest for Value*. Harper Business, 1991.

Stewart, Thomas A. *Intellectual Capital*. Doubleday/Currency, 1997.

Stone, M., A. Bond, and B. Foss. *Consumer Insight: How to Use Data and Market Research to Get Closer to Your Customer*. Kogan Page, London, 2004.

Strassmann, Paul A. *Information Payoff*. The Free Press, 1985.

———. *The Business Value of Computers*. The Information Economics Press, 1990.

Sullivan, Patrick H. *Value-Driven Intellectual Capital: How to Convert Intangible Corporate Assets into Market Value*. Wiley, 2000.

Sveiby, Karl E. *The New Organizational Wealth: Managing and Measuring Knowledge-Based Assets*. Berrett-Koehler, 1997.

Svendsen, Ann. *The Stakeholder Strategy*. Berrett-Koehler, 1998.

Tapscott, D. and D. Ticoll. *The Naked Corporation: How the Age of Transparency Will Revolutionize Business*. Free Press, 2003.

Taylor, David A. *Supply Chains*. Addison-Wesley, 2004.

Thakor, A.V. *Becoming a Better Value Creator*. Jossey-Bass, 2000.

Thoreson, J.D. and J.H. Blankenship. *Information Secrets*. Valuable Information, 1966.

Thorp, John. *The Information Paradox*. McGraw-Hill, 1998.

Turney, Peter B.B. *Common Cents: The ABC Performance Breakthrough*. Cost Technology, Hillsboro, Ore., 1991.

Ulrich, D. and N. Smallwood. *Why the Bottom Line Isn't! How to Build Value Through People and Organization*. Wiley, 2003.

Underhill, Paco. *Why We Buy: The Science of Shopping*. Simon and Schuster, 1999.

Underwood, Jim. *What's Your Corporate IQ? How the Smartest Companies Learn, Transform, Lead*. Dearborn, 2004.

Walker, S.F. and J.W. Marr. *Stakeholder Power*. Perseus Publishing, 2001.

Walters, Jonathan. *Measuring Up*. Governing Books, 1998.

Wheeler, D.J. and D.S. Chambers. *Understanding Statistical Process Control*. Statistical Process Controls, Knoxville, Tenn., 1986.

Whiteley, R.C. *The Customer-Driven Company*. Addison-Wesley, 1991.

Yankelovich, Daniel *The Magic of Dialogue*. Simon and Schuster, 1999.

Zuboff, S. and J. Maxmin. *The Support Economy*. Penguin Books, 2004.

# Index

accountability
  defined, 45
  as key to self-management, 62
  measurable, 46
  positive *vs.* negative, 16, 45–46
Acelera Group, 201
Activity-Based Costing (ABC), 83,
    240–242
  change to from traditional account-
    ing, 127
  as example of transformational
    thinking, 198
  methodology, 241
activity measures, 31
Alexeyev, Vasili, 24
Allied Signal, 135
Almquist, Eric, 224
Amidon, Debra, 78
Archimedes, 79
Argyris, Chris, 147
assets, intangible, *see* intangible assets
Autonomous Teams concept, 125

Bain, David, 130
Balanced Scorecard, 91–92, 129, *see
    also* scorecards
  *vs.* dynamic business scorecards,
    171
  principles, 92

baseline measurement, 156
Beane, Billy, as measurement leader,
    138–139
Benko, C., 32, 87
Bennett, Steve, as measurement
    leader, 136–137
Berry, Leonard, 223
betweenness centrality, 255
Blenko, Marcia, 18
Bossidy, Larry, 17, 104, 116, 123,
    128, 187
  as measurement leader, 135–136
Boulton, R. E. S., 79
Brache, A., 89
Brand Equity, 223–225
  measurable factors, 224
Brath, Richard, 170
Brunell, Tom, 230
Buckholtz, Thomas, 253–254
Buffer Index, 245
Burke, Dan, 87
business architecture, *see* business
    strategy
business models
  components, 75
  enhancement, 75
  generic, 75
  and strategy, 74–75
Business Performance Measurement
    (BPM), 163–164

business strategy
  and business model, 74–75
  conversion into practice, 92
  need for understanding of, 164

Carey, Chris, 221
Case, John, 63
Caulkin, Simon, 32
Champy, James, 42
Charan, Ram, 74, 104, 116, 123, 128, 187
cheating, *see* measurement cheating
Cheskin, Louis, 206
chief measurement officer (CMO)
  need for, 102
  role of, 139
closeness centrality, 256
Cohill, Andrew, 175
Collaboration, 233–234
collaborative learning, 187
Collins, Jim, 109, 212
communication, *see* dialogue
CompStat program, 137
conformity, 148
context of measurement, 4
  challenges, 101
  and communications, 59
  and constraints, 59
  as continuum, 61
  and expectations, 57–58
  and history of measurement, 58–59
  and human factor, 60–61
  improvement of, 181–183
  increasing positive change, 62, 63–67
  as key to transformational measurement, 52
  and leadership, 58
  and organizational climate, 57
  positive *vs.* negative, 40–41, 67
  recommendations for improvement, 258–259
  and resources, 59
  transforming power of, 67

Cook, Susan, 35, 125, 206, 218
Corporate Intangible Value, 243
Critelli, Michael J., as measurement leader, 135
"Critical Chain" method, 245
cross-functional measures, 53, 99–101, 156, 185, 209
  opportunities for, 209
Customer Delight, 216–217
*Customer Delight Index,* 217
Customer Engagement, 214–215
  measuring instrument (Gallup), 215
Customer Experience, 83, 214–215
  *vs.* customer service, 215
Customer Lifetime Value (CLV), 83, 222
Customer Loyalty, 217–218
customer measurement framework, 212
Customer Profitability, 221–222
  shifts in thinking about, 82–83
Customer Relationship, 83, 218–219
  measurable indicators, 219
Customer Relationship Management (CRM), 219
customer satisfaction, 84
Customer Satisfaction Index, 158

dashboards
  as exception reports, 169–170
  future of, 171
  shortcomings, 170
  use of "idiot lights," 170
data
  conversion to wisdom, 105–109
  disintegration of, 90
  disparate quality of, 90
  gaining maximum benefit from, 187
  increasing integration of, 185
  *vs.* information, 105
  lack of insights from, 164
  quality problems with, 90
Dauphinais, G. W., 228

Davila, T., 162, 227
Day, George, 218
decision making, improved by measurement, 18
de Geus, Arie, 179
Dell Computer Corporation
  "cash conversion cycle time" as key measure, 78
  "Dell direct" business model, 77
Dell, Michael, 77
Deming, W. Edwards, 19, 20, 26, 27, 101, 114, 153, 154
dialogue
  defined, 115, 116
  vs. discussion, 115
  and diversity of perspective, 115–116
  importance of, 187
  as interactivity, 115–116
DiPiazza, Samuel A., Jr., 91, 95, 113, 209
DiRomualdo, Tony, 199
disintegration
  of data, 90
  of measurement, 89–90
  of organizations, 87–88
distrust, of measurement, 45
Dockar-Drysdale, Barbara, 122
double-loop learning, 143–145
  example of, 157
Dow, Roger, 35, 125, 206, 218
Drucker, Peter, 71, 242
Dubner, Stephen, 33
dysfunctional measurement, see measurement dysfunction

Eccles, Robert, 70, 95, 113, 209
Economic Value Added (EVA), 242–243
  formula, 242
Edwards, Darrel, 217
Einstein, Albert, 98
Ekvall, Goran, 227
Eliot, T. S., 98

emergent measures, 81–82, see also transformational measures
  automation of, 166–167
  trial use of, 201
Emotional Intelligence (EI), 247–248
  competencies, 247–248
  tests, 248
emotions, as obstacles to decision making, 107
"Employee Acid Test" (Satmetrix), 246–247
"Employee Commitment Assessment" (Mercer), 247
Employee Engagement, 245–247
Employee Presenteeism, 250–251
employees
  attitudes about measurement, 60–61
  capabilities of, 61
  disempowerment of, 43–44
  empowerment of, 49
  fear of measurement, 45
  resistance to measurement, 46
Employee Safety, 249–250
Enterprise Resource Planning (ERP), 90
Epstein, M. J., 162, 227
estimating
  acceptability of, 206
  accuracy vs. appropriateness, 207
Euske, Ken, 95
evaluation
  defined, 41
  judgment as outcome of, 41
  vs. measurement, 41–42

fear, of measurement, 45
FedEx, 139
feedback, facilitated by measurement, 17
filtering, 147
Finton, Doug, 118
fixed mindsets, 147
focus of measurement
  importance of, 68–69

focus of measurement (*continued*)
  improvement of, 183–184, 259
  as key to transformational measure-
    ment, 52–53
Fonvielle, William, 171
Friedman, L., 232
Frost, Bob, 16

Galvin, Bob, as measurement leader,
  135
General Electric, 135
Geniat, Edward J., 11
Ghosn, Carlos, as measurement
  leader, 136
Giniat, Edward, 260
Giuliani, Rudolph, 104
  as measurement leader, 137
goal-setting
  measurement as basis for, 17
  and SMART acronym, 17
*Goal, The* (Goldratt), 238–239
Goldratt, Eliyahu, 15, 41, 76, 159,
  234, 239, 245
Goleman, Daniel, 247
Govindarajan, Vijay, 43
Greenhalgh, Leonard, 38, 232
Grove, Andy, 113, 133
Grumbar, John, 247
Gupta, Sunil, 222

habit, 148
Hamel, Gary, 62
Hammer, Michael, 22, 35, 62, 95,
  145, 152
Harrah's Entertainment, 138
Harrington, H. James, 18, 19
Harry, Mikel, 135
Hart, Christopher, 125
Hawken, Paul, 73, 74
high-leverage measurement, 79–81
Hoffman, Debra, 177
horizontal integration, 86–87
Hronec, Steven, 125
Hunter, Peter, 40

IC Rating methodology, 225
Immelt, Jeff, 33
information
  acquisition of *vs.* learning, 141
  and data, 105
  and knowledge, 142
informational measurement, 23
Information Behaviors and Values
  (IBV), 253
Information Management Practices
  (IMP), 252–253
Information Orientation (IO),
  252–253
Information Proficiency, 253–255
  sample questions, 254
Innovation Climate, 227–228
Innovation Climate Questionnaire
  (ICQ), 227
in-process measurement, 156
Input-Process-Output-Outcome
  model, 155
inquiry, *vs.* advocacy, 150
intangible assets, *see also* Intellectual
  Capital (IC); Strategic Readiness
  of Intangibles
  difficulty of measuring, 202–203
  intellectual capital as, 203–204
  qualitative measurement of,
    205–206
  and Skandia Intangible Assets Nav-
    igator, 203
  subjective measurement of,
    207–208
  transformational measurement of,
    78–79, 204–211
  and Value Creation Index, 203
integration of measurement, *see also*
    cross-functional measures
  encouragement of, 133–134
  improvement of, 184–186, 259
  as key to transformational measure-
    ment, 53
  types of, 86–87
  use of cross-functional measures,
    99–101

Intellectual Capital (IC), 225
interactivity of measurement
  and data-to-wisdom transforma-
    tion, 109–110
  dialogue as key, 115–116, 119
  importance of, 104–105
  improvement of, 186–188
  as key to transformational measure-
    ment, 54
  recommendations for improve-
    ment, 260
  in today's environment, 118–119
Intuit, 136–137
intuition, *vs.* measurement, 122
intuitive leader, myth of, 123
Inventory, 238–240
Inventory Dollar days (IDD),
  239–240
IT Practices (ITP), 252
Ittner, Christopher, 96

James, William, 148
Jaques, Elliott, 34
Johnson & Johnson, 137
Jones, Daniel, 238
judgment, separation from measurement, 131
justification, 147–148
"just in time" manufacturing model,
  239

Kaplan, Robert, 91, 93, 99, 104, 133,
  169, 186, 226
Kaydos, Will, 18
Kelleher, Herb, 202
Kelley, D. Lynn, 205
Kelvin, Lord, 19
Kettinger, William, 252
key performance indicators (KPIs),
  145
Kleiner, Art, 35
Klein, Herbert Arthur, 10
Klopp, Happ, 85
knowledge, *vs.* information, 106, 142
Knowledge Flow, 255–256

Kohn, Alfie, 44
Kraines, Gerald, 123
Krueger, David, 61
Kuhn, Thomas, 81

labeling, 147
Landes, David, 10
Larcker, David, 96
Larson, Mary, 165
Leadbeater, Charles, 253
"lean" movement, 238
learning, *see also* transformational
    learning
  and accommodation, 142
  and assimilation, 142
  collaborative, 187
  double-loop, 143–145
  effectiveness *vs.* activity, 251
  informal, 142–143
  in spite of curriculum, 141
  organizational, 145–147
  process, 140–143
  single-loop, 143–144
"learning disabilities," individual *vs.*
    organizational, 147
Learning Effectiveness, 251–252
Learning Effectiveness Measurement
    (Spitzer), 251
learning loop, 142–143
Lebas, Michel, 95
LeBoeuf, Michael, 12
Lehmann, Donald, 222
leverage, 79
Levitt, Arthur, 31
Levitt, Steven, 33
Lewis, Michael M., 138
Libert, B., 79, 260
Libert, Edward D., 11
Linux operating system, 36
Lloyd's Bank, 138
Loveman, Gary, as measurement
    leader, 138
"lovemarks," 224

Machiavelli, 127
Malone, Michael, 204

management, measurement as foundation of, 13
Marchand, Donald, 252
Marr, Bernard, 164
maturity, see performance measurement maturity
Maxmin, J., 168
McCaw, Craig, 33
McClure, Ben, 243–244
McDaniel, Rich, 68, 73, 197
McFarland, F. W., 32, 87
McGee, Kenneth, 170
McInerny, D. Q., 206
McMinn, Steve, 167
Meador, David, 45, 80, 127
Means, G., 228
measurement, see also measures; performance measurement
  as basis for goal-setting, 17
  cheating, see measurement cheating
  to clarify expectations, 16
  context of, see context of measurement
  creativity in, 84
  disintegration of, 89–90
  as driver of behavior, 15
  dysfunction, see measurement dysfunction
  early tools, 10
  employee attitude toward, 39–40
  employee resistance, 46
  employees' attitudes toward, 39–40, 60–61
  to enable accountability, 16
  to enable prediction, 20
  vs. evaluation, 41–42
  to facilitate feedback, 17
  to focus attention, 16, 68
  focus of, see focus of measurement
  as foundation of management, 13–14
  high-leverage, 79–81
  history of, 58–59
  importance of dialogue, 105
  to improve decision making, 18
  to improve execution, 17
  to improve integration, 184–186
  to improve interactivity, 186–188
  to improve problem solving, 18
  to increase alignment, 18
  to increase objectivity, 16–17
  as instigator of informed action, 11
  integration of, see integration of measurement
  interactivity of, see interactivity of measurement
  vs. intuition, 122
  knowing the limits of, 44
  management's uses of, 39–40, 47
  motivational use of, 20, 44, 46–47
  negative experiences with, 38
  origins of, 9
  pervasiveness of, 10–11
  phases of, 156–157
  positive vs. negative context, 40–41
  potential for distortion, 21
  to promote consistency, 17
  to provide early warning signals, 19
  purpose of, 42
  qualitative, 205–206
  of the right things, 52–53, 69–71
  separation from rewards, 131–132
  social nature of, 9
  as steering vs. grading tool, 43
  strategic, 90–91
  subjective, 207–208
  as task, 40
  types of, 22
  and visibility of performance, 15–16
  of what matters most, 76
measurement change
  creating environment for, 128–132
  resistance to, 127–128
measurement cheating, 33–34
  examples of, 34
  "Roger Jones Phenomenon," 34
measurement communications, 59

measurement constraints, 59
measurement conversations, support
    of, 151–152
measurement dysfunction
  cause of, 23
  and conspiracy of silence, 37
  defined, 22
  and employees, 35
  examples, 22, 24–26, 27–29
  fear-induced, 26–29
  incentive-based, 25–26
  measuring too much, 34–35
  measuring what "looks good,"
    30–31
  measuring wrong things, 29–30,
    52–53
  motive for, 37
  opportunity for, 36
  responses to, 37
measurement expectations, 57–58
measurement frameworks
  alternative format, 100
  continual improvement of, 187
  conversations around, 152
  for customer relationships, 212
  development of, 97–99, 185
  to improve decision making, 95
  to increase visibility, 94
  initial hypotheses, 97, 100–101
  to manage the future, 95–96
  need for innovation, 100–101
  performance vs. cost trade-offs,
    96–97
  and relationships, 94
  sample format, 98
  strategy map approach, 93, 99
measurement incidents, 10
measurement innovation
  encouragement of, 134
  incentives tied to, 43
measurement leaders
  creating environment for change,
    128–132
  need for commitment, 130

need for truth, 131
  profiles of, 134–139
measurement leadership, 58
  absence of, 123–126
  importance of, 121
  lack of, 122
  to transform context of measure-
    ment, 183
"measurement literacy," 107
measurement process, as component
    of measurement system, 59
measurement resources, 59
measurement systems
  and cheating, 33–34
  dealing with defects in, 36
  lack of integration, 14
  need for effectiveness, 71
  unfocused, 71
measurement technology, see also
    technology
  automation of emergent measures,
    166–167
  designing in social interaction,
    173–174
  capability of staff, 173
  client-supplier relationship as key,
    171–172
  and cultural constraints, 168
  failure rate, 171–172
  involvement of stakeholders in, 175
  need for due diligence, 174
  need for house cleaning, 168
  and organizational integration,
    167–168
  readiness of measurement system,
    173
  steps for successful investment in,
    174–176
  successful adoption of, 171–174
  total cost of ownership, 172
measures, see also measurement; per-
    formance measurement
  as component of measurement sys-
    tem, 59

measures (*continued*)
  emergent, 81–82
  multiple, 210–211
  proper usage of term, 69–70
  routine, 69
  subjective, 158
  transformational, *see* transforma-
    tional measures
Men's Wearhouse, 74
metrics
  avoiding institutionalization, 200
  development *vs.* implementation,
    232
  usage of term, 69–70
Meyer, Christopher, 187
Mezirow, Jack, 140
Mittlestaedt, Robert, 123
Moore, Geoffrey, 68
Morrison, David, 148
motivational measurement, 20, 23, 44
Motorola, 135
"multiple-gate" assessment, 50
multiple measures, 210–211

Napier, Rod, 68, 73, 197
negative accountability, 16, 45–46
negative measurement, 38, *see also*
    measurement dysfunction
Net Promoter Score (NPS), 217
Nissan Motor Co., 136
Nohria, Nitin, 70
Norton, David, 91, 93, 99, 104, 133,
    169, 186, 226
numbers, *see* statistics
Nutt, Paul, 18

Oakland Athletics, 138
O'Brien, Daniel Patrick, 249
Ohno, Taiichi, 237
Olve, Nils-Goran, 92, 169
Omni Institute, 233
Open Book Management, 64, 136
O'Reilly, Charles, 196
Organizational Agility, 235–237

Organizational Agility Questionnaire,
    235–237
organizational climate, dimensions of,
    57
Organizational Intangible Value,
    243–244
organizational learning, 145–147
  examples of, 146
  to foster transformational measure-
    ment, 146
organizational measurement systems,
    *see also* measurement systems
  disparate "silos" in, 31
  negative aspects, 21–22
Organizational Trust, 229–231
Organizational Trust Questionnaire,
    230–231
organizations
  complexity of, 11
  disintegrated, 87–88
  effect of poor measurement on,
    14–15
  history of measurement, 58–59
  importance of alignment, 89–90
  key to success of, 1, 72–74
  measuring capability of, 116
  need for business architecture, 164
  need for excellence in measure-
    ment, 11–12
  wasteful activities in, 125

Palmisano, Sam, 43
paradigms
  defined, 2
  shift in, 2
Parasuraman, A., 223
Parker, Marilyn, 81
Parkinson, Cyril Northcote, 124
Partner Relationships, 232
Pasteur, Louis, 10
Pate, Carter, 228
Penzias, Arno, 168, 206
performance dashboards, *see* dash-
    boards

performance measurement, *see also*
    measurement; transformational
    performance measurement
  building trust, 182
  change in paradigm, 2
  to combat bias and habits, 148–149
  context of, 4
  employee attitude toward, 3
  increased involvement in, 182
  of intangibles, 99
  and learning, 182
  as lens for viewing organization, 2
  major functions of, 15–20
  need for excellence in, 11
  and openness, 182
  optimal environment for, 4
  programmatic, 189
  purposes of, 182
  relevance, 181
  resources for, 182–183
  role of technology, 163–164
  specialized, 189
  transformation cycle, 179–180
performance measurement cycle
  Analyze phase, 112
  Collect phase, 112
  Commit phase, 114
  Decide phase, 113–114
  defined, 110
  Interpret phase, 113
  Plan phase, 111
  Review phase, 114–115
  role of technology in, 164–165
  sample capability assessment,
    117–118
  Select phase, 111–112
  Take Action phase, 114
performance measurement maturity
  assessment, *see* Transformational
    Measurement Maturity Assess-
    ment
  concepts associated with, 178
  *vs.* human development maturity,
    178

social aspects as key, 180
  transformation process, 179–180
Performance Measurement Maturity
  Model, 188–189
performance measurement system
  components, 59–60
  technical infrastructure, 60
Perkin-Elmer, 81
Peters, Michael, 170
Pfeffer, Jeffrey, 126, 205
Phelps, Bob, 69, 86
Pitman, Brian, as measurement
  leader, 138
Pitney Bowes, 135
Plan-Do-Check-Act cycle, 101
Platt, Harlan, 228
positive accountability, 16, 45–46
positive work measurement, examples, 63–67
Prahalad, C. K., 62
prediction, as key to management,
  154–155
predictive measurement, 156,
  209–210
presenteeism, *see* Employee Presenteeism
Price, C., 228
problem solving
  improved by measurement, 18
  need to find root causes, 19
process measurement control charts,
  80
Productivity, 234–235
Project Scheduling, 244–245
Pujals, Leo, as measurement leader,
  137
Puts, Pierre, 167

$Q^{12}$ survey (Gallup), 246
qualitative measurement, 80, 157–
  158, 205–206
Quinn, Feargal, 156
Quinn, James Brian, 197, 257

Rackham, N., 232
Rangan, V. K., 88

rating scales, 208
Reichheld, Frederick, 13, 23, 80, 127, 217
Renault S. A., 136
Renwick, Glen, as measurement leader, 137–138
Reputation, 228–229
Reputation Quotient (RQ), 228–229
Resney, Romney, 165
retrospective measurement, 156
"reverse synergy," 147
rewards
  and measurement dysfunction, 23
  power of, 12–13
  role of measurement systems, 13
  separation from measurement, 131
Rodin, Robert, 162
Rogers, Paul, 18
Rollins, John, 252
Ruff, R., 232
Rummler, G., 89

Safe Behavior measure, 249–250
Samek, S. M., 79
Sayles, Leonard, 88
Schragenheim, Eli, 235
Schwartz, Peter, 147
scorecards
  balanced, see Balanced Scorecard
  future of, 171
  need for interactivity, 169
  perspectives, 169
score keeping, in sports vs. at work, 3
Sedden, John, 39
Segil, Larraine, 232
self-management, as indicator of positive change, 62–63
Senge, Peter, 19, 95, 125, 147, 150, 180
Service Quality, 222–223
Service Quality Indicator (SQI), 139
SERVQUAL, 213, 223
Shapiro, Benson, 88

Shelton, R., 162, 227
Shewhart, Walter, 101
Shingo, Shigeo, 237–238
silo phenomenon, 31, 88
Simon, Herbert, 96
single-loop learning, 143–144
Six Sigma, 104, 129, 135, 145
  vs. transformational measures, 71–72
Skandia Intangible Assets Navigator, 203
Skyrme, David, 202
Slater, Philip, 26
Slywotsky, Adrian, 75, 148
SMART acronym, 17
Smith, Bill, 135
Smith, Frederick W., 166
  as measurement leader, 139
Social Network Analysis (SNA), 255
Southwest Airlines
  business model, 76
  "turnaround time" as key measure, 77
Stack, Jack, as measurement leader, 136
Statistical Process Control (SPC), 63
statistics
  correlation vs. causation, 154
  interpretation of, 153–154
Sterman, John, 201
Stern Stewart and Co., 33, 242
Stoll, Clifford, 107
Strassman, Paul, 67
strategic measurement, 90–91
Strategic Readiness of Intangibles, 226–227
strategy maps, 93, 99
subjective measurement, 207–208
suboptimization
  defined, 31
  examples of, 32–33
  and project proliferation, 32
Sunbeam Corporation, 34

*Supermotivation* (Spitzer), 40, 41
Survey/Feedback/Action (SFA), 139
Sutton, Robert, 205
Sveiby, Karl-Erik, 200, 203, 207
Sviokla, John J., 88
"system thinking," 155

target fixation, 148
technical infrastructure, as component of measurement system, 60
technology, *see also* measurement technology
   appropriate uses, 188
   design *vs.* adoption process, 166
   and human factor, 162, 165–166
   inappropriate uses, 161
   infatuation with, 161–162
   knowing when to use, 120
   "measurement system gaming," 163
   role in performance measurement, 163–164
   search for quick fix, 160–161
   unrealistic expectations, 166
   viewed as panacea, 119–120
Theory of Constraints (Goldratt), 245
throughput, as measure of productivity, 234–235
Thurber, James, 111
Tichy, Noel, 16
Timmerman, Tim, 162
Total Cost of Ownership, 240
Total Quality Management (TQM), 104
Toyota Production System (TPS), 237–238
transformational learning, *see also* learning
   changing what and how we measure, 159
   defined, 140
   and double-loop learning, 144–145
   keys to, 150–158

willingness to experiment, 151–152
willingness to question, 150–151
Transformational Measurement Action Plans (TMAPs)
   of emergent measures, 214–256
   overview, 211–212
Transformational Measurement Maturity Assessment, 191–195
Transformational Measurement Questionnaire (TMQ), 5–7
transformational measures, 82–84, *see also* measures
   alignment with strategies, 53
   cross-functional, 209
   defined, 196, 201
   *vs.* emergent measures, 201
   to facilitate organizational learning, 146
   focus on critical few, 53
   multiple, 210–211
   need for different perspective, 196
   need to change traditional thinking, 197–198
   positive effect of, 4
   predictive, 209–210
   qualitative, 205–206
   subjective, 207–208
transformational performance measurement, *see also* performance measurement
   context as key to, 52
   creating environment for change, 128–132
   example of, 157
   focus as key to, 52–53
   ideal implementation, 48–51
   importance of four keys, 54–55
   integration as key to, 53
   interactivity as key to, 54
   recognizing accomplishments, 134
   resistance to change, 127–128
   role of CMO, 139
   *vs.* routine measurement, 126–127

transformational performance
   measurement (*continued*)
  as search for new truths, 200
  separation from judgment, 58
  skepticism as barrier, 200
  as social process, 54
  steps to aid implementation,
   132–134
  usefulness as key, 200
  as visionary destination, 48–51
transformational performance measurement maturity, 177
Treagus, Matthew, 172
trust, *see also* Organizational Trust
  defined, 229
tunnel vision, 147
Twain, Mark, 111

Valley Stream Mapping, 238
value creation, 72–74
  *vs.* destruction, 73
  measurement as key in, 74
  missed opportunities, 123–124
  visibility of, 152–153
Value Creation Index, 203

value destruction, 124
  inadvertent, 153
vertical integration, 86–87
Voice of the Customer, 219–221

waste, unchecked existence of,
  124–125
Welch, Jack, 32, 69
  as measurement leader, 135
Wells, H.G., 153
Weston, Josh, as measurement leader,
  136
Whitney, John, 125
*Wilder Collaboration Factors Inven-
  tory,* 233
Winter, Nicholas, 224
wisdom
  *vs.* knowledge, 106
  transformation from data, 108–109
*Wizard of Oz,* 162
Womack, James, 238
Woods, Jeff, 174
work, "dumbing down" of, 119, 161

Zeithaml, Valarie, 223
Zero Based Budgeting concept, 125
Zuboff, S., 168